T&P BOOKS

I0168807

ARABIC
VOCABULARY

FOR ENGLISH SPEAKERS

ENGLISH-
ARABIC

The most useful words
To expand your lexicon and sharpen
your language skills

9000 words

Arabic vocabulary for English speakers - 9000 words

By Andrey Taranov

T&P Books vocabularies are intended for helping you learn, memorize and review foreign words. The dictionary is divided into themes, covering all major spheres of everyday activities, business, science, culture, etc.

The process of learning words using T&P Books' theme-based dictionaries gives you the following advantages:

- Correctly grouped source information predetermines success at subsequent stages of word memorization
- Availability of words derived from the same root allowing memorization of word units (rather than separate words)
- Small units of words facilitate the process of establishing associative links needed for consolidation of vocabulary
- Level of language knowledge can be estimated by the number of learned words

T&P Books Publishing
www.tpbooks.com

ISBN: 978-1-78716-694-3

This book is also available in E-book formats.
Please visit www.tpbooks.com or the major online bookstores.

ARABIC VOCABULARY
for English speakers

T&P Books vocabularies are intended to help you learn, memorize, and review foreign words. The vocabulary contains over 9000 commonly used words arranged thematically.

- Vocabulary contains the most commonly used words
- Recommended as an addition to any language course
- Meets the needs of beginners and advanced learners of foreign languages
- Convenient for daily use, revision sessions, and self-testing activities
- Allows you to assess your vocabulary

Special features of the vocabulary

- Words are organized according to their meaning, not alphabetically
- Words are presented in three columns to facilitate the reviewing and self-testing processes
- Words in groups are divided into small blocks to facilitate the learning process
- The vocabulary offers a convenient and simple transcription of each foreign word

The vocabulary has 256 topics including:

Basic Concepts, Numbers, Colors, Months, Seasons, Units of Measurement, Clothing & Accessories, Food & Nutrition, Restaurant, Family Members, Relatives, Character, Feelings, Emotions, Diseases, City, Town, Sightseeing, Shopping, Money, House, Home, Office, Working in the Office, Import & Export, Marketing, Job Search, Sports, Education, Computer, Internet, Tools, Nature, Countries, Nationalities and more ...

T&P BOOKS' THEME-BASED DICTIONARIES

The Correct System for Memorizing Foreign Words

Acquiring vocabulary is one of the most important elements of learning a foreign language, because words allow us to express our thoughts, ask questions, and provide answers. An inadequate vocabulary can impede communication with a foreigner and make it difficult to understand a book or movie well.

The pace of activity in all spheres of modern life, including the learning of modern languages, has increased. Today, we need to memorize large amounts of information (grammar rules, foreign words, etc.) within a short period. However, this does not need to be difficult. All you need to do is to choose the right training materials, learn a few special techniques, and develop your individual training system.

Having a system is critical to the process of language learning. Many people fail to succeed in this regard; they cannot master a foreign language because they fail to follow a system comprised of selecting materials, organizing lessons, arranging new words to be learned, and so on. The lack of a system causes confusion and eventually, lowers self-confidence.

T&P Books' theme-based dictionaries can be included in the list of elements needed for creating an effective system for learning foreign words. These dictionaries were specially developed for learning purposes and are meant to help students effectively memorize words and expand their vocabulary.

Generally speaking, the process of learning words consists of three main elements:

- Reception (creation or acquisition) of a training material, such as a word list
- Work aimed at memorizing new words
- Work aimed at reviewing the learned words, such as self-testing

All three elements are equally important since they determine the quality of work and the final result. All three processes require certain skills and a well-thought-out approach.

New words are often encountered quite randomly when learning a foreign language and it may be difficult to include them all in a unified list. As a result, these words remain written on scraps of paper, in book margins, textbooks, and so on. In order to systematize such words, we have to create and continually update a "book of new words." A paper notebook, a netbook, or a tablet PC can be used for these purposes.

This "book of new words" will be your personal, unique list of words. However, it will only contain the words that you came across during the learning process. For example, you might have written down the words "Sunday," "Tuesday," and "Friday." However, there are additional words for days of the week, for example, "Saturday," that are missing, and your list of words would be incomplete. Using a theme dictionary, in addition to the "book of new words," is a reasonable solution to this problem.

The theme-based dictionary may serve as the basis for expanding your vocabulary.

It will be your big "book of new words" containing the most frequently used words of a foreign language already included. There are quite a few theme-based dictionaries available, and you should ensure that you make the right choice in order to get the maximum benefit from your purchase.

Therefore, we suggest using theme-based dictionaries from T&P Books Publishing as an aid to learning foreign words. Our books are specially developed for effective use in the sphere of vocabulary systematization, expansion and review.

Theme-based dictionaries are not a magical solution to learning new words. However, they can serve as your main database to aid foreign-language acquisition. Apart from theme dictionaries, you can have copybooks for writing down new words, flash cards, glossaries for various texts, as well as other resources; however, a good theme dictionary will always remain your primary collection of words.

T&P Books' theme-based dictionaries are specialty books that contain the most frequently used words in a language.

The main characteristic of such dictionaries is the division of words into themes. For example, the *City* theme contains the words "street," "crossroads," "square," "fountain," and so on. The *Talking* theme might contain words like "to talk," "to ask," "question," and "answer".

All the words in a theme are divided into smaller units, each comprising 3–5 words. Such an arrangement improves the perception of words and makes the learning process less tiresome. Each unit contains a selection of words with similar meanings or identical roots. This allows you to learn words in small groups and establish other associative links that have a positive effect on memorization.

The words on each page are placed in three columns: a word in your native language, its translation, and its transcription. Such positioning allows for the use of techniques for effective memorization. After closing the translation column, you can flip through and review foreign words, and vice versa. "This is an easy and convenient method of review – one that we recommend you do often."

Our theme-based dictionaries contain transcriptions for all the foreign words. Unfortunately, none of the existing transcriptions are able to convey the exact nuances of foreign pronunciation. That is why we recommend using the transcriptions only as a supplementary learning aid. Correct pronunciation can only be acquired with the help of sound. Therefore our collection includes audio theme-based dictionaries.

The process of learning words using T&P Books' theme-based dictionaries gives you the following advantages:

- You have correctly grouped source information, which predetermines your success at subsequent stages of word memorization
- Availability of words derived from the same root (lazy, lazily, lazybones), allowing you to memorize word units instead of separate words
- Small units of words facilitate the process of establishing associative links needed for consolidation of vocabulary
- You can estimate the number of learned words and hence your level of language knowledge
- The dictionary allows for the creation of an effective and high-quality revision process
- You can revise certain themes several times, modifying the revision methods and techniques
- Audio versions of the dictionaries help you to work out the pronunciation of words and develop your skills of auditory word perception

The T&P Books' theme-based dictionaries are offered in several variants differing in the number of words: 1.500, 3.000, 5.000, 7.000, and 9.000 words. There are also dictionaries containing 15,000 words for some language combinations. Your choice of dictionary will depend on your knowledge level and goals.

We sincerely believe that our dictionaries will become your trusty assistant in learning foreign languages and will allow you to easily acquire the necessary vocabulary.

TABLE OF CONTENTS

Education

Arts

Rest. Entertainment. Travel

TECHNICAL EQUIPMENT. TRANSPORTATION

Technical equipment

MISCELLANEOUS

MAIN 500 VERBS

PRONUNCIATION GUIDE

T&P phonetic alphabet	Arabic example	English example
[a]	طفَّى [ṭaffa]	shorter than in ask
[ā]	إختار [iχtār]	calf, palm
[e]	هامبورجر [hamburger]	elm, medal
[i]	زفاف [zifāf]	shorter than in feet
[ī]	أبريل [abrīl]	feet, meter
[u]	كلكتا [kalkutta]	book
[ū]	جاموس [ʒāmūs]	fuel, tuna
[b]	بداية [bidāya]	baby, book
[d]	سعادة [saʿāda]	day, doctor
[ḍ]	وضع [waḍʾ]	[d] pharyngeal
[ʒ]	الأرجنتين [arʒantīn]	forge, pleasure
[ð]	تذكار [tiðkār]	pharyngealized th
[ẓ]	ظهر [ẓahar]	[z] pharyngeal
[f]	خفيف [χafīf]	face, food
[g]	جولف [gūlf]	game, gold
[h]	إتّجاه [ittiʒāh]	home, have
[ḥ]	أحبّ [aḥabb]	[h] pharyngeal
[y]	ذهبيّ [ðahabíy]	yes, New York
[k]	كرسيّ [kursiy]	clock, kiss
[l]	لمح [lamaḥ]	lace, people
[m]	مرصد [marṣad]	magic, milk
[n]	جنوب [ʒanūb]	sang, thing
[p]	كابتشينو [kaputʃīnu]	pencil, private
[q]	وثق [waθiq]	king, club
[r]	روح [rūḥ]	rice, radio
[s]	سخريّة [suχriyya]	city, boss
[ṣ]	معصم [miʿṣam]	[s] pharyngeal
[ʃ]	عشاء [ʿaʃāʾ]	machine, shark
[t]	تنّوب [tannūb]	tourist, trip
[ṭ]	خريطة [χarīṭa]	[t] pharyngeal
[θ]	ماموث [mamūθ]	month, tooth
[v]	فيتنام [vitnām]	very, river
[w]	ودّع [waddaʾ]	vase, winter
[χ]	بخيل [baχīl]	as in Scots 'loch'
[ɣ]	تغدّى [taɣadda]	between [g] and [h]
[z]	ماعز [māʿiz]	zebra, please

T&P phonetic alphabet	Arabic example	English example
['] (ayn)	سبعة [sab'a]	voiced pharyngeal fricative
['] (hamza)	سأل [sa'al]	glottal stop

ABBREVIATIONS
used in the vocabulary

Arabic abbreviations

du	-	plural noun (double)
f	-	feminine noun
m	-	masculine noun
pl	-	plural

English abbreviations

ab.	-	about
adj	-	adjective
adv	-	adverb
anim.	-	animate
as adj	-	attributive noun used as adjective
e.g.	-	for example
etc.	-	et cetera
fam.	-	familiar
fem.	-	feminine
form.	-	formal
inanim.	-	inanimate
masc.	-	masculine
math	-	mathematics
mil.	-	military
n	-	noun
pl	-	plural
pron.	-	pronoun
sb	-	somebody
sing.	-	singular
sth	-	something
v aux	-	auxiliary verb
vi	-	intransitive verb
vi, vt	-	intransitive, transitive verb
vt	-	transitive verb

BASIC CONCEPTS

Basic concepts. Part 1

1. Pronouns

I, me	ana	أنا
you (masc.)	anta	أنت
you (fem.)	anti	أنت
he	huwa	هو
she	hiya	هي
we	naḥnu	نحن
you (to a group)	antum	أنتم
they	hum	هم

2. Greetings. Salutations. Farewells

Hello! (form.)	as salāmu 'alaykum!	السلام عليكم!
Good morning!	ṣabāḥ al xayr!	صباح الخير!
Good afternoon!	nahārak saʿīd!	نهارك سعيد!
Good evening!	masā' al xayr!	مساء الخير!
to say hello	sallam	سلّم
Hi! (hello)	salām!	سلام!
greeting (n)	salām (m)	سلام
to greet (vt)	sallam 'ala	سلّم على
How are you?	kayfa ḥāluka?	كيف حالك؟
What's new?	ma axbārak?	ما أخبارك؟
Bye-Bye! Goodbye!	maʿ as salāma!	مع السلامة!
See you soon!	ilal liqā'!	إلى اللقاء!
Farewell!	maʿ as salāma!	مع السلامة!
to say goodbye	waddaʿ	ودّع
So long!	bay bay!	باي باي!
Thank you!	ʃukran!	شكرًا!
Thank you very much!	ʃukran ʒazīlan!	شكرًا جزيلًا!
You're welcome	'afwan	عفوا
Don't mention it!	la ʃukr 'ala wāʒib	لا شكر على واجب
It was nothing	al 'afw	العفو
Excuse me! (fam.)	'an iðnak!	عن أذنك!
Excuse me! (form.)	'afwan!	عفوًا!

to excuse (forgive)	ʻaðar	عذر
to apologize (vi)	iʻtaðar	إعتذر
My apologies	ana ʾāsif	أنا آسف
I'm sorry!	la tuʾāxiðōni!	لا تؤاخذني!
to forgive (vt)	ʻafa	عفا
please (adv)	min faḍlak	من فضلك

Don't forget!	la tansa!	لا تنس!
Certainly!	ṭabʻan!	طبعًا!
Of course not!	abadan!	أبدًا!
Okay! (I agree)	ittafaqna!	إتّفقنا!
That's enough!	kifāya!	كفاية!

3. How to address

mister, sir	ya sayyid	يا سيّد
ma'am	ya sayyida	يا سيدة
miss	ya ʾānisa	يا آنسة
young man	ya ustāð	يا أستاذ
young man (little boy, kid)	ya bni	يا بني
miss (little girl)	ya binti	يا بنتي

4. Cardinal numbers. Part 1

0 zero	ṣifr	صفر
1 one	wāḥid	واحد
1 one (fem.)	wāḥida	واحدة
2 two	iθnān	إثنان
3 three	θalāθa	ثلاثة
4 four	arbaʻa	أربعة

5 five	xamsa	خمسة
6 six	sitta	ستّة
7 seven	sabʻa	سبعة
8 eight	θamāniya	ثمانية
9 nine	tisʻa	تسعة

10 ten	ʻaʃara	عشرة
11 eleven	ahad ʻaʃar	أحد عشر
12 twelve	iθnā ʻaʃar	إثنا عشر
13 thirteen	θalāθat ʻaʃar	ثلاثة عشر
14 fourteen	arbaʻat ʻaʃar	أربعة عشر

15 fifteen	xamsat ʻaʃar	خمسة عشر
16 sixteen	sittat ʻaʃar	ستّة عشر
17 seventeen	sabʻat ʻaʃar	سبعة عشر
18 eighteen	θamāniyat ʻaʃar	ثمانية عشر
19 nineteen	tisʻat ʻaʃar	تسعة عشر

20 twenty	'iʃrūn	عشرون
21 twenty-one	wāḥid wa 'iʃrūn	واحد وعشرون
22 twenty-two	iθnān wa 'iʃrūn	إثنان وعشرون
23 twenty-three	θalāθa wa 'iʃrūn	ثلاثة وعشرون
30 thirty	θalāθīn	ثلاثون
31 thirty-one	wāḥid wa θalāθūn	واحد وثلاثون
32 thirty-two	iθnān wa θalāθūn	إثنان وثلاثون
33 thirty-three	θalāθa wa θalāθūn	ثلاثة وثلاثون
40 forty	arba'ūn	أربعون
41 forty-one	wāḥid wa arba'ūn	واحد وأربعون
42 forty-two	iθnān wa arba'ūn	إثنان وأربعون
43 forty-three	θalāθa wa arba'ūn	ثلاثة وأربعون
50 fifty	χamsūn	خمسون
51 fifty-one	wāḥid wa χamsūn	واحد وخمسون
52 fifty-two	iθnān wa χamsūn	إثنان وخمسون
53 fifty-three	θalāθa wa χamsūn	ثلاثة وخمسون
60 sixty	sittūn	ستّون
61 sixty-one	wāḥid wa sittūn	واحد وستّون
62 sixty-two	iθnān wa sittūn	إثنان وستّون
63 sixty-three	θalāθa wa sittūn	ثلاثة وستّون
70 seventy	sab'ūn	سبعون
71 seventy-one	wāḥid wa sab'ūn	واحد وسبعون
72 seventy-two	iθnān wa sab'ūn	إثنان وسبعون
73 seventy-three	θalāθa wa sab'ūn	ثلاثة وسبعون
80 eighty	θamānūn	ثمانون
81 eighty-one	wāḥid wa θamānūn	واحد وثمانون
82 eighty-two	iθnān wa θamānūn	إثنان وثمانون
83 eighty-three	θalāθa wa θamānūn	ثلاثة وثمانون
90 ninety	tis'ūn	تسعون
91 ninety-one	wāḥid wa tis'ūn	واحد وتسعون
92 ninety-two	iθnān wa tis'ūn	إثنان وتسعون
93 ninety-three	θalāθa wa tis'ūn	ثلاثة وتسعون

5. Cardinal numbers. Part 2

100 one hundred	mi'a	مائة
200 two hundred	mi'atān	مائتان
300 three hundred	θalāθumi'a	ثلاثمائة
400 four hundred	rub'umi'a	أربعمائة
500 five hundred	χamsumi'a	خمسمائة
600 six hundred	sittumi'a	ستّمائة
700 seven hundred	sab'umi'a	سبعمائة

| 800 eight hundred | θamānimi'a | ثمانمائة |
| 900 nine hundred | tis'umi'a | تسعمائة |

1000 one thousand	alf	ألف
2000 two thousand	alfān	ألفان
3000 three thousand	θalāθat 'ālāf	ثلاثة آلاف
10000 ten thousand	'aʃarat 'ālāf	عشرة آلاف
one hundred thousand	mi'at alf	مائة ألف
million	milyūn (m)	مليون
billion	milyār (m)	مليار

6. Ordinal numbers

first (adj)	awwal	أوّل
second (adj)	θāni	ثان
third (adj)	θāliθ	ثالث
fourth (adj)	rābi'	رابع
fifth (adj)	χāmis	خامس

sixth (adj)	sādis	سادس
seventh (adj)	sābi'	سابع
eighth (adj)	θāmin	ثامن
ninth (adj)	tāsi'	تاسع
tenth (adj)	'āʃir	عاشر

7. Numbers. Fractions

fraction	kasr (m)	كسر
one half	niṣf	نصف
one third	θulθ	ثلث
one quarter	rub'	ربع

one eighth	θumn	ثمن
one tenth	'uʃr	عشر
two thirds	θulθān	ثلثان
three quarters	talātit arbā'	ثلاثة أرباع

8. Numbers. Basic operations

subtraction	ṭarḥ (m)	طرح
to subtract (vi, vt)	ṭaraḥ	طرح
division	qisma (f)	قسمة
to divide (vt)	qasam	قسم

| addition | ʒam' (m) | جمع |
| to add up (vt) | ʒama' | جمع |

to add (vi, vt)	ʒamaʿ	جمع
multiplication	ḍarb (m)	ضرب
to multiply (vt)	ḍarab	ضرب

9. Numbers. Miscellaneous

digit, figure	raqm (m)	رقم
number	ʿadad (m)	عدد
numeral	ism al ʿadad (m)	إسم العدد
minus sign	nāqiṣ (m)	ناقص
plus sign	zāʼid (m)	زائد
formula	ṣīɣa (f)	صيغة

calculation	ḥisāb (m)	حساب
to count (vi, vt)	ʿadd	عدّ
to count up	ḥasab	حسب
to compare (vt)	qāran	قارن

How much?	kam?	كم؟
sum, total	maʒmūʿ (m)	مجموع
result	natīʒa (f)	نتيجة
remainder	al bāqi (m)	الباقي

a few (e.g., ~ years ago)	ʿiddat	عدّة
little (I had ~ time)	qalīl	قليل
the rest	al bāqi (m)	الباقي
one and a half	wāḥid wa niṣf (m)	واحد ونصف
dozen	iθnā ʿaʃar (f)	إثنا عشر

in half (adv)	ila ʃaṭrayn	إلى شطرين
equally (evenly)	bit tasāwi	بالتساوى
half	niṣf (m)	نصف
time (three ~s)	marra (f)	مرّة

10. The most important verbs. Part 1

to advise (vt)	naṣaḥ	نصح
to agree (say yes)	ittafaq	إتفق
to answer (vi, vt)	aʒāb	أجاب
to apologize (vi)	iʿtaðar	إعتذر
to arrive (vi)	waṣal	وصل

to ask (~ oneself)	sa'al	سأل
to ask (~ sb to do sth)	ṭalab	طلب
to be (vi)	kān	كان

| to be afraid | χāf | خاف |
| to be hungry | arād an ya'kul | أراد أن يأكل |

to be interested in …	ihtamm	إهتمّ
to be needed	kān maṭlūb	كان مطلوبا
to be surprised	indahaʃ	إندهش

to be thirsty	arād an yaʃrab	أراد أن يشرب
to begin (vt)	bada'	بدأ
to belong to …	χaṣṣ	خصّ
to boast (vi)	tabāha	تباهى
to break (split into pieces)	kasar	كسر

to call (~ for help)	istaɣāθ	إستغاث
can (v aux)	istaṭā'	إستطاع
to catch (vt)	amsak	أمسك
to change (vt)	ɣayyar	غيّر
to choose (select)	iχtār	إختار

to come down (the stairs)	nazil	نزل
to compare (vt)	qāran	قارن
to complain (vi, vt)	ʃaka	شكا
to confuse (mix up)	iχtalaṭ	إختلط
to continue (vt)	istamarr	إستمرّ
to control (vt)	taḥakkam	تحكّم

to cook (dinner)	ḥaḍḍar	حضّر
to cost (vt)	kallaf	كلّف
to count (add up)	'add	عدّ
to count on …	i'tamad 'ala …	إعتمد على…
to create (vt)	χalaq	خلق
to cry (weep)	baka	بكى

11. The most important verbs. Part 2

to deceive (vi, vt)	χada'	خدع
to decorate (tree, street)	zayyan	زيّن
to defend (a country, etc.)	dāfa'	دافع
to demand (request firmly)	ṭālib	طالب
to dig (vt)	ḥafar	حفر

to discuss (vt)	nāqaʃ	ناقش
to do (vt)	'amal	عمل
to doubt (have doubts)	ʃakk fi	شكّ في
to drop (let fall)	awqa'	أوقع
to enter (room, house, etc.)	daχal	دخل

to exist (vi)	kān mawʒūd	كان موجودًا
to expect (foresee)	tanabba'	تنبّأ
to explain (vt)	ʃaraḥ	شرح
to fall (vi)	saqaṭ	سقط
to find (vt)	waʒad	وجد

to finish (vt)	atamm	أتمَّ
to fly (vi)	ṭār	طار
to follow ... (come after)	taba'	تبع
to forget (vi, vt)	nasiy	نسي

to forgive (vt)	'afa	عفا
to give (vt)	a'ṭa	أعطى
to give a hint	a'ṭa talmīḥ	أعطى تلميحًا
to go (on foot)	maʃa	مشى

to go for a swim	sabaḥ	سبح
to go out (for dinner, etc.)	xaraʒ	خرج
to guess (the answer)	xamman	خمّن

to have (vt)	malak	ملك
to have breakfast	afṭar	أفطر
to have dinner	ta'aʃʃa	تعشّى
to have lunch	taɣadda	تغدّى
to hear (vt)	sami'	سمع

to help (vt)	sā'ad	ساعد
to hide (vt)	xaba'	خبأ
to hope (vi, vt)	tamanna	تمنّى
to hunt (vi, vt)	iṣṭād	إصطاد
to hurry (vi)	ista'ʒal	إستعجل

12. The most important verbs. Part 3

to inform (vt)	axbar	أخبر
to insist (vi, vt)	aṣarr	أصرَّ
to insult (vt)	ahān	أهان
to invite (vt)	da'a	دعا
to joke (vi)	mazaḥ	مزح

to keep (vt)	ḥafaẓ	حفظ
to keep silent	sakat	سكت
to kill (vt)	qatal	قتل
to know (sb)	'araf	عرف
to know (sth)	'araf	عرف
to laugh (vi)	ḍaḥik	ضحك

to liberate (city, etc.)	ḥarrar	حرّر
to like (I like ...)	a'ʒab	أعجب
to look for ... (search)	baḥaθ	بحث
to love (sb)	aḥabb	أحبَّ
to make a mistake	axṭa'	أخطأ

to manage, to run	adār	أدار
to mean (signify)	'ana	عنى
to mention (talk about)	ðakar	ذكر

to miss (school, etc.)	ɣāb	غاب
to notice (see)	lāḥaẓ	لاحظ
to object (vi, vt)	i'taraḍ	إعترض
to observe (see)	rāqab	راقب
to open (vt)	fataḥ	فتح
to order (meal, etc.)	ṭalab	طلب
to order (mil.)	amar	أمر
to own (possess)	malak	ملك
to participate (vi)	iʃtarak	إشترك
to pay (vi, vt)	dafa'	دفع
to permit (vt)	raxxaṣ	رخّص
to plan (vt)	xaṭṭaṭ	خطّط
to play (children)	la'ib	لعب
to pray (vi, vt)	ṣalla	صلّى
to prefer (vt)	faḍḍal	فضّل
to promise (vt)	wa'ad	وعد
to pronounce (vt)	naṭaq	نطق
to propose (vt)	iqtaraḥ	إقترح
to punish (vt)	'āqab	عاقب

13. The most important verbs. Part 4

to read (vi, vt)	qara'	قرأ
to recommend (vt)	naṣaḥ	نصح
to refuse (vi, vt)	rafaḍ	رفض
to regret (be sorry)	nadim	ندم
to rent (sth from sb)	ista'ʒar	إستأجر
to repeat (say again)	karrar	كرّر
to reserve, to book	ḥaʒaz	حجز
to run (vi)	ʒara	جرى
to save (rescue)	anqað	أنقذ
to say (~ thank you)	qāl	قال
to scold (vt)	wabbax	وبّخ
to see (vt)	ra'a	رأى
to sell (vt)	bā'	باع
to send (vt)	arsal	أرسل
to shoot (vi)	aṭlaq an nār	أطلق النار
to shout (vi)	ṣarax	صرخ
to show (vt)	'araḍ	عرض
to sign (document)	waqqa'	وقّع
to sit down (vi)	ʒalas	جلس
to smile (vi)	ibtasam	إبتسم
to speak (vi, vt)	takallam	تكلّم

25

to steal (money, etc.)	saraq	سرق
to stop (for pause, etc.)	waqaf	وقف
to stop (please ~ calling me)	tawaqqaf	توقّف

to study (vt)	daras	درس
to swim (vi)	sabaḥ	سبح
to take (vt)	aχað	أخذ
to think (vi, vt)	ẓann	ظنّ
to threaten (vt)	haddad	هدّد

to touch (with hands)	lamas	لمس
to translate (vt)	tarʒam	ترجم
to trust (vt)	waθiq	وثق
to try (attempt)	ḥāwal	حاول
to turn (e.g., ~ left)	inʿaṭaf	إنعطف

to underestimate (vt)	istaχaff	إستخفّ
to understand (vt)	fahim	فهم
to unite (vt)	waḥḥad	وحّد
to wait (vt)	intazar	إنتظر

to want (wish, desire)	arād	أراد
to warn (vt)	ḥaððar	حذّر
to work (vi)	ʿamal	عمل
to write (vt)	katab	كتب
to write down	katab	كتب

14. Colors

color	lawn (m)	لون
shade (tint)	daraʒat al lawn (m)	درجة اللون
hue	ṣabɣit lūn (f)	لون
rainbow	qaws quzaḥ (m)	قوس قزح

white (adj)	abyaḍ	أبيض
black (adj)	aswad	أسود
gray (adj)	ramādiy	رماديّ

green (adj)	aχḍar	أخضر
yellow (adj)	aṣfar	أصفر
red (adj)	aḥmar	أحمر

blue (adj)	azraq	أزرق
light blue (adj)	azraq fātiḥ	أزرق فاتح
pink (adj)	wardiy	ورديّ
orange (adj)	burtuqāliy	برتقاليّ
violet (adj)	banafsaʒiy	بنفسجيّ
brown (adj)	bunniy	بنّيّ
golden (adj)	ðahabiy	ذهبيّ

silvery (adj)	fiḍḍiy	فضّي
beige (adj)	bɛ:ʒ	بيج
cream (adj)	'āʒiy	عاجي
turquoise (adj)	fayrūziy	فيروزي
cherry red (adj)	karaziy	كرزي
lilac (adj)	laylakiy	ليلكي
crimson (adj)	qirmiziy	قرمزي
light (adj)	fātiḥ	فاتح
dark (adj)	ɣāmiq	غامق
bright, vivid (adj)	zāhi	زاه
colored (pencils)	mulawwan	ملوّن
color (e.g., ~ film)	mulawwan	ملوّن
black-and-white (adj)	abyaḍ wa aswad	أبيض وأسود
plain (one-colored)	waḥīd al lawn, sāda	وحيد اللون, سادة
multicolored (adj)	muta'addid al alwān	متعدّد الألوان

15. Questions

Who?	man?	من؟
What?	māða?	ماذا؟
Where? (at, in)	ayna?	أين؟
Where (to)?	ila ayna?	إلى أين؟
From where?	min ayna?	من أين؟
When?	mata?	متى؟
Why? (What for?)	li māða?	لماذا؟
Why? (~ are you crying?)	li māða?	لماذا؟
What for?	li māða?	لماذا؟
How? (in what way)	kayfa?	كيف؟
What? (What kind of ...?)	ay?	أي؟
Which?	ay?	أي؟
To whom?	li man?	لمن؟
About whom?	'amman?	عمّن؟
About what?	'amma?	عمّا؟
With whom?	ma' man?	مع من؟
How many? How much?	kam?	كم؟
Whose?	li man?	لمن؟

16. Prepositions

with (accompanied by)	ma'	مع
without	bi dūn	بدون
to (indicating direction)	ila	إلى
about (talking ~ ...)	'an	عن

| before (in time) | qabl | قبل |
| in front of ... | amām | أمام |

under (beneath, below)	taḥt	تحت
above (over)	fawq	فوق
on (atop)	'ala	على
from (off, out of)	min	من
of (made from)	min	من

| in (e.g., ~ ten minutes) | ba'd | بعد |
| over (across the top of) | 'abr | عبر |

17. Function words. Adverbs. Part 1

Where? (at, in)	ayna?	أين؟
here (adv)	huna	هنا
there (adv)	hunāk	هناك

| somewhere (to be) | fi makānin ma | في مكان ما |
| nowhere (not anywhere) | la fi ay makān | لا في أي مكان |

| by (near, beside) | bi ʒānib | بجانب |
| by the window | bi ʒānib aʃ ʃubbāk | بجانب الشبّاك |

Where (to)?	ila ayna?	إلى أين؟
here (e.g., come ~!)	huna	هنا
there (e.g., to go ~)	hunāk	هناك
from here (adv)	min huna	من هنا
from there (adv)	min hunāk	من هناك

| close (adv) | qarīban | قريبًا |
| far (adv) | ba'īdan | بعيدًا |

near (e.g., ~ Paris)	'ind	عند
nearby (adv)	qarīban	قريبًا
not far (adv)	ɣayr ba'īd	غير بعيد

left (adj)	al yasār	اليسار
on the left	'alaʃ ʃimāl	على الشمال
to the left	ilaʃ ʃimāl	إلى الشمال

right (adj)	al yamīn	اليمين
on the right	'alal yamīn	على اليمين
to the right	llal yamīn	إلى اليمين

in front (adv)	min al amām	من الأمام
front (as adj)	amāmiy	أمامي
ahead (the kids ran ~)	ilal amām	إلى الأمام
behind (adv)	warā'	وراء
from behind	min al warā'	من الوراء

back (towards the rear)	ilal warā'	إلى الوراء
middle	wasaṭ (m)	وسط
in the middle	fil wasaṭ	في الوسط
at the side	bi ʒānib	بجانب
everywhere (adv)	fi kull makān	في كل مكان
around (in all directions)	ḥawl	حول
from inside	min ad dāχil	من الداخل
somewhere (to go)	ila ayy makān	إلى أيّ مكان
straight (directly)	bi aqṣar ṭarīq	بأقصر طريق
back (e.g., come ~)	'īyāban	إيابًا
from anywhere	min ayy makān	من أي مكان
from somewhere	min makānin ma	من مكان ما
firstly (adv)	awwalan	أوّلًا
secondly (adv)	θāniyan	ثانيًا
thirdly (adv)	θāliθan	ثالثًا
suddenly (adv)	faʒ'a	فجأة
at first (in the beginning)	fil bidāya	في البداية
for the first time	li 'awwal marra	لأوّل مرّة
long before …	qabl … bi mudda ṭawīla	قبل...بمدّة طويلة
anew (over again)	min ʒadīd	من جديد
for good (adv)	ilal abad	إلى الأبد
never (adv)	abadan	أبدًا
again (adv)	min ʒadīd	من جديد
now (adv)	al 'ān	الآن
often (adv)	kaθīran	كثيرًا
then (adv)	fi ðalika al waqt	في ذلك الوقت
urgently (quickly)	'āʒilan	عاجلًا
usually (adv)	kal 'āda	كالعادة
by the way, …	'ala fikra …	على فكرة...
possible (that is ~)	min al mumkin	من الممكن
probably (adv)	la'alla	لعلّ
maybe (adv)	min al mumkin	من الممكن
besides …	bil iḍāfa ila ðalik …	بالإضافة إلى...
that's why …	li ðalik	لذلك
in spite of …	bir raγm min …	بالرغم من...
thanks to …	bi faḍl …	بفضل...
what (pron.)	allaði	الذي
that (conj.)	anna	أنّ
something	ʃay' (m)	شيء
anything (something)	ʃay' (m)	شيء
nothing	la ʃay'	لا شيء
who (pron.)	allaði	الذي
someone	aḥad	أحد

29

somebody	aḥad	أحد
nobody	la aḥad	لا أحد
nowhere (a voyage to ~)	la ila ay makān	لا إلى أي مكان
nobody's	la yaxuṣṣ aḥad	لا يخص أحدًا
somebody's	li aḥad	لأحد

so (I'm ~ glad)	hakaða	هكذا
also (as well)	kaðalika	كذلك
too (as well)	ayḍan	أيضًا

18. Function words. Adverbs. Part 2

Why?	li māða?	لماذا؟
for some reason	li sababin ma	لسبب ما
because ...	li'anna ...	لأنَّ...
for some purpose	li amr mā	لأمر ما

and	wa	و
or	aw	أو
but	lakin	لكن
for (e.g., ~ me)	li	لـ

too (~ many people)	kaθīran ʒiddan	كثير جدًّا
only (exclusively)	faqaṭ	فقط
exactly (adv)	biḍ ḍabṭ	بالضبط
about (more or less)	naḥw	نحو

approximately (adv)	taqrīban	تقريبًا
approximate (adj)	taqrībiy	تقريبيّ
almost (adv)	taqrīban	تقريبًا
the rest	al bāqi (m)	الباقي

each (adj)	kull	كلّ
any (no matter which)	ayy	أيّ
many, much (a lot of)	kaθīr	كثير
many people	kaθīr min an nās	كثير من الناس
all (everyone)	kull an nās	كل الناس

in return for ...	muqābil ...	مقابل...
in exchange (adv)	muqābil	مقابل
by hand (made)	bil yad	باليد
hardly (negative opinion)	hayhāt	هيهات

probably (adv)	la'alla	لعلّ
on purpose (intentionally)	qaṣdan	قصدا
by accident (adv)	ṣudfa	صدفة

very (adv)	ʒiddan	جدًّا
for example (adv)	maθalan	مثلا
between	bayn	بين

among	bayn	بين
so much (such a lot)	haðihi al kammiyya	هذه الكمية
especially (adv)	χāṣṣa	خاصّة

Basic concepts. Part 2

19. Weekdays

Monday	yawm al iθnayn (m)	يوم الإثنين
Tuesday	yawm aθ θulāθā' (m)	يوم الثلاثاء
Wednesday	yawm al arbi'ā' (m)	يوم الأربعاء
Thursday	yawm al xamīs (m)	يوم الخميس
Friday	yawm al ʒum'a (m)	يوم الجمعة
Saturday	yawm as sabt (m)	يوم السبت
Sunday	yawm al aḥad (m)	يوم الأحد
today (adv)	al yawm	اليوم
tomorrow (adv)	ɣadan	غدًا
the day after tomorrow	ba'd ɣad	بعد غد
yesterday (adv)	ams	أمس
the day before yesterday	awwal ams	أوّل أمس
day	yawm (m)	يوم
working day	yawm 'amal (m)	يوم عمل
public holiday	yawm al 'uṭla ar rasmiyya (m)	يوم العطلة الرسمية
day off	yawm 'uṭla (m)	يوم عطلة
weekend	ayyām al 'uṭla (pl)	أيام العطلة
all day long	ṭūl al yawm	طول اليوم
the next day (adv)	fil yawm at tāli	في اليوم التالي
two days ago	min yawmayn	قبل يومين
the day before	fil yawm as sābiq	في اليوم السابق
daily (adj)	yawmiy	يومي
every day (adv)	yawmiyyan	يوميًا
week	usbū' (m)	أسبوع
last week (adv)	fil isbū' al māḍi	في الأسبوع الماضي
next week (adv)	fil isbū' al qādim	في الأسبوع القادم
weekly (adj)	usbū'iy	أسبوعي
every week (adv)	usbū'iyyan	أسبوعيًا
twice a week	marratayn fil usbū'	مرّتين في الأسبوع
every Tuesday	kull yawm aθ θulaθā'	كل يوم الثلاثاء

20. Hours. Day and night

morning	ṣabāḥ (m)	صباح
in the morning	fiṣ ṣabāḥ	في الصباح

noon, midday	ẓuhr (m)	ظهر
in the afternoon	ba'd aẓ ẓuhr	بعد الظهر
evening	masā' (m)	مساء
in the evening	fil masā'	في المساء
night	layl (m)	ليل
at night	bil layl	بالليل
midnight	muntaṣif al layl (m)	منتصف الليل
second	θāniya (f)	ثانية
minute	daqīqa (f)	دقيقة
hour	sā'a (f)	ساعة
half an hour	niṣf sā'a (m)	نصف ساعة
a quarter-hour	rub' sā'a (f)	ربع ساعة
fifteen minutes	xamsat 'aʃar daqīqa	خمس عشرة دقيقة
24 hours	yawm kāmil (m)	يوم كامل
sunrise	ʃurūq aʃ ʃams (m)	شروق الشمس
dawn	faȝr (m)	فجر
early morning	ṣabāḥ bākir (m)	صباح باكر
sunset	ɣurūb aʃ ʃams (m)	غروب الشمس
early in the morning	fis ṣabāḥ al bākir	في الصباح الباكر
this morning	al yawm fiṣ ṣabāḥ	اليوم في الصباح
tomorrow morning	ɣadan fiṣ ṣabāḥ	غدًا في الصباح
this afternoon	al yawm ba'd aẓ ẓuhr	اليوم بعد الظهر
in the afternoon	ba'd aẓ ẓuhr	بعد الظهر
tomorrow afternoon	ɣadan ba'd aẓ ẓuhr	غدًا بعد الظهر
tonight (this evening)	al yawm fil masā'	اليوم في المساء
tomorrow night	ɣadan fil masā'	غدًا في المساء
at 3 o'clock sharp	fis sā'a aθ θāliθa tamāman	في الساعة الثالثة تماما
about 4 o'clock	fis sā'a ar rābi'a taqrīban	في الساعة الرابعة تقريبا
by 12 o'clock	ḥattas sā'a aθ θāniya 'aʃara	حتى الساعة الثانية عشرة
in 20 minutes	ba'd 'iʃrīn daqīqa	بعد عشرين دقيقة
in an hour	ba'd sā'a	بعد ساعة
on time (adv)	fi maw'idih	في موعده
a quarter of ...	illa rub'	إلا ربع
within an hour	ṭiwāl sā'a	طوال الساعة
every 15 minutes	kull rub' sā'a	كل ربع ساعة
round the clock	layl nahār	ليل نهار

21. Months. Seasons

January	yanāyir (m)	يناير
February	fibrāyir (m)	فبراير

March	māris (m)	مارس
April	abrīl (m)	أبريل
May	māyu (m)	مايو
June	yūnyu (m)	يونيو
July	yūlyu (m)	يوليو
August	aɣusṭus (m)	أغسطس
September	sibtambar (m)	سبتمبر
October	uktūbir (m)	أكتوبر
November	nuvimbar (m)	نوفمبر
December	disimbar (m)	ديسمبر
spring	rabīʿ (m)	ربيع
in spring	fir rabīʿ	في الربيع
spring (as adj)	rabīʿiy	ربيعي
summer	ṣayf (m)	صيف
in summer	fiṣ ṣayf	في الصيف
summer (as adj)	ṣayfiy	صيفي
fall	xarīf (m)	خريف
in fall	fil xarīf	في الخريف
fall (as adj)	xarīfiy	خريفي
winter	ʃitāʾ (m)	شتاء
in winter	fiʃ ʃitāʾ	في الشتاء
winter (as adj)	ʃitawiy	شتوي
month	ʃahr (m)	شهر
this month	fi haða aʃ ʃahr	في هذا الشهر
next month	fiʃ ʃahr al qādim	في الشهر القادم
last month	fiʃ ʃahr al māḍi	في الشهر الماضي
a month ago	qabl ʃahr	قبل شهر
in a month (a month later)	baʿd ʃahr	بعد شهر
in 2 months (2 months later)	baʿd ʃahrayn	بعد شهرين
the whole month	ṭūl aʃ ʃahr	طول الشهر
all month long	ʃahr kāmil	شهر كامل
monthly (~ magazine)	ʃahriy	شهري
monthly (adv)	kull ʃahr	كل شهر
every month	kull ʃahr	كل شهر
twice a month	marratayn fiʃ ʃahr	مرّتين في الشهر
year	sana (f)	سنة
this year	fi haðihi as sana	في هذه السنة
next year	fis sana al qādima	في السنة القادمة
last year	fis sana al māḍiya	في السنة الماضية
a year ago	qabla sana	قبل سنة
in a year	baʿd sana	بعد سنة

in two years	ba'd sanatayn	بعد سنتين
the whole year	ṭūl as sana	طول السنة
all year long	sana kāmila	سنة كاملة
every year	kull sana	كل سنة
annual (adj)	sanawiy	سنويّ
annually (adv)	kull sana	كل سنة
4 times a year	arba' marrāt fis sana	أربع مرّات في السنة
date (e.g., today's ~)	tarīχ (m)	تاريخ
date (e.g., ~ of birth)	tarīχ (m)	تاريخ
calendar	taqwīm (m)	تقويم
half a year	niṣf sana (m)	نصف سنة
six months	niṣf sana (m)	نصف سنة
season (summer, etc.)	faṣl (m)	فصل
century	qarn (m)	قرن

22. Time. Miscellaneous

time	waqt (m)	وقت
moment	laḥẓa (f)	لحظة
instant (n)	laḥẓa (f)	لحظة
instant (adj)	χāṭif	خاطف
lapse (of time)	fatra (f)	فترة
life	ḥayāt (f)	حياة
eternity	abadiyya (f)	أبديّة
epoch	'ahd (m)	عهد
era	'aṣr (m)	عصر
cycle	dawra (f)	دورة
period	fatra (f)	فترة
term (short-~)	fatra (f)	فترة
the future	al mustaqbal (m)	المستقبل
future (as adj)	qādim	قادم
next time	fil marra al qādima	في المرّة القادمة
the past	al māḍi (m)	الماضي
past (recent)	māḍi	ماض
last time	fil marra al māḍiya	في المرّة الماضية
later (adv)	fima ba'd	فيما بعد
after (prep.)	ba'd	بعد
nowadays (adv)	fi haðihi al ayyām	في هذه الأيام
now (adv)	al 'ān	الآن
immediately (adv)	ḥālan	حالًا
soon (adv)	qarīban	قريبًا
in advance (beforehand)	muqaddaman	مقدّمًا
a long time ago	min zamān	من زمان
recently (adv)	min zaman qarīb	من زمان قريب

destiny	maṣīr (m)	مصير
memories (childhood ~)	ðikra (f)	ذكرى
archives	arʃīf (m)	أرشيف

during ...	aθnā'...	أثناء...
long, a long time (adv)	li mudda ṭawīla	لمدّة طويلة
not long (adv)	li mudda qaṣīra	لمدّة قصيرة
early (in the morning)	bākiran	باكرًا
late (not early)	muta'axxiran	متأخّرًا

forever (for good)	lil abad	للأبد
to start (begin)	bada'	بدأ
to postpone (vt)	aʒʒal	أجّل

at the same time	fi nafs al waqt	في نفس الوقت
permanently (adv)	dā'iman	دائمًا
constant (noise, pain)	mustamirr	مستمرّ
temporary (adj)	mu'aqqat	مؤقّت

sometimes (adv)	min ḥīn li 'āxar	من حين لآخر
rarely (adv)	nādiran	نادرًا
often (adv)	kaθīran	كثيرًا

23. Opposites

| rich (adj) | ɣaniy | غنيّ |
| poor (adj) | faqīr | فقير |

| ill, sick (adj) | marīḍ | مريض |
| well (not sick) | salīm | سليم |

| big (adj) | kabīr | كبير |
| small (adj) | ṣaɣīr | صغير |

| quickly (adv) | bi sur'a | بسرعة |
| slowly (adv) | bi buṭ' | ببطء |

| fast (adj) | sarī‘ | سريع |
| slow (adj) | baṭī' | بطيء |

| glad (adj) | farḥān | فرحان |
| sad (adj) | ḥazīn | حزين |

| together (adv) | ma‘an | معًا |
| separately (adv) | bi mufradih | بمفرده |

aloud (to read)	bi ṣawt 'āli	بصوت عال
silently (to oneself)	sirran	سرًا
tall (adj)	'āli	عال
low (adj)	munxafiḍ	منخفض

deep (adj)	ʿamīq	عميق
shallow (adj)	ḍaḥl	ضحل
yes	naʿam	نعم
no	la	لا
distant (in space)	baʿīd	بعيد
nearby (adj)	qarīb	قريب
far (adv)	baʿīdan	بعيدًا
nearby (adv)	qarīban	قريبًا
long (adj)	ṭawīl	طويل
short (adj)	qaṣīr	قصير
good (kindhearted)	ṭayyib	طيّب
evil (adj)	ʃarīr	شرير
married (adj)	mutazawwiʒ	متزوّج
single (adj)	aʿzab	أعزب
to forbid (vt)	manaʿ	منع
to permit (vt)	samaḥ	سمح
end	nihāya (f)	نهاية
beginning	bidāya (f)	بداية
left (adj)	al yasār	اليسار
right (adj)	al yamīn	اليمين
first (adj)	awwal	أوّل
last (adj)	ʾāχir	آخر
crime	ʒarīma (f)	جريمة
punishment	ʿuqūba (f), ʿiqāb (m)	عقوبة، عقاب
to order (vt)	amar	أمر
to obey (vi, vt)	ṭāʿ	طاع
straight (adj)	mustaqīm	مستقيم
curved (adj)	munḥani	منحن
paradise	al ʒanna (f)	الجنّة
hell	al ʒaḥīm (f)	الجحيم
to be born	wulid	وُلد
to die (vi)	māt	مات
strong (adj)	qawiy	قويّ
weak (adj)	ḍaʿīf	ضعيف
old (adj)	ʿaʒūz	عجوز
young (adj)	ʃābb	شابّ

| old (adj) | qadīm | قديم |
| new (adj) | ʒadīd | جديد |

| hard (adj) | ṣalb | صلب |
| soft (adj) | ṭariy | طري |

| warm (tepid) | dāfiʼ | دافئ |
| cold (adj) | bārid | بارد |

| fat (adj) | θaχīn | ثخين |
| thin (adj) | naḥīf | نحيف |

| narrow (adj) | ḍayyiq | ضيق |
| wide (adj) | wāsiʻ | واسع |

| good (adj) | ʒayyid | جيّد |
| bad (adj) | sayyiʼ | سيّئ |

| brave (adj) | ʃuʒāʻ | شجاع |
| cowardly (adj) | ʒabān | جبان |

24. Lines and shapes

square	murabbaʻ (m)	مربّع
square (as adj)	murabbaʻ	مربّع
circle	dāʼira (f)	دائرة
round (adj)	mudawwar	مدوّر
triangle	muθallaθ (m)	مثلّث
triangular (adj)	muθallaθ	مثلّث

oval	bayḍawiy (m)	بيضويّ
oval (as adj)	bayḍawiy	بيضويّ
rectangle	mustaṭīl (m)	مستطيل
rectangular (adj)	mustaṭīliy	مستطيليّ

pyramid	haram (m)	هرم
rhombus	muʻayyan (m)	معيّن
trapezoid	murabbaʻ munḥarif (m)	مربّع منحرف
cube	mukaʻʻab (m)	مكعّب
prism	manʃūr (m)	منشور

| circumference | muḥīṭ munḥanan muɣlaq (m) | محيط منحنى مغلق |

sphere	kura (f)	كرة
ball (solid sphere)	kura (f)	كرة
diameter	quṭr (m)	قطر
radius	niṣf qaṭr (m)	نصف قطر
perimeter (circle's ~)	muḥīṭ (m)	محيط
center	wasaṭ (m)	وسط
horizontal (adj)	ufuqiy	أفقيّ

vertical (adj)	ʿamūdiy	عمودي
parallel (n)	χaṭṭ mutawāzi (m)	خط متواز
parallel (as adj)	mutawāzi	متواز

line	χaṭṭ (m)	خط
stroke	ḥaraka (m)	حركة
straight line	χaṭṭ mustaqīm (m)	خط مستقيم
curve (curved line)	χaṭṭ munḥani (m)	خط منحن
thin (line, etc.)	rafīʿ	رفيع
contour (outline)	kuntūr (m)	كنتور

intersection	taqāṭuʿ (m)	تقاطع
right angle	zāwya mustaqīma (f)	زاوية مستقيمة
segment	qiṭʿa (f)	قطعة
sector	qiṭāʿ (m)	قطاع
side (of triangle)	ḍilʿ (m)	ضلع
angle	zāwiya (f)	زاوية

25. Units of measurement

weight	wazn (m)	وزن
length	ṭūl (m)	طول
width	ʿarḍ (m)	عرض
height	irtifāʿ (m)	إرتفاع
depth	ʿumq (m)	عمق
volume	ḥaʒm (m)	حجم
area	misāḥa (f)	مساحة

gram	grām (m)	جرام
milligram	milliɣrām (m)	مليغرام
kilogram	kiluɣrām (m)	كيلوغرام
ton	ṭunn (m)	طن
pound	raṭl (m)	رطل
ounce	ūnṣa (f)	أونصة

meter	mitr (m)	متر
millimeter	millimitr (m)	مليمتر
centimeter	santimitr (m)	سنتيمتر
kilometer	kilumitr (m)	كيلومتر
mile	mīl (m)	ميل

inch	būṣa (f)	بوصة
foot	qadam (f)	قدم
yard	yārda (f)	ياردة

| square meter | mitr murabbaʿ (m) | متر مربّع |
| hectare | hiktār (m) | هكتار |

| liter | litr (m) | لتر |
| degree | daraʒa (f) | درجة |

volt	vūlt (m)	فولت
ampere	ambīr (m)	أمبير
horsepower	ḥiṣān (m)	حصان

quantity	kammiyya (f)	كمّية
a little bit of ...	qalīl ...	قليل...
half	niṣf (m)	نصف
dozen	iθnā 'aʃar (f)	إثنا عشر
piece (item)	waḥda (f)	وحدة

| size | ḥaзm (m) | حجم |
| scale (map ~) | miqyās (m) | مقياس |

minimal (adj)	al adna	الأدنى
the smallest (adj)	al aṣyar	الأصغر
medium (adj)	mutawassiṭ	متوسّط
maximal (adj)	al aqṣa	الأقصى
the largest (adj)	al akbar	الأكبر

26. Containers

| canning jar (glass ~) | barṭamān (m) | برطمان |
| can | tanaka (f) | تنكة |

| bucket | зardal (m) | جردل |
| barrel | barmīl (m) | برميل |

wash basin (e.g., plastic ~)	ḥawḍ lil yasīl (m)	حوض للغسيل
tank (100L water ~)	xazzān (m)	خزّان
hip flask	zamzamiyya (f)	زمزمية
jerrycan	зirikan (m)	جركن
tank (e.g., tank car)	xazzān (m)	خزّان

mug	māgg (m)	ماجّ
cup (of coffee, etc.)	finзān (m)	فنجان
saucer	ṭabaq finзān (m)	طبق فنجان

glass (tumbler)	kubbāya (f)	كبّاية
wine glass	ka's (f)	كأس
stock pot (soup pot)	kassirūlla (f)	كاسرولة

| bottle (~ of wine) | zuзāзa (f) | زجاجة |
| neck (of the bottle, etc.) | 'unq (m) | عنق |

carafe (decanter)	dawraq zuзāзiy (m)	دورق زجاجيّ
pitcher	ibrīq (m)	إبريق
vessel (container)	inā' (m)	إناء
pot (crock, stoneware ~)	aṣīṣ (m)	أصيص
vase	vāza (f)	فازة
bottle (perfume ~)	zuзāзa (f)	زجاجة

vial, small bottle	zuʒāʒa (f)	زجاجة
tube (of toothpaste)	umbūba (f)	أنبوبة
sack (bag)	kīs (m)	كيس
bag (paper ~, plastic ~)	kīs (m)	كيس
pack (of cigarettes, etc.)	'ulba (f)	علبة
box (e.g., shoebox)	'ulba (f)	علبة
crate	şundū' (m)	صندوق
basket	salla (f)	سلة

27. Materials

material	mādda (f)	مادّة
wood (n)	xaʃab (m)	خشب
wood-, wooden (adj)	xaʃabiy	خشبيّ
glass (n)	zuʒāʒ (m)	زجاج
glass (as adj)	zuʒāʒiy	زجاجيّ
stone (n)	haʒar (m)	حجر
stone (as adj)	haʒariy	حجريّ
plastic (n)	blastīk (m)	بلاستيك
plastic (as adj)	min al blastīk	من البلاستيك
rubber (n)	maṭṭāṭ (m)	مطّاط
rubber (as adj)	maṭṭāṭiy	مطّاطيّ
cloth, fabric (n)	qumāʃ (m)	قماش
fabric (as adj)	min al qumāʃ	من القماش
paper (n)	waraq (m)	ورق
paper (as adj)	waraqiy	ورقيّ
cardboard (n)	kartūn (m)	كرتون
cardboard (as adj)	kartūniy	كرتونيّ
polyethylene	buli iθilīn (m)	بولي إثيلين
cellophane	silufān (m)	سيلوفان
plywood	ablakāʃ (m)	أبلكاش
porcelain (n)	bursilān (m)	بورسلان
porcelain (as adj)	min il bursilān	من البورسلان
clay (n)	ṭīn (m)	طين
clay (as adj)	faxxāry	فخّاري
ceramic (n)	siramīk (m)	سيراميك
ceramic (as adj)	siramīkiy	سيراميكيّ

28. Metals

metal (n)	ma'dan (m)	معدن
metal (as adj)	ma'daniy	معدني
alloy (n)	sabīka (f)	سبيكة
gold (n)	ðahab (m)	ذهب
gold, golden (adj)	ðahabiy	ذهبي
silver (n)	fiḍḍa (f)	فضة
silver (as adj)	fiḍḍiy	فضي
iron (n)	ḥadīd (m)	حديد
iron-, made of iron (adj)	ḥadīdiy	حديدي
steel (n)	fūlāð (m)	فولاذ
steel (as adj)	fulāðiy	فولاذي
copper (n)	nuḥās (m)	نحاس
copper (as adj)	nuḥāsiy	نحاسي
aluminum (n)	alumīniyum (m)	الومينيوم
aluminum (as adj)	alumīniyum	الومينيوم
bronze (n)	brūnz (m)	برونز
bronze (as adj)	brūnziy	برونزي
brass	nuḥās aṣfar (m)	نحاس أصفر
nickel	nikil (m)	نيكل
platinum	blatīn (m)	بلاتين
mercury	zi'baq (m)	زئبق
tin	qaṣdīr (m)	قصدير
lead	ruṣāṣ (m)	رصاص
zinc	zink (m)	زنك

HUMAN BEING

Human being. The body

29. Humans. Basic concepts

human being	insān (m)	إنسان
man (adult male)	raӡul (m)	رجل
woman	imra'a (f)	إمرأة
child	ṭifl (m)	طفل
girl	bint (f)	بنت
boy	walad (m)	ولد
teenager	murāhiq (m)	مراهق
old man	ʻaӡūz (m)	عجوز
old woman	ʻaӡūza (f)	عجوزة

30. Human anatomy

organism (body)	ӡism (m)	جسم
heart	qalb (m)	قلب
blood	dam (m)	دم
artery	ʃaryān (m)	شريان
vein	ʻirq (m)	عرق
brain	muχχ (m)	مخّ
nerve	ʻaṣab (m)	عصب
nerves	a'ṣāb (pl)	أعصاب
vertebra	faqra (f)	فقرة
spine (backbone)	ʻamūd faqriy (m)	عمود فقريّ
stomach (organ)	ma'ida (f)	معدة
intestines, bowels	am'ā' (pl)	أمعاء
intestine (e.g., large ~)	mi'an (m)	معى
liver	kibd (f)	كبد
kidney	kilya (f)	كلية
bone	ʻaӡm (m)	عظم
skeleton	haykal ʻaӡmiy (m)	هيكل عظميّ
rib	ḍil' (m)	ضلع
skull	ӡumӡuma (f)	جمجمة
muscle	ʻaḍala (f)	عضلة
biceps	ʻaḍala ðāt ra'sayn (f)	عضلة ذات رأسين

43

triceps	'aḍla θulāθiyyat ar ru'ūs (f)	عضلة ثلاثية الرءوس
tendon	watar (m)	وتر
joint	mafṣil (m)	مفصل
lungs	ri'atān (du)	رئتان
genitals	a'ḍā' ʒinsiyya (pl)	أعضاء جنسيّة
skin	buʃra (m)	بشرة

31. Head

head	ra's (m)	رأس
face	waʒh (m)	وجه
nose	anf (m)	أنف
mouth	fam (m)	فم

eye	'ayn (f)	عين
eyes	'uyūn (pl)	عيون
pupil	ḥadaqa (f)	حدقة
eyebrow	ḥāʒib (m)	حاجب
eyelash	rimʃ (m)	رمش
eyelid	ʒafn (m)	جفن

tongue	lisān (m)	لسان
tooth	sinn (f)	سنّ
lips	ʃifāh (pl)	شفاه
cheekbones	'iẓām waʒhiyya (pl)	عظام وجهيّة
gum	liθθa (f)	لثة
palate	ḥanak (m)	حنك

nostrils	minxarān (du)	منخران
chin	ðaqan (m)	ذقن
jaw	fakk (m)	فكّ
cheek	xadd (m)	خدّ

forehead	ʒabha (f)	جبهة
temple	ṣudɣ (m)	صدغ
ear	uðun (f)	أذن
back of the head	qafa (m)	قفا
neck	raqaba (f)	رقبة
throat	ḥalq (m)	حلق

hair	ʃa'r (m)	شعر
hairstyle	tasrīḥa (f)	تسريحة
haircut	tasrīḥa (f)	تسريحة
wig	barūka (f)	باروكة

mustache	ʃawārib (pl)	شوارب
beard	liḥya (f)	لحية
to have (a beard, etc.)	'indahu	عنده
braid	ḍifīra (f)	ضفيرة
sideburns	sawālif (pl)	سوالف

red-haired (adj)	aḥmar aʃ ʃaʼr	أحمر الشعر
gray (hair)	abyaḍ	أبيض
bald (adj)	aṣlaʻ	أصلع
bald patch	ṣalaʻ (m)	صلع
ponytail	ðayl ḥiṣān (m)	ذيل حصان
bangs	quṣṣa (f)	قصّة

32. Human body

hand	yad (m)	يد
arm	ðirāʻ (f)	ذراع
finger	iṣbaʻ (m)	إصبع
toe	iṣbaʻ al qadam (m)	إصبع القدم
thumb	ibhām (m)	إبهام
little finger	χunṣur (m)	خنصر
nail	ẓufr (m)	ظفر
fist	qabḍa (f)	قبضة
palm	kaff (f)	كفّ
wrist	miʻṣam (m)	معصم
forearm	sāʻid (m)	ساعد
elbow	mirfaq (m)	مرفق
shoulder	katf (f)	كتف
leg	riʒl (f)	رجل
foot	qadam (f)	قدم
knee	rukba (f)	ركبة
calf (part of leg)	sammāna (f)	سمّانة
hip	faχð (f)	فخذ
heel	ʻaqb (m)	عقب
body	ʒism (m)	جسم
stomach	baṭn (m)	بطن
chest	ṣadr (m)	صدر
breast	θady (m)	ثدي
flank	ʒamb (m)	جنب
back	ẓahr (m)	ظهر
lower back	asfal aẓ ẓahr (m)	أسفل الظهر
waist	χaṣr (m)	خصر
navel (belly button)	surra (f)	سرّة
buttocks	ardāf (pl)	أرداف
bottom	dubr (m)	دبر
beauty mark	ʃāma (f)	شامة
birthmark (café au lait spot)	waḥma	وحمة
tattoo	waʃm (m)	وشم
scar	nadba (f)	ندبة

Clothing & Accessories

33. Outerwear. Coats

clothes	malābis (pl)	ملابس
outerwear	malābis fawqāniyya (pl)	ملابس فوقانيّة
winter clothing	malābis ʃitawiyya (pl)	ملابس شتويّة
coat (overcoat)	miʿṭaf (m)	معطف
fur coat	miʿṭaf farw (m)	معطف فرو
fur jacket	ʒakīt farw (m)	جاكيت فرو
down coat	ḥaʃiyyat rīʃ (m)	حشية ريش
jacket (e.g., leather ~)	ʒakīt (m)	جاكيت
raincoat (trenchcoat, etc.)	miʿṭaf lil maṭar (m)	معطف للمطر
waterproof (adj)	ṣāmid lil māʾ	صامد للماء

34. Men's & women's clothing

shirt (button shirt)	qamīṣ (m)	قميص
pants	banṭalūn (m)	بنطلون
jeans	ʒīnz (m)	جينز
suit jacket	sutra (f)	سترة
suit	badla (f)	بدلة
dress (frock)	fustān (m)	فستان
skirt	tannūra (f)	تنّورة
blouse	blūza (f)	بلوزة
knitted jacket (cardigan, etc.)	kardigān (m)	كارديجان
jacket (of woman's suit)	ʒakīt (m)	جاكيت
T-shirt	ti ʃirt (m)	تي شيرت
shorts (short trousers)	ʃūrt (m)	شورت
tracksuit	badlat at tadrīb (f)	بدلة التدريب
bathrobe	θawb ḥammām (m)	ثوب حمّام
pajamas	biʒāma (f)	بيجاما
sweater	bulūvir (m)	بلوفر
pullover	bulūvir (m)	بلوفر
vest	ṣudayriy (m)	صديريّ
tailcoat	badlat sahra (f)	بدلة سهرة
tuxedo	smūkin (m)	سموكن

uniform	zayy muwaḥḥad (m)	زي موحّد
workwear	θiyāb al ʻamal (m)	ثياب العمل
overalls	uvirūl (m)	اوفرول
coat (e.g., doctor's smock)	θawb (m)	ثوب

35. Clothing. Underwear

underwear	malābis dāχiliyya (pl)	ملابس داخليّة
boxers, briefs	sirwāl dāχiliy riǧaliy (m)	سروال داخلي رجاليّ
panties	sirwāl dāχiliy nisāʼiy (m)	سروال داخلي نسائي
undershirt (A-shirt)	qamīṣ bila aqmām (m)	قميص بلا أكمام
socks	ʒawārib (pl)	جوارب

nightgown	qamīṣ nawm (m)	قميص نوم
bra	ḥammālat ṣadr (f)	حمّالة صدر
knee highs (knee-high socks)	ʒawārib ṭawīla (pl)	جوارب طويلة

pantyhose	ʒawārib kulūn (pl)	جوارب كولون
stockings (thigh highs)	ʒawārib nisāʼiyya (pl)	جوارب نسائية
bathing suit	libās sibāḥa (m)	لباس سباحة

36. Headwear

hat	qubbaʻa (f)	قبّعة
fedora	burnayṭa (f)	برنيطة
baseball cap	kāb baysbūl (m)	كاب بيسبول
flatcap	qubbaʻa musaṭṭaḥa (f)	قبّعة مسطحة

beret	birīh (m)	بيريه
hood	γiṭāʼ (m)	غطاء
panama hat	qubbaʻat banāma (f)	قبّعة بناما
knit cap (knitted hat)	qubbāʻa maḥbūka (m)	قبّعة محبوكة

headscarf	ʼīǧārb (m)	إيشارب
women's hat	burnayṭa (f)	برنيطة
hard hat	χūða (f)	خوذة
garrison cap	kāb (m)	كاب
helmet	χūða (f)	خوذة

| derby | qubbaʻat dirbi (f) | قبّعة ديربي |
| top hat | qubbaʻa ʻāliya (f) | قبّعة عالية |

37. Footwear

| footwear | aḥðiya (pl) | أحذية |
| shoes (men's shoes) | ʒazma (f) | جزمة |

shoes (women's shoes)	ʒazma (f)	جزمة
boots (e.g., cowboy ~)	būt (m)	بوت
slippers	ʃibʃib (m)	شبشب
tennis shoes (e.g., Nike ~)	ḥiðāʼ riyāḍiy (m)	حذاء رياضيّ
sneakers	kutʃi (m)	كوتشي
(e.g., Converse ~)		
sandals	ṣandal (pl)	صندل
cobbler (shoe repairer)	iskāfiy (m)	إسكافيّ
heel	kaʻb (m)	كعب
pair (of shoes)	zawʒ (m)	زوج
shoestring	ʃarīṭ (m)	شريط
to lace (vt)	rabaṭ	ربط
shoehorn	labbāsat ḥiðāʼ (f)	لبّاسة حذاء
shoe polish	warnīʃ al ḥiðāʼ (m)	ورنيش الحذاء

38. Textile. Fabrics

cotton (n)	quṭn (m)	قطن
cotton (as adj)	min al quṭn	من القطن
flax (n)	kattān (m)	كتّان
flax (as adj)	min il kattān	من الكتّان
silk (n)	ḥarīr (m)	حرير
silk (as adj)	min al ḥarīr	من الحرير
wool (n)	ṣūf (m)	صوف
wool (as adj)	min aṣ ṣūf	من الصوف
velvet	muxmal (m)	مخمل
suede	ʒild ʃāmwāh (m)	جلد شامواه
corduroy	quṭn qaṭīfa (f)	قطن قطيفة
nylon (n)	naylūn (m)	نايلون
nylon (as adj)	min an naylūn	من النيلون
polyester (n)	bulyistir (m)	بوليستر
polyester (as adj)	min al bulyastar	من البوليستر
leather (n)	ʒild (m)	جلد
leather (as adj)	min al ʒild	من الجلد
fur (n)	farw (m)	فرو
fur (e.g., ~ coat)	min al farw	من الفرو

39. Personal accessories

gloves	quffāz (m)	قفّاز
mittens	quffāz muɣlaq (m)	قفّاز مغلق

scarf (muffler)	ʃārb (m)	إيشارب
glasses (eyeglasses)	nazzāra (f)	نظّارة
frame (eyeglass ~)	iṭār (m)	إطار
umbrella	ʃamsiyya (f)	شمسيّة
walking stick	'aṣa (f)	عصا
hairbrush	furʃat ʃa'r (f)	فرشة شعر
fan	mirwaha yadawiyya (f)	مروحة يدويّة

tie (necktie)	karavatta (f)	كرافتة
bow tie	babyūn (m)	بيبون
suspenders	hammāla (f)	حمّالة
handkerchief	mandīl (m)	منديل

comb	miʃṭ (m)	مشط
barrette	dabbūs (m)	دبّوس
hairpin	bansa (m)	بنسة
buckle	bukla (f)	بكلة

| belt | hizām (m) | حزام |
| shoulder strap | hammalat al katf (f) | حمّالة الكتف |

bag (handbag)	ʃanṭa (f)	شنطة
purse	ʃanṭat yad (f)	شنطة يد
backpack	haqībat zahr (f)	حقيبة ظهر

40. Clothing. Miscellaneous

fashion	mūḍa (f)	موضة
in vogue (adj)	fil mūḍa	في الموضة
fashion designer	muṣammim azyā' (m)	مصمّم أزياء

collar	yāqa (f)	ياقة
pocket	ʒayb (m)	جيب
pocket (as adj)	ʒayb	جيب
sleeve	kumm (m)	كمّ
hanging loop	'allāqa (f)	علّاقة
fly (on trousers)	lisān (m)	لسان

zipper (fastener)	zimām munzaliq (m)	زمام منزلق
fastener	miʃbak (m)	مشبك
button	zirr (m)	زرّ
buttonhole	'urwa (f)	عروة
to come off (ab. button)	waqa'	وقع

to sew (vi, vt)	xāṭ	خاط
to embroider (vi, vt)	ṭarraz	طرّز
embroidery	taṭrīz (m)	تطريز
sewing needle	ibra (f)	إبرة
thread	xayṭ (m)	خيط
seam	darz (m)	درز

to get dirty (vi)	tawassaχ	توسّخ
stain (mark, spot)	buqʻa (f)	بقعة
to crease, crumple (vi)	takarmaʃ	تكرمش
to tear, to rip (vt)	qaṭṭaʻ	قطّع
clothes moth	ʻuθθa (f)	عثّة

41. Personal care. Cosmetics

toothpaste	maʻʒūn asnān (m)	معجون أسنان
toothbrush	furʃat asnān (f)	فرشة أسنان
to brush one's teeth	nazzaf al asnān	نظّف الأسنان
razor	mūs ḥilāqa (m)	موس حلاقة
shaving cream	krīm ḥilāqa (m)	كريم حلاقة
to shave (vi)	ḥalaq	حلق
soap	ṣābūn (m)	صابون
shampoo	ʃāmbū (m)	شامبو
scissors	maqaṣṣ (m)	مقصّ
nail file	mibrad (m)	مبرد
nail clippers	milqaṭ (m)	ملقط
tweezers	milqaṭ (m)	ملقط
cosmetics	mawādd at taʒmīl (pl)	موادّ التجميل
face mask	mask (m)	ماسك
manicure	manikūr (m)	مانيكور
to have a manicure	ʻamal manikūr	عمل مانيكور
pedicure	badikīr (m)	باديكير
make-up bag	ḥaqībat adawāt at taʒmīl (f)	حقيبة أدوات التجميل
face powder	budrat waʒh (f)	بودرة وجه
powder compact	ʻulbat būdra (f)	علبة بودرة
blusher	aḥmar χudūd (m)	أحمر خدود
perfume (bottled)	ʻiṭr (m)	عطر
toilet water (lotion)	kulūnya (f)	كولونيا
lotion	lusiyun (m)	لوسيون
cologne	kulūniya (f)	كولونيا
eyeshadow	ay ʃaduw (m)	اي شادو
eyeliner	kuḥl al ʻuyūn (m)	كحل العيون
mascara	maskara (f)	ماسكارا
lipstick	aḥmar ʃifāh (m)	أحمر شفاه
nail polish, enamel	mulammiʻ al aẓāfir (m)	ملمّع الاظافر
hair spray	muθabbit aʃ ʃaʻr (m)	مثبّت الشعر
deodorant	muzīl rawāʼiḥ (m)	مزيل روائح
cream	krīm (m)	كريم
face cream	krīm lil waʒh (m)	كريم للوجه

hand cream	krīm lil yadayn (m)	كريم لليدين
anti-wrinkle cream	krīm muḍādd lit taǧā'īd (m)	كريم مضادّ للتجاعيد
day cream	krīm an nahār (m)	كريم النهار
night cream	krīm al layl (m)	كريم الليل
day (as adj)	nahāriy	نهاريّ
night (as adj)	layliy	ليليّ

tampon	tambūn (m)	تانبون
toilet paper (toilet roll)	waraq ḥammām (m)	ورق حمّام
hair dryer	muǧaffif ʃaʻr (m)	مجفف شعر

42. Jewelry

jewelry	muǧawharāt (pl)	مجوهرات
precious (e.g., ~ stone)	karīm	كريم
hallmark stamp	damɣa (f)	دمغة

ring	xātim (m)	خاتم
wedding ring	diblat al xuṭūba (m)	دبلة الخطوبة
bracelet	siwār (m)	سوار

earrings	ḥalaq (m)	حلق
necklace (~ of pearls)	ʻaqd (m)	عقد
crown	tāǧ (m)	تاج
bead necklace	ʻaqd xaraz (m)	عقد خرز

diamond	almās (m)	الماس
emerald	zumurrud (m)	زمرّد
ruby	yāqūt aḥmar (m)	ياقوت أحمر
sapphire	yāqūt azraq (m)	ياقوت أزرق
pearl	luʼluʼ (m)	لؤلؤ
amber	kahramān (m)	كهرمان

43. Watches. Clocks

watch (wristwatch)	sāʻa (f)	ساعة
dial	waǧh as sāʻa (m)	وجه الساعة
hand (of clock, watch)	ʻaqrab as sāʻa (m)	عقرب الساعة
metal watch band	siwār sāʻa maʻdaniyya (m)	سوار ساعة معدنية
watch strap	siwār sāʻa (m)	سوار ساعة

battery	baṭṭāriyya (f)	بطّاريّة
to be dead (battery)	tafarraɣ	تفرّغ
to change a battery	ɣayyar al baṭṭāriyya	غيّر البطّاريّة
to run fast	sabaq	سبق
to run slow	taʼaxxar	تأخّر
wall clock	sāʻat ḥāʼiṭ (f)	ساعة حائط
hourglass	sāʻa ramliyya (f)	ساعة رمليّة

sundial	sā'a ʃamsiyya (f)	ساعة شمسيّة
alarm clock	munabbih (m)	منبّه
watchmaker	sa'ātiy (m)	ساعاتيَ
to repair (vt)	aṣlaḥ	أصلح

Food. Nutricion

44. Food

meat	laḥm (m)	لحم
chicken	daʒāʒ (m)	دجاج
Rock Cornish hen (poussin)	farrūʒ (m)	فروج
duck	baṭṭa (f)	بطة
goose	iwazza (f)	إوزة
game	ṣayd (m)	صيد
turkey	daʒāʒ rūmiy (m)	دجاج رومي
pork	laḥm al ximzīr (m)	لحم الخنزير
veal	laḥm il ʻiʒl (m)	لحم العجل
lamb	laḥm aḍ ḍa'n (m)	لحم الضأن
beef	laḥm al baqar (m)	لحم البقر
rabbit	arnab (m)	أرنب
sausage (bologna, pepperoni, etc.)	suʒuq (m)	سجق
vienna sausage (frankfurter)	suʒuq (m)	سجق
bacon	bikūn (m)	بيكون
ham	hām (m)	هام
gammon	faxð ximzīr (m)	فخذ خنزير
pâté	ma'ʒūn laḥm (m)	معجون لحم
liver	kibda (f)	كبدة
hamburger (ground beef)	haʃwa (f)	حشوة
tongue	lisān (m)	لسان
egg	bayḍa (f)	بيضة
eggs	bayḍ (m)	بيض
egg white	bayāḍ al bayḍ (m)	بياض البيض
egg yolk	ṣafār al bayḍ (m)	صفار البيض
fish	samak (m)	سمك
seafood	fawākih al baḥr (pl)	فواكه البحر
caviar	kaviyār (m)	كافيار
crab	salṭaʻūn (m)	سلطعون
shrimp	ʒambari (m)	جمبري
oyster	maḥār (m)	محار
spiny lobster	karkand ʃāik (m)	كركند شائك
octopus	uxṭubūṭ (m)	أخطبوط

squid	kalmāri (m)	كالماري
sturgeon	samak al ḥaʃʃ (m)	سمك الحفش
salmon	salmūn (m)	سلمون
halibut	samak al halbūt (m)	سمك الهلبوت
cod	samak al qudd (m)	سمك القدّ
mackerel	usqumriy (m)	أسقمريّ
tuna	tūna (f)	تونة
eel	ḥankalīs (m)	حنكليس
trout	salmūn muraqqaṭ (m)	سلمون مرقّط
sardine	sardīn (m)	سردين
pike	samak al karāki (m)	سمك الكراكي
herring	rinʒa (f)	رنجة
bread	xubz (m)	خبز
cheese	ʒubna (f)	جبنة
sugar	sukkar (m)	سكّر
salt	milḥ (m)	ملح
rice	urz (m)	أرز
pasta (macaroni)	makarūna (f)	مكرونة
noodles	nūdlis (f)	نودلز
butter	zubda (f)	زبدة
vegetable oil	zayt (m)	زيت
sunflower oil	zayt ʿabīd aʃ ʃams (m)	زيت عبيد الشمس
margarine	marɣarīn (m)	مرغرين
olives	zaytūn (m)	زيتون
olive oil	zayt az zaytūn (m)	زيت الزيتون
milk	ḥalīb (m)	حليب
condensed milk	ḥalīb mukaθθaf (m)	حليب مكثّف
yogurt	yūɣurt (m)	يوغورت
sour cream	krīma ḥāmiḍa (f)	كريمة حامضة
cream (of milk)	krīma (f)	كريمة
mayonnaise	mayunīz (m)	مايونيز
buttercream	krīmat zubda (f)	كريمة زبدة
cereal grains (wheat, etc.)	ḥubūb (pl)	حبوب
flour	daqīq (m)	دقيق
canned food	muʿallabāt (pl)	معلّبات
cornflakes	kurn fliks (m)	كورن فليكس
honey	ʿasal (m)	عسل
jam	murabba (m)	مربّى
chewing gum	ʿilk (m)	علك

45. Drinks

water	mā' (m)	ماء
drinking water	mā' ʃurb (m)	ماء شرب
mineral water	mā' maʿdaniy (m)	ماء معدنيّ

still (adj)	bi dūn ɣāz	بدون غاز
carbonated (adj)	mukarban	مكربن
sparkling (adj)	bil ɣāz	بالغاز
ice	θalʒ (m)	ثلج
with ice	biθ θalʒ	بالثلج

non-alcoholic (adj)	bi dūn kuḥūl	بدون كحول
soft drink	maʃrūb ɣāziy (m)	مشروب غازي
refreshing drink	maʃrūb muθallaʒ (m)	مشروب مثلج
lemonade	ʃarāb laymūn (m)	شراب ليمون

liquors	maʃrūbāt kuḥūliyya (pl)	مشروبات كحوليّة
wine	nabīð (f)	نبيذ
white wine	nibīð abyaḍ (m)	نبيذ أبيض
red wine	nabīð aḥmar (m)	نبيذ أحمر

liqueur	liqiūr (m)	ليكيور
champagne	ʃambāniya (f)	شمبانيا
vermouth	virmut (m)	فيرموث

whiskey	wiski (m)	وسكي
vodka	vudka (f)	فودكا
gin	ʒīn (m)	جين
cognac	kunyāk (m)	كونياك
rum	rum (m)	رم

coffee	qahwa (f)	قهوة
black coffee	qahwa sāda (f)	قهوة سادة
coffee with milk	qahwa bil ḥalīb (f)	قهوة بالحليب
cappuccino	kaputʃīnu (m)	كابتشينو
instant coffee	niskafi (m)	نيسكافيه

milk	ḥalīb (m)	حليب
cocktail	kuktayl (m)	كوكتيل
milkshake	milk ʃiyk (m)	ميلك شيك

juice	ʿaṣīr (m)	عصير
tomato juice	ʿaṣīr ṭamāṭim (m)	عصير طماطم
orange juice	ʿaṣīr burtuqāl (m)	عصير برتقال
freshly squeezed juice	ʿaṣīr ṭāziʒ (m)	عصير طازج

beer	bīra (f)	بيرة
light beer	bīra xafīfa (f)	بيرة خفيفة
dark beer	bīra ɣāmiqa (f)	بيرة غامقة
tea	ʃāy (m)	شاي

| black tea | ʃāy aswad (m) | شاي أسود |
| green tea | ʃāy axḍar (m) | شاي أخضر |

46. Vegetables

| vegetables | xuḍār (pl) | خضار |
| greens | xuḍrawāt waraqiyya (pl) | خضروات ورقيّة |

tomato	ṭamāṭim (f)	طماطم
cucumber	xiyār (m)	خيار
carrot	ʒazar (m)	جزر
potato	baṭāṭis (f)	بطاطس
onion	baṣal (m)	بصل
garlic	θūm (m)	ثوم

cabbage	kurumb (m)	كرنب
cauliflower	qarnabīṭ (m)	قرنبيط
Brussels sprouts	kurumb brūksil (m)	كرنب بروكسل
broccoli	brukuli (m)	بركولي

beetroot	banʒar (m)	بنجر
eggplant	bātinʒān (m)	باذنجان
zucchini	kūsa (f)	كوسة
pumpkin	qarʿ (m)	قرع
turnip	lift (m)	لفت

parsley	baqdūnis (m)	بقدونس
dill	ʃabat (m)	شبت
lettuce	xass (m)	خسّ
celery	karafs (m)	كرفس
asparagus	halyūn (m)	هليون
spinach	sabānix (m)	سبانخ

pea	bisilla (f)	بسلة
beans	fūl (m)	فول
corn (maize)	ðura (f)	ذرّة
kidney bean	faṣūliya (f)	فاصوليا

bell pepper	filfil (m)	فلفل
radish	fiʒl (m)	فجل
artichoke	xurʃūf (m)	خرشوف

47. Fruits. Nuts

fruit	fākiha (f)	فاكهة
apple	tuffāḥa (f)	تفّاحة
pear	kummaθra (f)	كمّثرى
lemon	laymūn (m)	ليمون

orange	burtuqāl (m)	برتقال
strawberry (garden ~)	farawla (f)	فراولة
mandarin	yūsufiy (m)	يوسفي
plum	barqūq (m)	برقوق
peach	durrāq (m)	دراق
apricot	miʃmiʃ (f)	مشمش
raspberry	tūt al ʻullayq al aḥmar (m)	توت العليق الأحمر
pineapple	ananās (m)	أناناس
banana	mawz (m)	موز
watermelon	baṭṭīχ aḥmar (m)	بطيخ أحمر
grape	ʻinab (m)	عنب
cherry	karaz (m)	كرز
melon	baṭṭīχ aṣfar (f)	بطيخ أصفر
grapefruit	zinbāʻ (m)	زنباع
avocado	avukādu (f)	افوكاتو
papaya	babāya (m)	بابايا
mango	mangu (m)	مانجو
pomegranate	rummān (m)	رمان
redcurrant	kiʃmiʃ aḥmar (m)	كشمش أحمر
blackcurrant	ʻinab aθ θaʻlab al aswad (m)	عنب الثعلب الأسود
gooseberry	ʻinab aθ θaʻlab (m)	عنب الثعلب
bilberry	ʻinab al aḥrāʒ (m)	عنب الأحراج
blackberry	θamar al ʻullayk (m)	ثمر العليق
raisin	zabīb (m)	زبيب
fig	tīn (m)	تين
date	tamr (m)	تمر
peanut	fūl sudāniy (m)	فول سوداني
almond	lawz (m)	لوز
walnut	ʻayn al ʒamal (f)	عين الجمل
hazelnut	bunduq (m)	بندق
coconut	ʒawz al hind (m)	جوز هند
pistachios	fustuq (m)	فستق

48. Bread. Candy

bakers' confectionery (pastry)	ḥalawiyyāt (pl)	حلويّات
bread	χubz (m)	خبز
cookies	baskawīt (m)	بسكويت
chocolate (n)	ʃukulāta (f)	شكولاتة
chocolate (as adj)	biʃ ʃukulāta	بالشكولاتة
candy (wrapped)	bumbūn (m)	بونبون

cake (e.g., cupcake)	ka'k (m)	كعك
cake (e.g., birthday ~)	tūrta (f)	تورتة
pie (e.g., apple ~)	faṭīra (f)	فطيرة
filling (for cake, pie)	haʃwa (f)	حشوة
jam (whole fruit jam)	murabba (m)	مربّى
marmalade	marmalād (f)	مرملاد
waffles	wāfil (m)	وافل
ice-cream	muθallaʒāt (pl)	مثلّجات
pudding	būding (m)	بودنج

49. Cooked dishes

course, dish	waʒba (f)	وجبة
cuisine	maṭbax (m)	مطبخ
recipe	waṣfa (f)	وصفة
portion	waʒba (f)	وجبة
salad	sulṭa (f)	سلطة
soup	ʃūrba (f)	شوربة
clear soup (broth)	maraq (m)	مرق
sandwich (bread)	sandawitʃ (m)	ساندويتش
fried eggs	bayḍ maqliy (m)	بيض مقليّ
hamburger (beefburger)	hamburger (m)	هامبورجر
beefsteak	biftīk (m)	بفتيك
side dish	ṭabaq ʒānibiy (m)	طبق جانبيّ
spaghetti	spaɣitti (m)	سباغيتي
mashed potatoes	harīs baṭāṭis (m)	هريس بطاطس
pizza	bītza (f)	بيتزا
porridge (oatmeal, etc.)	'aṣīda (f)	عصيدة
omelet	bayḍ maxfūq (m)	بيض مخفوق
boiled (e.g., ~ beef)	maslūq	مسلوق
smoked (adj)	mudaxxin	مدخّن
fried (adj)	maqliy	مقليّ
dried (adj)	muʒaffaf	مجفّف
frozen (adj)	muʒammad	مجمّد
pickled (adj)	muxallil	مخلّل
sweet (sugary)	musakkar	مسكّر
salty (adj)	māliḥ	مالح
cold (adj)	bārid	بارد
hot (adj)	sāxin	ساخن
bitter (adj)	murr	مرّ
tasty (adj)	laðīð	لذيذ
to cook in boiling water	ṭabax	طبخ

to cook (dinner)	ḥaḍḍar	حضّر
to fry (vt)	qala	قلى
to heat up (food)	saxxan	سخّن

to salt (vt)	mallaḥ	ملّح
to pepper (vt)	falfal	فلفل
to grate (vt)	baʃar	بشر
peel (n)	qiʃra (f)	قشرة
to peel (vt)	qaʃʃar	قشّر

50. Spices

salt	milḥ (m)	ملح
salty (adj)	māliḥ	مالح
to salt (vt)	mallaḥ	ملّح

black pepper	filfil aswad (m)	فلفل أسود
red pepper (milled ~)	filfil aḥmar (m)	فلفل أحمر
mustard	ṣalṣat al xardal (f)	صلصة الخردل
horseradish	fiɉl ḥārr (m)	فجل حارّ

condiment	tābil (m)	تابل
spice	bahār (m)	بهار
sauce	ṣalṣa (f)	صلصة
vinegar	xall (m)	خلّ

anise	yānsūn (m)	يانسون
basil	rīḥān (m)	ريحان
cloves	qurumful (m)	قرنفل
ginger	zanɉabīl (m)	زنجبيل
coriander	kuzbara (f)	كزبرة
cinnamon	qirfa (f)	قرفة

sesame	simsim (m)	سمسم
bay leaf	awrāq al ɣār (pl)	أوراق الغار
paprika	babrika (f)	بابريكا
caraway	karāwiya (f)	كراوية
saffron	za'farān (m)	زعفران

51. Meals

| food | akl (m) | أكل |
| to eat (vi, vt) | akal | أكل |

breakfast	fuṭūr (m)	فطور
to have breakfast	afṭar	أفطر
lunch	ɣadā' (m)	غداء
to have lunch	taɣadda	تغدّى

dinner	'aʃā' (m)	عشاء
to have dinner	ta'aʃʃa	تعشّى
appetite	ʃahiyya (f)	شهيّة
Enjoy your meal!	hanīʾan marīʾan!	هنيئًا مريئًا!
to open (~ a bottle)	fataḥ	فتح
to spill (liquid)	dalaq	دلق
to spill out (vi)	indalaq	إندلق
to boil (vi)	ɣala	غلى
to boil (vt)	ɣala	غلى
boiled (~ water)	maɣliy	مغليّ
to chill, cool down (vt)	barrad	برّد
to chill (vi)	tabarrad	تبرّد
taste, flavor	ṭaʿm (m)	طعم
aftertaste	al maðāq al 'āliq fil fam (m)	المذاق العالق في الفم
to slim down (lose weight)	faqad al wazn	فقد الوزن
diet	ḥimya ɣaðā'iyya (f)	حمية غذائية
vitamin	vitamīn (m)	فيتامين
calorie	su'ra ḥarāriyya (f)	سعرة حراريّة
vegetarian (n)	nabātiy (m)	نباتيّ
vegetarian (adj)	nabātiy	نباتيّ
fats (nutrient)	duhūn (pl)	دهون
proteins	brutināt (pl)	بروتينات
carbohydrates	naʃawiyyāt (pl)	نشويّات
slice (of lemon, ham)	ʃarīḥa (f)	شريحة
piece (of cake, pie)	qiṭ'a (f)	قطعة
crumb (of bread, cake, etc.)	futāta (f)	فتاتة

52. Table setting

spoon	mil'aqa (f)	ملعقة
knife	sikkīn (m)	سكّين
fork	ʃawka (f)	شوكة
cup (e.g., coffee ~)	finʒān (m)	فنجان
plate (dinner ~)	ṭabaq (m)	طبق
saucer	ṭabaq finʒān (m)	طبق فنجان
napkin (on table)	mandīl (m)	منديل
toothpick	xallat asnān (f)	خلّة أسنان

53. Restaurant

restaurant	maṭ'am (m)	مطعم
coffee house	kafé (m), maqha (m)	كافيه، مقهى

pub, bar	bār (m)	بار
tearoom	ṣālun ʃāy (m)	صالون شاي
waiter	nādil (m)	نادل
waitress	nādila (f)	نادلة
bartender	bārman (m)	بارمان
menu	qāʾimat aṭ ṭaʿām (f)	قائمة طعام
wine list	qāʾimat al χumūr (f)	قائمة خمور
to book a table	ḥaɀaz māʾida	حجز مائدة
course, dish	waɀba (f)	وجبة
to order (meal)	ṭalab	طلب
to make an order	ṭalab	طلب
aperitif	ʃarāb (m)	شراب
appetizer	muqabbilāt (pl)	مقبّلات
dessert	ḥalawiyyāt (pl)	حلويّات
check	ḥisāb (m)	حساب
to pay the check	dafaʿ al ḥisāb	دفع الحساب
to give change	aʿṭa al bāqi	أعطى الباقي
tip	baqʃiʃ (m)	بقشيش

Family, relatives and friends

54. Personal information. Forms

name (first name)	ism (m)	إسم
surname (last name)	ism al 'ā'ila (m)	إسم العائلة
date of birth	tarīx al mīlād (m)	تاريخ الميلاد
place of birth	makān al mīlād (m)	مكان الميلاد
nationality	ʒinsiyya (f)	جنسية
place of residence	maqarr al iqāma (m)	مقر الإقامة
country	balad (m)	بلد
profession (occupation)	mihna (f)	مهنة
gender, sex	ʒins (m)	جنس
height	ṭūl (m)	طول
weight	wazn (m)	وزن

55. Family members. Relatives

mother	umm (f)	أمّ
father	ab (m)	أب
son	ibn (m)	إبن
daughter	ibna (f)	إبنة
younger daughter	al ibna aṣ ṣaɣīra (f)	الإبنة الصغيرة
younger son	al ibn aṣ ṣaɣīr (m)	الابن الصغير
eldest daughter	al ibna al kabīra (f)	الإبنة الكبيرة
eldest son	al ibn al kabīr (m)	الإبن الكبير
brother	ax (m)	أخ
elder brother	al ax al kabīr (m)	الأخ الكبير
younger brother	al ax aṣ ṣaɣīr (m)	الأخ الصغير
sister	uxt (f)	أخت
elder sister	al uxt al kabīra (f)	الأخت الكبيرة
younger sister	al uxt aṣ ṣaɣīra (f)	الأخت الصغيرة
cousin (masc.)	ibn 'amm (m), ibn xāl (m)	إبن عمّ, إبن خال
cousin (fem.)	ibnat 'amm (f), ibnat xāl (f)	إبنة عمّ, إبنة خال
mom, mommy	mama (f)	ماما
dad, daddy	baba (m)	بابا
parents	wālidān (du)	والدان
child	ṭifl (m)	طفل
children	aṭfāl (pl)	أطفال

grandmother	ӡidda (f)	جدّة
grandfather	ӡadd (m)	جدّ
grandson	ḥafīd (m)	حفيد
granddaughter	ḥafīda (f)	حفيدة
grandchildren	aḥfād (pl)	أحفاد
uncle	'amm (m), χāl (m)	عمّ، خال
aunt	'amma (f), χāla (f)	عمّة، خالة
nephew	ibn al aχ (m), ibn al uχt (m)	إبن الأخ، إبن الأخت
niece	ibnat al aχ (f), ibnat al uχt (f)	إبنة الأخ، إبنة الأخت
mother-in-law (wife's mother)	ḥamātt (f)	حماة
father-in-law (husband's father)	ḥamm (m)	حم
son-in-law (daughter's husband)	zawӡ al ibna (m)	زوج الأبنة
stepmother	zawӡat al ab (f)	زوجة الأب
stepfather	zawӡ al umm (m)	زوج الأمّ
infant	ṭifl raḍī' (m)	طفل رضيع
baby (infant)	mawlūd (m)	مولود
little boy, kid	walad ṣaγīr (m)	ولد صغير
wife	zawӡa (f)	زوجة
husband	zawӡ (m)	زوج
spouse (husband)	zawӡ (m)	زوج
spouse (wife)	zawӡa (f)	زوجة
married (masc.)	mutazawwiӡ	متزوّج
married (fem.)	mutazawwiӡa	متزوّجة
single (unmarried)	a'zab	أعزب
bachelor	a'zab (m)	أعزب
divorced (masc.)	muṭallaq (m)	مطلّق
widow	armala (f)	أرملة
widower	armal (m)	أرمل
relative	qarīb (m)	قريب
close relative	nasīb qarīb (m)	نسيب قريب
distant relative	nasīb ba'īd (m)	نسيب بعيد
relatives	aqārib (pl)	أقارب
orphan (boy or girl)	yatīm (m)	يتيم
guardian (of a minor)	waliyy amr (m)	وليّ أمر
to adopt (a boy)	tabanna	تبنّى
to adopt (a girl)	tabanna	تبنّى

56. Friends. Coworkers

friend (masc.)	ṣadīq (m)	صديق
friend (fem.)	ṣadīqa (f)	صديقة

| friendship | ṣadāqa (f) | صداقة |
| to be friends | ṣādaq | صادق |

buddy (masc.)	ṣāḥib (m)	صاحب
buddy (fem.)	ṣaḥiba (f)	صاحبة
partner	rafīq (m)	رفيق

chief (boss)	raʾīs (m)	رئيس
superior (n)	raʾīs (m)	رئيس
owner, proprietor	ṣāḥib (m)	صاحب
subordinate (n)	tābiʿ (m)	تابع
colleague	zamīl (m)	زميل

acquaintance (person)	maʿruf (m)	معروف
fellow traveler	rafīq safar (m)	رفيق سفر
classmate	zamīl fiṣ ṣaff (m)	زميل في الصفّ

neighbor (masc.)	ʒār (m)	جار
neighbor (fem.)	ʒāra (f)	جارة
neighbors	ʒirān (pl)	جيران

57. Man. Woman

woman	imraʾa (f)	إمرأة
girl (young woman)	fatāt (f)	فتاة
bride	ʿarūsa (f)	عروسة

beautiful (adj)	ʒamīla	جميلة
tall (adj)	ṭawīla	طويلة
slender (adj)	raʃīqa	رشيقة
short (adj)	qaṣīra	قصيرة

| blonde (n) | ʃaqrāʾ (f) | شقراء |
| brunette (n) | sawdāʾ aʃ ʃaʿr (f) | سوداء الشعر |

ladies' (adj)	sayyidāt	سيّدات
virgin (girl)	ʿaðrāʾ (f)	عذراء
pregnant (adj)	ḥāmil	حامل

man (adult male)	raʒul (m)	رجل
blond (n)	aʃqar (m)	أشقر
brunet (n)	aswad aʃ ʃaʿr (m)	أسود الشعر
tall (adj)	ṭawīl	طويل
short (adj)	qaṣīr	قصير

rude (rough)	waqiḥ	وقح
stocky (adj)	malyān	مليان
robust (adj)	matīn	متين
strong (adj)	qawiy	قويّ
strength	quwwa (f)	قوّة

stout, fat (adj)	θaxīn	ثخين
swarthy (adj)	asmar	أسمر
slender (well-built)	rajīq	رشيق
elegant (adj)	anīq	أنيق

58. Age

age	'umr (m)	عمر
youth (young age)	ʃabāb (m)	شباب
young (adj)	ʃābb	شاب
younger (adj)	aṣɣar	أصغر
older (adj)	akbar	أكبر
young man	ʃābb (m)	شاب
teenager	murāhiq (m)	مراهق
guy, fellow	ʃābb (m)	شاب
old man	'aʒūz (m)	عجوز
old woman	'aʒūza (f)	عجوزة
adult (adj)	bāliɣ (m)	بالغ
middle-aged (adj)	fi muntaṣaf al 'umr	في منتصف العمر
elderly (adj)	'aʒūz	عجوز
old (adj)	'aʒūz	عجوز
retirement	ma'āʃ (m)	معاش
to retire (from job)	uḥīl 'alal ma'āʃ	أحيل على المعاش
retiree	mutaqā'id (m)	متقاعد

59. Children

child	ṭifl (m)	طفل
children	aṭfāl (pl)	أطفال
twins	taw'amān (du)	توأمان
cradle	mahd (m)	مهد
rattle	xaʃxīʃa (f)	خشخيشة
diaper	ḥifāẓ aṭfāl (m)	حفاظ أطفال
pacifier	bazzāza (f)	بزّازة
baby carriage	'arabat aṭfāl (f)	عربة أطفال
kindergarten	rawḍat aṭfāl (f)	روضة أطفال
babysitter	murabbiyat aṭfāl (f)	مربّية الأطفال
childhood	ṭufūla (f)	طفولة
doll	dumya (f)	دمية
toy	lu'ba (f)	لعبة

construction set (toy)	muka‘abāt (pl)	مكعّبات
well-bred (adj)	mu'addab	مؤدّب
ill-bred (adj)	qalīl al adab	قليل الأدب
spoiled (adj)	mutdalli‘	متدلّع

to be naughty	la‘ib	لعب
mischievous (adj)	la‘ūb	لعوب
mischievousness	iz‘āʒ (m)	إزعاج
mischievous child	ṭifl la‘ūb (m)	طفل لعوب

| obedient (adj) | muṭī‘ | مطيع |
| disobedient (adj) | ‘āq | عاقّ |

docile (adj)	‘āqil	عاقل
clever (smart)	ðakiy	ذكيّ
child prodigy	ṭifl mu‘ʒiza (m)	طفل معجزة

60. Married couples. Family life

to kiss (vt)	bās	باس
to kiss (vi)	bās	باس
family (n)	‘ā'ila (f)	عائلة
family (as adj)	‘ā'iliy	عائليّ
couple	zawʒān (du)	زوجان
marriage (state)	zawāʒ (m)	زواج
hearth (home)	bayt (m)	بيت
dynasty	sulāla (f)	سلالة

| date | maw‘id (m) | موعد |
| kiss | būsa (f) | بوسة |

love (for sb)	ḥubb (m)	حبّ
to love (sb)	aḥabb	أحبّ
beloved	ḥabīb	حبيب

tenderness	ḥanān (m)	حنان
tender (affectionate)	ḥanūn	حنون
faithfulness	iҳlāṣ (m)	إخلاص
faithful (adj)	muҳliṣ	مخلص
care (attention)	‘ināya (f)	عناية
caring (~ father)	muhtamm	مهتمّ

newlyweds	‘arūsān (du)	عروسان
honeymoon	ʃahr al ‘asal (m)	شهر العسل
to get married (ab. woman)	tazawwaʒ	تزوّج
to get married (ab. man)	tazawwaʒ	تزوّج
wedding	zifāf (m)	زفاف
golden wedding	al yubīl að ðahabiy liz zawāʒ (m)	اليوبيل الذهبي للزواج

anniversary	ðikra sanawiyya (f)	ذكرى سنويّة
lover (masc.)	ḥabīb (m)	حبيب
mistress (lover)	ḥabība (f)	حبيبة
adultery	χiyāna zawʒiyya (f)	خيانة زوجية
to cheat on ... (commit adultery)	χān	خان
jealous (adj)	ɣayūr	غيور
to be jealous	ɣār	غار
divorce	ṭalāq (m)	طلاق
to divorce (vi)	ṭallaq	طلق
to quarrel (vi)	taʃāʒar	تشاجر
to be reconciled (after an argument)	taṣālaḥ	تصالح
together (adv)	maʿan	معًا
sex	ʒins (m)	جنس
happiness	saʿāda (f)	سعادة
happy (adj)	saʿīd	سعيد
misfortune (accident)	muṣība (m)	مصيبة
unhappy (adj)	taʿis	تعس

Character. Feelings. Emotions

61. Feelings. Emotions

feeling (emotion)	ʃuʿūr (m)	شعور
feelings	maʃāʿir (pl)	مشاعر
to feel (vt)	ʃaʿar	شعر
hunger	ʒawʿ (m)	جوع
to be hungry	arād an yaʾkul	أراد أن يأكل
thirst	ʿataʃ (m)	عطش
to be thirsty	arād an yaʃrab	أراد أن يشرب
sleepiness	nuʿās (m)	نعاس
to feel sleepy	arād an yanām	أراد أن ينام
tiredness	taʿab (m)	تعب
tired (adj)	taʿbān	تعبان
to get tired	taʿib	تعب
mood (humor)	ḥāla nafsiyya, mazāʒ (m)	حالة نفسيّة، مزاج
boredom	malal (m)	ملل
to be bored	ʃaʿar bil malal	شعر بالملل
seclusion	ʿuzla (f)	عزلة
to seclude oneself	inzawa	إنزوى
to worry (make anxious)	aqlaq	أقلق
to be worried	qalaq	قلق
worrying (n)	qalaq (m)	قلق
anxiety	qalaq (m)	قلق
preoccupied (adj)	maʃɣūl al bāl	مشغول البال
to be nervous	qalaq	قلق
to panic (vi)	uṣīb bið ðaʿr	أصيب بالذعر
hope	amal (m)	أمل
to hope (vi, vt)	tamanna	تمنّى
certainty	yaqīn (m)	يقين
certain, sure (adj)	mutaʾakkid	متأكّد
uncertainty	ʿadam at taʾakkud (m)	عدم التأكّد
uncertain (adj)	ɣayr mutaʾakkid	غير متأكّد
drunk (adj)	sakrān	سكران
sober (adj)	ṣāḥi	صاح
weak (adj)	daʿīf	ضعيف
happy (adj)	saʿīd	سعيد
to scare (vt)	arhab	أرهب

| fury (madness) | ɣaḍab ʃadīd (m) | غضب شديد |
| rage (fury) | ɣaḍab (m) | غضب |

depression	ikti'āb (m)	إكتئاب
discomfort (unease)	'adam irtiyāḥ (m)	عدم إرتياح
comfort	rāḥa (f)	راحة
to regret (be sorry)	nadim	ندم
regret	nadam (m)	ندم
bad luck	sū' al ḥazz (m)	سوء الحظ
sadness	ḥuzn (f)	حزن

shame (remorse)	xaʒal (m)	خجل
gladness	faraḥ (m)	فرح
enthusiasm, zeal	ḥamās (m)	حماس
enthusiast	mutaḥammis (m)	متحمس
to show enthusiasm	taḥammas	تحمس

62. Character. Personality

character	ṭab' (m)	طبع
character flaw	'ayb (m)	عيب
mind, reason	'aql (m)	عقل

conscience	ḍamīr (m)	ضمير
habit (custom)	'āda (f)	عادة
ability (talent)	qudra (f)	قدرة
can (e.g., ~ swim)	'araf	عرف

patient (adj)	ṣābir	صابر
impatient (adj)	qalīl aṣ ṣabr	قليل الصبر
curious (inquisitive)	fuḍūliy	فضولي
curiosity	fuḍūl (m)	فضول

modesty	tawāḍu' (m)	تواضع
modest (adj)	mutawāḍi'	متواضع
immodest (adj)	ɣayr mutawāḍi'	غير متواضع

laziness	kasal (m)	كسل
lazy (adj)	kaslān	كسلان
lazy person (masc.)	kaslān (m)	كسلان

cunning (n)	makr (m)	مكر
cunning (as adj)	mākir	ماكر
distrust	'adam aθ θiqa (m)	عدم الثقة
distrustful (adj)	ʃakūk	شكوك

generosity	karam (m)	كرم
generous (adj)	karīm	كريم
talented (adj)	mawhūb	موهوب
talent	mawhiba (f)	موهبة

courageous (adj)	ʃuʒāʿ	شجاع
courage	ʃaʒāʿa (f)	شجاعة
honest (adj)	amīn	أمين
honesty	amāna (f)	أمانة

careful (cautious)	ḥāðir	حاذر
brave (courageous)	ʃuʒāʿ	شجاع
serious (adj)	ʒādd	جادّ
strict (severe, stern)	ṣārim	صارم

decisive (adj)	ḥazīm	حزيم
indecisive (adj)	mutaraddid	متردد
shy, timid (adj)	xaʒūl	خجول
shyness, timidity	xaʒal (m)	خجل

confidence (trust)	θiqa (f)	ثقة
to believe (trust)	waθiq	وثق
trusting (credulous)	sarīʿ at taṣdīq	سريع التصديق

sincerely (adv)	bi ṣarāḥa	بصراحة
sincere (adj)	muxliṣ	مخلص
sincerity	ixlāṣ (m)	إخلاص
open (person)	ṣarīḥ	صريح

calm (adj)	hādi'	هادئ
frank (sincere)	ṣarīḥ	صريح
naïve (adj)	sāðiʒ	ساذج
absent-minded (adj)	ʃārid al fikr	شارد الفكر
funny (odd)	muḍḥik	مضحك

greed	buxl (m)	بخل
greedy (adj)	baxīl	بخيل
stingy (adj)	baxīl	بخيل
evil (adj)	ʃarīr	شرير
stubborn (adj)	ʿanīd	عنيد
unpleasant (adj)	karīh	كريه

selfish person (masc.)	anāniy (m)	أنانيّ
selfish (adj)	anāniy	أنانيّ
coward	ʒabān (m)	جبان
cowardly (adj)	ʒabān	جبان

63. Sleep. Dreams

to sleep (vi)	nām	نام
sleep, sleeping	nawm (m)	نوم
dream	ḥulm (m)	حلم
to dream (in sleep)	ḥalam	حلم
sleepy (adj)	naʿsān	نعسان
bed	sarīr (m)	سرير

mattress	martaba (f)	مرتبة
blanket (comforter)	baṭṭāniyya (f)	بطّانيّة
pillow	wisāda (f)	وسادة
sheet	milāya (f)	ملاية

insomnia	araq (m)	أرق
sleepless (adj)	ariq	أرِق
sleeping pill	munawwim (m)	منوّم
to take a sleeping pill	tanāwal munawwim	تناول منوّمًا

to feel sleepy	arād an yanām	أراد أن ينام
to yawn (vi)	taθā'ab	تثاءب
to go to bed	ðahab ila n nawm	ذهب إلى النوم
to make up the bed	a'add as sarīr	أعدّ السرير
to fall asleep	nām	نام

nightmare	kābūs (m)	كابوس
snore, snoring	ʃaxīr (m)	شخير
to snore (vi)	ʃaxxar	شخّر

alarm clock	munabbih (m)	منبّه
to wake (vt)	ayqaẓ	أيقظ
to wake up	istayqaẓ	إستيقظ
to get up (vi)	qām	قام
to wash up (wash face)	ɣasal waʒhah	غسل وجهه

64. Humour. Laughter. Gladness

humor (wit, fun)	fukāha (f)	فكاهة
sense of humor	ḥiss (m)	حس
to enjoy oneself	istamta'	إستمتع
cheerful (merry)	farḥān	فرحان
merriment (gaiety)	faraḥ (m)	فرح

smile	ibtisāma (f)	إبتسامة
to smile (vi)	ibtasam	إبتسم
to start laughing	ḍaḥik	ضحك

| to laugh (vi) | ḍaḥik | ضحك |
| laugh, laughter | ḍaḥka (f) | ضحكة |

anecdote	ḥikāya muḍḥika (f)	حكاية مضحكة
funny (anecdote, etc.)	muḍḥik	مضحك
funny (odd)	muḍḥik	مضحك

to joke (vi)	mazaḥ	مزح
joke (verbal)	nukta (f)	نكتة
joy (emotion)	sa'āda (f)	سعادة
to rejoice (vi)	mariḥ	مرح
joyful (adj)	sa'īd	سعيد

65. Discussion, conversation. Part 1

| communication | tawāṣul (m) | تواصل |
| to communicate | tawāṣal | تواصل |

conversation	muḥādaθa (f)	محادثة
dialog	ḥiwār (m)	حوار
discussion (discourse)	munāqaʃa (f)	مناقشة
dispute (debate)	munāẓara (f)	مناظرة
to dispute	χālaf	خالف

interlocutor	muḥāwir (m)	محاور
topic (theme)	mawḍū' (m)	موضوع
point of view	wiʒhat naẓar (f)	وجهة نظر
opinion (point of view)	ra'y (m)	رأي
speech (talk)	χiṭāb (m)	خطاب

discussion (of report, etc.)	munāqaʃa (f)	مناقشة
to discuss (vt)	nāqaʃ	ناقش
talk (conversation)	ḥadīs (m)	حديث
to talk (to chat)	taḥādaθ	تحادث
meeting	liqā' (m)	لقاء
to meet (vi, vt)	qābal	قابل

proverb	maθal (m)	مثل
saying	qawl ma'θūr (m)	قول مأثور
riddle (poser)	luɣz (m)	لغز
to pose a riddle	alqa luɣz	ألقى لغزًا
password	kalimat al murūr (f)	كلمة مرور
secret	sirr (m)	سرّ

oath (vow)	qasam (m)	قسم
to swear (an oath)	aqsam	أقسم
promise	wa'd (m)	وعد
to promise (vt)	wa'ad	وعد

advice (counsel)	naṣīḥa (f)	نصيحة
to advise (vt)	naṣaḥ	نصح
to follow one's advice	intaṣaḥ	إنتصح
to listen to ... (obey)	aṭā'	أطاع

news	χabar (m)	خبر
sensation (news)	ḍaʒʒa (f)	ضجّة
information (data)	ma'lūmāt (pl)	معلومات
conclusion (decision)	istintāʒ (f)	إستنتاج
voice	ṣawt (m)	صوت
compliment	madḥ (m)	مدح
kind (nice)	laṭīf	لطيف

| word | kalima (f) | كلمة |
| phrase | 'ibāra (f) | عبارة |

answer	ʒawāb (m)	جواب
truth	ḥaqīqa (f)	حقيقة
lie	kiðb (m)	كذب
thought	fikra (f)	فكرة
idea (inspiration)	fikra (f)	فكرة
fantasy	χayāl (m)	خيال

66. Discussion, conversation. Part 2

respected (adj)	muḥtaram	محترم
to respect (vt)	iḥtaram	إحترم
respect	iḥtirām (m)	إحترام
Dear ... (letter)	ʿazīzi ...	عزيزي...
to introduce (sb to sb)	ʿarraf	عرّف
to make acquaintance	taʿarraf	تعرّف
intention	niyya (f)	نيّة
to intend (have in mind)	nawa	نوى
wish	tamanni (m)	تمنٍ
to wish (~ good luck)	tamanna	تمنّى
surprise (astonishment)	ʿaʒab (m)	عجب
to surprise (amaze)	adhaʃ	أدهش
to be surprised	indahaʃ	إندهش
to give (vt)	aʿṭa	أعطى
to take (get hold of)	aχað	أخذ
to give back	radd	ردّ
to return (give back)	arʒaʿ	أرجع
to apologize (vi)	iʿtaðar	إعتذر
apology	iʿtiðār (m)	إعتذار
to forgive (vt)	ʿafa	عفا
to talk (speak)	taḥaddaθ	تحدّث
to listen (vi)	istamaʿ	إستمع
to hear out	samiʿ	سمع
to understand (vt)	fahim	فهم
to show (to display)	ʿaraḍ	عرض
to look at ...	naẓar	نظر
to call (yell for sb)	nāda	نادى
to distract (disturb)	ʃaɣal	شغل
to disturb (vt)	azʿaʒ	أزعج
to pass (to hand sth)	sallam	سلّم
demand (request)	ṭalab (m)	طلب
to request (ask)	ṭalab	طلب
demand (firm request)	maṭlab (m)	مطلب

to demand (request firmly)	ṭālib	طالب
to tease (call names)	ɣāẓ	غاظ
to mock (make fun of)	saxar	سخر
mockery, derision	suxriyya (f)	سخرية
nickname	laqab (m)	لقب
insinuation	talmīḥ (m)	تلميح
to insinuate (imply)	lamaḥ	لمح
to mean (vt)	qaṣad	قصد
description	waṣf (m)	وصف
to describe (vt)	waṣaf	وصف
praise (compliments)	madḥ (m)	مدح
to praise (vt)	madaḥ	مدح
disappointment	xaybat amal (f)	خيبة أمل
to disappoint (vt)	xayyab	خيب
to be disappointed	xābat 'āmāluh	خابت آماله
supposition	iftirāḍ (m)	إفتراض
to suppose (assume)	iftaraḍ	إفترض
warning (caution)	taḥðīr (m)	تحذير
to warn (vt)	ḥaððar	حذّر

67. Discussion, conversation. Part 3

to talk into (convince)	aqna'	أقنع
to calm down (vt)	ṭam'an	طمأن
silence (~ is golden)	sukūt (m)	سكوت
to be silent (not speaking)	sakat	سكت
to whisper (vi, vt)	hamas	همس
whisper	hamsa (f)	همسة
frankly, sincerely (adv)	bi ṣarāḥa	بصراحة
in my opinion ...	fi ra'yi ...	في رأيي...
detail (of the story)	tafṣīl (m)	تفصيل
detailed (adj)	mufaṣṣal	مفصّل
in detail (adv)	bit tafāṣīl	بالتفاصيل
hint, clue	iʃāra (f), talmīḥ (m)	إشارة, تلميح
to give a hint	a'ṭa talmīḥ	أعطى تلميحًا
look (glance)	naẓra (f)	نظرة
to have a look	alqa naẓra	ألقى نظرة
fixed (look)	θābit	ثابت
to blink (vi)	ramaʃ	رمش
to wink (vi)	ɣamaz	غمز
to nod (in assent)	hazz ra'sah	هزّ رأسه

sigh	tanahhuda (f)	تنهّدة
to sigh (vi)	tanahhad	تنهّد
to shudder (vi)	irta'aʃ	إرتعش
gesture	iʃārat yad (f)	إشارة يد
to touch (one's arm, etc.)	lamas	لمس
to seize (e.g., ~ by the arm)	amsak	أمسك
to tap (on the shoulder)	ṣafaq	صفق

Look out!	χuð bālak!	خذ بالك!
Really?	wallahi?	والله؟
Are you sure?	hal anta muta'akkid?	هل أنت متأكّد؟
Good luck!	bit tawfīq!	بالتوفيق!
I see!	wāḍiḥ!	واضح!
What a pity!	ya lil asaf!	يا للأسف!

68. Agreement. Refusal

consent	muwāfaqa (f)	موافقة
to consent (vi)	wāfa'	وافق
approval	istiḥsān (m)	إستحسان
to approve (vt)	istiḥsan	إستحسن
refusal	rafḍ (m)	رفض
to refuse (vi, vt)	rafaḍ	رفض

Great!	'aẓīm!	!عظيم
All right!	ittafaqna!	!إتّفقنا
Okay! (I agree)	ittafaqna!	!إتّفقنا

forbidden (adj)	mamnū'	ممنوع
it's forbidden	mamnū'	ممنوع
it's impossible	mustaḥīl	مستحيل
incorrect (adj)	ɣalaṭ	غلط

to reject (~ a demand)	rafaḍ	رفض
to support (cause, idea)	ayyad	أيّد
to accept (~ an apology)	qabil	قبل

to confirm (vt)	aθbat	أثبت
confirmation	iθbāt (m)	إثبات
permission	samāḥ (m)	سماح
to permit (vt)	samaḥ	سمح
decision	qarār (m)	قرار
to say nothing (hold one's tongue)	ṣamat	صمت

condition (term)	ʃarṭ (m)	شرط
excuse (pretext)	'uðr (m)	عذر
praise (compliments)	madḥ (m)	مدح
to praise (vt)	madaḥ	مدح

69. Success. Good luck. Failure

success	naʒāḥ (m)	نجاح
successfully (adv)	bi naʒāḥ	بنجاح
successful (adj)	nāʒiḥ	ناجح
luck (good luck)	ḥazz (m)	حظ
Good luck!	bit tawfīq!	بالتوفيق!
lucky (e.g., ~ day)	murawaffiq	متوفق
lucky (fortunate)	maḥzūz	محظوظ
failure	faʃl (m)	فشل
misfortune	sū' al ḥazz (m)	سوء الحظ
bad luck	sū' al ḥazz (m)	سوء الحظ
unsuccessful (adj)	fāʃil	فاشل
catastrophe	kāriθa (f)	كارثة
pride	faxr (m)	فخر
proud (adj)	faxūr	فخور
to be proud	iftaxar	إفتخر
winner	fā'iz (m)	فائز
to win (vi)	fāz	فاز
to lose (not win)	xasir	خسر
try	muḥāwala (f)	محاولة
to try (vi)	ḥāwal	حاول
chance (opportunity)	furṣa (f)	فرصة

70. Quarrels. Negative emotions

shout (scream)	ṣarxa (f)	صرخة
to shout (vi)	ṣarax	صرخ
to start to cry out	ṣarax	صرخ
quarrel	muʃāʒara (f)	مشاجرة
to quarrel (vi)	taʃāʒar	تشاجر
fight (squabble)	muʃāʒara (f)	مشاجرة
to make a scene	taʃāʒar	تشاجر
conflict	xilāf (m)	خلاف
misunderstanding	sū'at tafāhum (m)	سوء التفاهم
insult	ihāna (f)	إهانة
to insult (vt)	ahān	أهان
insulted (adj)	muhān	مهان
resentment	ḍaym (m)	ضيم
to offend (vt)	asā'	أساء
to take offense	istā'	إستاء
indignation	istiyā' (m)	إستياء
to be indignant	istā'	إستاء

complaint	ʃakwa (f)	شكوى
to complain (vi, vt)	ʃaka	شكا
apology	iʿtiðār (m)	إعتذار
to apologize (vi)	iʿtaðar	إعتذر
to beg pardon	iʿtaðar	إعتذر
criticism	naqd (m)	نقد
to criticize (vt)	naqad	نقد
accusation	ittihām (m)	إتهام
to accuse (vt)	ittaham	إتهم
revenge	intiqām (m)	إنتقام
to avenge (get revenge)	intaqam	إنتقم
to pay back	radd	ردّ
disdain	iḥtiqār (m)	إحتقار
to despise (vt)	iḥtaqar	إحتقر
hatred, hate	karāha (f)	كراهة
to hate (vt)	karah	كره
nervous (adj)	ʿaṣabiy	عصبيّ
to be nervous	qalaq	قلق
angry (mad)	zaʿlān	زعلان
to make angry	azʿal	أزعل
humiliation	iðlāl (m)	إذلال
to humiliate (vt)	ðallal	ذلّل
to humiliate oneself	taðallal	تذلّل
shock	ṣadma (f)	صدمة
to shock (vt)	ṣadam	صدم
trouble (e.g., serious ~)	muʃkila (f)	مشكلة
unpleasant (adj)	karīh	كريه
fear (dread)	χawf (m)	خوف
terrible (storm, heat)	ʃadīd	شديد
scary (e.g., ~ story)	muχīf	مخيف
horror	ruʿb (m)	رعب
awful (crime, news)	murʿib	مرعب
to begin to tremble	irtaʿaʃ	إرتعش
to cry (weep)	baka	بكى
to start crying	baka	بكى
tear	damaʿa (f)	دمعة
fault	ɣalṭa (f)	غلطة
guilt (feeling)	ðamb (m)	ذنب
dishonor (disgrace)	ʿār (m)	عار
protest	iḥtiʒāʒ (m)	إحتجاج
stress	tawattur (m)	توتّر

to disturb (vt)	az'aʒ	أزعج
to be furious	yaḍib	غضب
mad, angry (adj)	yaḍbān	غضبان
to end (~ a relationship)	anha	أنهى
to swear (at sb)	ʃātam	شاتم
to scare (become afraid)	χāf	خاف
to hit (strike with hand)	ḍarab	ضرب
to fight (street fight, etc.)	ta'ārak	تعارك
to settle (a conflict)	sawwa	سوّى
discontented (adj)	yayr rāḍi	غير راض
furious (adj)	'anīf	عنيف
It's not good!	laysa haða amr ʒayyid!	ليس هذا أمرًا جيّدًا!
It's bad!	haða amr sayyi'!	هذا أمر سيّء!

Medicine

71. Diseases

sickness	maraḍ (m)	مرض
to be sick	maraḍ	مرض
health	ṣiḥḥa (f)	صحّة
runny nose (coryza)	zukām (m)	زكام
tonsillitis	iltihāb al lawzatayn (m)	التهاب اللوزتين
cold (illness)	bard (m)	برد
to catch a cold	aṣābahu al bard	أصابه البرد
bronchitis	iltihāb al qaṣabāt (m)	إلتهاب القصبات
pneumonia	iltihāb ar ri'atayn (m)	إلتهاب الرئتين
flu, influenza	inflūnza (f)	إنفلونزا
nearsighted (adj)	qaṣīr an naẓar	قصير النظر
farsighted (adj)	baʿīd an naẓar	بعيد النظر
strabismus (crossed eyes)	ḥawal (m)	حول
cross-eyed (adj)	aḥwal	أحول
cataract	katarakt (f)	كاتاراكت
glaucoma	glawkūma (f)	جلوكوما
stroke	sakta (f)	سكتة
heart attack	iḥtijā' (m)	إحتشاء
myocardial infarction	nawba qalbiya (f)	نوبة قلبية
paralysis	ʃalal (m)	شلل
to paralyze (vt)	ʃall	شلّ
allergy	ḥassāsiyya (f)	حسّاسيّة
asthma	rabw (m)	ربو
diabetes	ad dā' as sukkariyʲ (m)	الداء السكّريّ
toothache	alam al asnān (m)	ألم الأسنان
caries	naxar al asnān (m)	نخر الأسنان
diarrhea	ishāl (m)	إسهال
constipation	imsāk (m)	إمساك
stomach upset	ʿusr al haḍm (m)	عسر الهضم
food poisoning	tasammum (m)	تسمّم
to get food poisoning	tasammam	تسمّم
arthritis	iltihāb al mafāṣil (m)	إلتهاب المفاصل
rickets	kusāḥ al aṭfāl (m)	كساح الأطفال
rheumatism	riumatizm (m)	روماتزم

atherosclerosis	taṣṣallub aʃ ʃarayīn (m)	تصلّب الشرايين
gastritis	iltihāb al maʿida (m)	إلتهاب المعدة
appendicitis	iltihāb az zāʾida ad dūdiyya (m)	إلتهاب الزائدة الدوديّة
cholecystitis	iltihāb al marāra (m)	إلتهاب المرارة
ulcer	qurḥa (f)	قرحة

measles	maraḍ al ḥaṣba (m)	مرض الحصبة
rubella (German measles)	ḥaṣba almāniyya (f)	حصبة ألمانية
jaundice	yaraqān (m)	يرقان
hepatitis	iltihāb al kabd al vayrūsiy (m)	إلتهاب الكبد الفيروسيّ

schizophrenia	ʃizufrīniya (f)	شيزوفرينيا
rabies (hydrophobia)	dāʾ al kalb (m)	داء الكلب
neurosis	ʿiṣāb (m)	عصاب
concussion	irtiʒāʒ al muxx (m)	إرتجاج المخ

cancer	saraṭān (m)	سرطان
sclerosis	taṣṣallub (m)	تصلّب
multiple sclerosis	taṣṣallub mutaʿaddid (m)	تصلّب متعدد

alcoholism	idmān al xamr (m)	إدمان الخمر
alcoholic (n)	mudmin al xamr (m)	مدمن الخمر
syphilis	sifilis az zuhariy (m)	سفلس الزهري
AIDS	al aydz (m)	الايدز

tumor	waram (m)	ورم
malignant (adj)	xabīθ	خبيث
benign (adj)	ḥamīd (m)	حميد

fever	ḥumma (f)	حمّى
malaria	malāriya (f)	ملاريا
gangrene	ɣanɣrīna (f)	غنغرينا
seasickness	duwār al baḥr (m)	دوار البحر
epilepsy	maraḍ aṣ ṣarʿ (m)	مرض الصرع

epidemic	wabāʾ (m)	وباء
typhus	tīfus (m)	تيفوس
tuberculosis	maraḍ as sull (m)	مرض السلّ
cholera	kulīra (f)	كوليرا
plague (bubonic ~)	ṭāʿūn (m)	طاعون

72. Symptoms. Treatments. Part 1

symptom	ʿaraḍ (m)	عرض
temperature	ḥarāra (f)	حرارة
high temperature (fever)	ḥumma (f)	حمّى
pulse	nabḍ (m)	نبض
dizziness (vertigo)	dawxa (f)	دوخة

hot (adj)	ḥārr	حارّ
shivering	nafaḍān (m)	نفضان
pale (e.g., ~ face)	aṣfar	أصفر
cough	su'āl (m)	سعال
to cough (vi)	sa'al	سعل
to sneeze (vi)	'aṭas	عطس
faint	iɣmā' (m)	إغماء
to faint (vi)	ɣumiya 'alayh	غمي عليه
bruise (hématome)	kadma (f)	كدمة
bump (lump)	tawarrum (m)	تورّم
to bang (bump)	iṣṭadam	إصطدم
contusion (bruise)	raḍḍ (m)	رضّ
to get a bruise	taraḍḍaḍ	ترضّض
to limp (vi)	'araʒ	عرج
dislocation	χal' (m)	خلع
to dislocate (vt)	χala'	خلع
fracture	kasr (m)	كسر
to have a fracture	inkasar	إنكسر
cut (e.g., paper ~)	ʒurḥ (m)	جرح
to cut oneself	ʒaraḥ nafsah	جرح نفسه
bleeding	nazf (m)	نزف
burn (injury)	ḥarq (m)	حرق
to get burned	taʃayyat	تشيّط
to prick (vt)	waχaz	وخز
to prick oneself	waχaz nafsah	وخز نفسه
to injure (vt)	aṣāb	أصاب
injury	iṣāba (f)	إصابة
wound	ʒurḥ (m)	جرح
trauma	ṣadma (f)	صدمة
to be delirious	haða	هذى
to stutter (vi)	tala'sam	تلعثم
sunstroke	ḍarbat ʃams (f)	ضربة شمس

73. Symptoms. Treatments. Part 2

pain, ache	alam (m)	ألم
splinter (in foot, etc.)	ʃaẓiyya (f)	شظيّة
sweat (perspiration)	'irq (m)	عرق
to sweat (perspire)	'ariq	عرق
vomiting	taqayyu' (m)	تقيّؤ
convulsions	taʃannuʒāt (pl)	تشنّجات
pregnant (adj)	ḥāmil	حامل

to be born	wulid	وُلِد
delivery, labor	wilāda (f)	ولادة
to deliver (~ a baby)	walad	ولد
abortion	iʒhāḍ (m)	إجهاض
breathing, respiration	tanaffus (m)	تنفّس
in-breath (inhalation)	istinʃāq (m)	إستنشاق
out-breath (exhalation)	zafīr (m)	زفير
to exhale (breathe out)	zafar	زفر
to inhale (vi)	istanʃaq	إستنشق
disabled person	muʿāq (m)	معاق
cripple	muqʿad (m)	مقعد
drug addict	mudmin muχaddirāt (m)	مدمن مخدّرات
deaf (adj)	aṭraʃ	أطرش
mute (adj)	aχras	أخرس
deaf mute (adj)	aṭraʃ aχras	أطرش أخرس
mad, insane (adj)	maʒnūn (m)	مجنون
madman (demented person)	maʒnūn (m)	مجنون
madwoman	maʒnūna (f)	مجنونة
to go insane	ʒunn	جنّ
gene	ʒīn (m)	جين
immunity	manāʿa (f)	مناعة
hereditary (adj)	wirāθiy	وراثيّ
congenital (adj)	χilqiy munð al wilāda	خلقيّ منذ الولادة
virus	virūs (m)	فيروس
microbe	mikrūb (m)	ميكروب
bacterium	ʒurθūma (f)	جرئومة
infection	ʿadwa (f)	عدوى

74. Symptoms. Treatments. Part 3

hospital	mustaʃfa (m)	مستشفى
patient	marīḍ (m)	مريض
diagnosis	taʃχīṣ (m)	تشخيص
cure	ʿilāʒ (m)	علاج
medical treatment	ʿilāʒ (m)	علاج
to get treatment	taʿālaʒ	تعالج
to treat (~ a patient)	ʿālaʒ	عالج
to nurse (look after)	marraḍ	مرّض
care (nursing ~)	ʿināya (f)	عناية
operation, surgery	ʿamaliyya ʒaraḥiyya (f)	عمليّة جرحيّة
to bandage (head, limb)	ḍammad	ضمّد

bandaging	taḍmīd (m)	تضميد
vaccination	talqīḥ (m)	تلقيح
to vaccinate (vt)	laqqaḥ	لقح
injection, shot	ḥuqna (f)	حقنة
to give an injection	ḥaqan ibra	حقن إبرة

attack	nawba (f)	نوبة
amputation	batr (m)	بتر
to amputate (vt)	batar	بتر
coma	ɣaybūba (f)	غيبوبة
to be in a coma	kān fi ḥālat ɣaybūba	كان في حالة غيبوبة
intensive care	al 'ināya al murakkaza (f)	العناية المركزة

to recover (~ from flu)	ʃufiy	شفي
condition (patient's ~)	ḥāla (f)	حالة
consciousness	wa'y (m)	وعي
memory (faculty)	ðākira (f)	ذاكرة

to pull out (tooth)	xala'	خلع
filling	ḥaʃw (m)	حشو
to fill (a tooth)	ḥaʃa	حشا

| hypnosis | at tanwīm al maɣnaṭīsiy (m) | التنويم المغناطيسيّ |
| to hypnotize (vt) | nawwam | نوم |

75. Doctors

doctor	ṭabīb (m)	طبيب
nurse	mumarriḍa (f)	ممرضة
personal doctor	duktūr ʃaxṣiy (m)	دكتور شخصيّ

dentist	ṭabīb al asnān (m)	طبيب الأسنان
eye doctor	ṭabīb al 'uyūn (m)	طبيب العيون
internist	ṭabīb bāṭiniy (m)	طبيب باطنيّ
surgeon	ʒarrāḥ (m)	جرّاح

psychiatrist	ṭabīb nafsiy (m)	طبيب نفسيّ
pediatrician	ṭabīb al atfāl (m)	طبيب الأطفال
psychologist	sikulūʒiy (m)	سيكولوجيّ
gynecologist	ṭabīb an nisā' (m)	طبيب النساء
cardiologist	ṭabīb al qalb (m)	طبيب القلب

76. Medicine. Drugs. Accessories

medicine, drug	dawā' (m)	دواء
remedy	'ilāʒ (m)	علاج
to prescribe (vt)	waṣaf	وصف
prescription	waṣfa (f)	وصفة

tablet, pill	quṛ (m)	قرص
ointment	marham (m)	مرهم
ampule	ambūla (f)	أمبولة
mixture	dawā' ʃarāb (m)	دواء شراب
syrup	ʃarāb (m)	شراب
pill	ḥabba (f)	حبّة
powder	ðarūr (m)	ذرور
gauze bandage	ḍammāda (f)	ضمادة
cotton wool	quṭn (m)	قطن
iodine	yūd (m)	يود
Band-Aid	blāstir (m)	بلاستر
eyedropper	māṣṣat al bastara (f)	ماصّة البسترة
thermometer	tirmūmitr (m)	ترمومتر
syringe	miḥqana (f)	محقنة
wheelchair	kursiy mutaḥarrik (m)	كرسي متحرّك
crutches	ʿukkāzān (du)	عكّازان
painkiller	musakkin (m)	مسكّن
laxative	mulayyin (m)	ملين
spirits (ethanol)	iθanūl (m)	إيثانول
medicinal herbs	aʿʃāb ṭibbiyya (pl)	أعشاب طبية
herbal (~ tea)	ʿuʃbiy	عشبي

77. Smoking. Tobacco products

tobacco	tabɣ (m)	تبغ
cigarette	sīӡāra (f)	سيجارة
cigar	sīӡār (m)	سيجار
pipe	ɣalyūn (m)	غليون
pack (of cigarettes)	ʿulba (f)	علبة
matches	kibrīt (m)	كبريت
matchbox	ʿulbat kibrīt (f)	علبة كبريت
lighter	wallāʿa (f)	ولّاعة
ashtray	ṭaqṭūqa (f)	طقطوقة
cigarette case	ʿulbat saӡāʾir (f)	علبة سجائر
cigarette holder	ḥamilat siӡāra (f)	حاملة سيجارة
filter (cigarette tip)	filtir (m)	فلتر
to smoke (vi, vt)	daxxan	دخّن
to light a cigarette	aʃʿal siӡāra	أشعل سيجارة
smoking	tadxīn (m)	تدخين
smoker	mudaxxin (m)	مدخّن
stub, butt (of cigarette)	ʿuqb siӡāra (m)	عقب سيجارة
smoke, fumes	duxān (m)	دخان
ash	ramād (m)	رماد

HUMAN HABITAT

City

78. City. Life in the city

city, town	madīna (f)	مدينة
capital city	'āṣima (f)	عاصمة
village	qarya (f)	قرية
city map	xarīṭat al madīna (f)	خريطة المدينة
downtown	markaz al madīna (m)	مركز المدينة
suburb	ḍāḥiya (f)	ضاحية
suburban (adj)	aḍ ḍawāḥi	الضواحي
outskirts	aṭrāf al madīna (pl)	أطراف المدينة
environs (suburbs)	ḍawāḥi al madīna (pl)	ضواحي المدينة
city block	ḥayy (m)	حي
residential block (area)	ḥayy sakaniy (m)	حي سكني
traffic	ḥarakat al murūr (f)	حركة المرور
traffic lights	iʃārāt al murūr (pl)	إشارات المرور
public transportation	wasā'il an naql (pl)	وسائل النقل
intersection	taqāṭuʿ (m)	تقاطع
crosswalk	maʿbar al muʃāt (m)	معبر المشاة
pedestrian underpass	nafaq muʃāt (m)	نفق مشاة
to cross (~ the street)	ʿabar	عبر
pedestrian	māʃi (m)	ماش
sidewalk	raṣīf (m)	رصيف
bridge	ʒisr (m)	جسر
embankment (river walk)	kurnīʃ (m)	كورنيش
fountain	nāfūra (f)	نافورة
allée (garden walkway)	mamʃa (m)	ممشى
park	ḥadīqa (f)	حديقة
boulevard	bulvār (m)	بولفار
square	maydān (m)	ميدان
avenue (wide street)	ʃāriʿ (m)	شارع
street	ʃāriʿ (m)	شارع
side street	zuqāq (m)	زقاق
dead end	ṭarīq masdūd (m)	طريق مسدود
house	bayt (m)	بيت
building	mabna (m)	مبنى

skyscraper	nāṭiḥat saḥāb (f)	ناطمة سحاب
facade	wāžiha (f)	واجهة
roof	saqf (m)	سقف
window	ʃubbāk (m)	شبّاك
arch	qaws (m)	قوس
column	'amūd (m)	عمود
corner	zāwiya (f)	زاوية
store window	vatrīna (f)	فترينة
signboard (store sign, etc.)	lāfita (f)	لافتة
poster	mulṣaq (m)	ملصق
advertising poster	mulṣaq i'lāniy (m)	ملصق إعلاني
billboard	lawḥat i'lānāt (f)	لوحة إعلانات
garbage, trash	zubāla (f)	زبالة
trashcan (public ~)	ṣundūq zubāla (m)	صندوق زبالة
to litter (vi)	rama zubāla	رمى زبالة
garbage dump	mazbala (f)	مزبلة
phone booth	kuʃk tilifūn (m)	كشك تليفون
lamppost	'amūd al miṣbāḥ (m)	عمود المصباح
bench (park ~)	dikka (f), kursiy (m)	دكّة, كرسيّ
police officer	ʃurṭiy (m)	شرطيّ
police	ʃurṭa (f)	شرطة
beggar	ʃaḥḥāð (m)	شحّاذ
homeless (n)	mutaʃarrid (m)	متشرّد

79. Urban institutions

store	maḥall (m)	محلّ
drugstore, pharmacy	ṣaydaliyya (f)	صيدليّة
eyeglass store	al adawāt al baṣariyya (pl)	الأدوات البصريّة
shopping mall	markaz tižāriy (m)	مركز تجاريّ
supermarket	subirmarkit (m)	سوبرماركت
bakery	maxbaz (m)	مخبز
baker	xabbāz (m)	خبّاز
pastry shop	dukkān ḥalawāniy (m)	دكّان حلوانيّ
grocery store	baqqāla (f)	بقّالة
butcher shop	malḥama (f)	ملحمة
produce store	dukkān xuḍār (m)	دكّان خضار
market	sūq (f)	سوق
coffee house	kafé (m), maqha (m)	كافيه, مقهى
restaurant	maṭ'am (m)	مطعم
pub, bar	ḥāna (f)	حانة
pizzeria	maṭ'am pizza (m)	مطعم بيتزا
hair salon	ṣālūn ḥilāqa (m)	صالون حلاقة

post office	maktab al barīd (m)	مكتب البريد
dry cleaners	tanẓīf ӡāff (m)	تنظيف جافّ
photo studio	istūdiyu taṣwīr (m)	إستوديو تصوير
shoe store	maḥall aḥðiya (m)	محلّ أحذية
bookstore	maḥall kutub (m)	محلّ كتب
sporting goods store	maḥall riyāḍiy (m)	محلّ رياضيّ
clothes repair shop	maḥall ҳiyāṭat malābis (m)	محلّ خياطة ملابس
formal wear rental	maḥall ta'ӡīr malābis rasmiyya (m)	محلّ تأجير ملابس رسمية
video rental store	maḥal ta'ӡīr vidiyu (m)	محلّ تأجير فيديو
circus	sirk (m)	سيرك
zoo	ḥadīqat al ḥayawān (f)	حديقة حيوان
movie theater	sinima (f)	سينما
museum	matḥaf (m)	متحف
library	maktaba (f)	مكتبة
theater	masraḥ (m)	مسرح
opera (opera house)	ubra (f)	أوبرا
nightclub	malha layliy (m)	ملهى ليليّ
casino	kazinu (m)	كازينو
mosque	masӡid (m)	مسجد
synagogue	kanīs ma'bad yahūdiy (m)	كنيس معبد يهوديّ
cathedral	katidrā'iyya (f)	كاتدرائيّة
temple	ma'bad (m)	معبد
church	kanīsa (f)	كنيسة
college	kulliyya (m)	كلّيّة
university	ӡāmi'a (f)	جامعة
school	madrasa (f)	مدرسة
prefecture	muqāṭa'a (f)	مقاطعة
city hall	baladiyya (f)	بلديّة
hotel	funduq (m)	فندق
bank	bank (m)	بنك
embassy	safāra (f)	سفارة
travel agency	ʃarikat siyāḥa (f)	شركة سياحة
information office	maktab al isti'lāmāt (m)	مكتب الإستعلامات
currency exchange	ṣarrāfa (f)	صرّافة
subway	mitru (m)	مترو
hospital	mustaʃfa (m)	مستشفى
gas station	maḥaṭṭat banzīn (f)	محطّة بنزين
parking lot	mawqif as sayyārāt (m)	موقف السيّارات

80. Signs

signboard (store sign, etc.)	lāfita (f)	لافتة
notice (door sign, etc.)	bayān (m)	بيان
poster	mulṣaq i'lāniy (m)	ملصق إعلاني
direction sign	'alāmat ittiʒāh (f)	علامة إتّجاه
arrow (sign)	'alāmat iʃāra (f)	علامة إشارة
caution	taḥðīr (m)	تحذير
warning sign	lāfitat taḥðīr (f)	لافتة تحذير
to warn (vt)	ḥaððar	حذّر
rest day (weekly ~)	yawm 'uṭla (m)	يوم عطلة
timetable (schedule)	ʒadwal (m)	جدول
opening hours	awqāt al 'amal (pl)	أوقات العمل
WELCOME!	ahlan wa sahlan!	أهلًا وسهلًا
ENTRANCE	duχūl	دخول
EXIT	χurūʒ	خروج
PUSH	idfaʿ	إدفع
PULL	isḥab	إسحب
OPEN	maftūḥ	مفتوح
CLOSED	muɣlaq	مغلق
WOMEN	lis sayyidāt	للسيدات
MEN	lir riʒāl	للرجال
DISCOUNTS	χaṣm	خصم
SALE	taχfīḍāt	تخفيضات
NEW!	ʒadīd!	جديد!
FREE	maʒʒānan	مجّانًا
ATTENTION!	intibāh!	إنتباه!
NO VACANCIES	kull al amākin maḥʒūza	كل الأماكن محجوزة
RESERVED	maḥʒūz	محجوز
ADMINISTRATION	idāra	إدارة
STAFF ONLY	lil 'āmilīn faqaṭ	للعاملين فقط
BEWARE OF THE DOG!	iḥðar wuʒūd al kalb	إحذر وجود الكلب
NO SMOKING	mamnūʿ at tadχīn	ممنوع التدخين
DO NOT TOUCH!	'adam al lams	عدم اللمس
DANGEROUS	χaṭīr	خطير
DANGER	χaṭar	خطر
HIGH VOLTAGE	tayyār 'āli	تيّار عالي
NO SWIMMING!	as sibāḥa mamnū'a	السباحة ممنوعة
OUT OF ORDER	mu'aṭṭal	معطّل
FLAMMABLE	sarī' al iʃti'āl	سريع الإشتعال
FORBIDDEN	mamnūʿ	ممنوع

| NO TRESPASSING! | mamnūʿ al murūr | ممنوع المرور |
| WET PAINT | iḥðar ṭilāʾ ɣayr ӡāff | إحذر طلاء غير جاف |

81. Urban transportation

bus	bāṣ (m)	باص
streetcar	trām (m)	ترام
trolley bus	truli bāṣ (m)	ترولي باص
route (of bus, etc.)	χaṭṭ (m)	خط
number (e.g., bus ~)	raqm (m)	رقم
to go by ...	rakib ...	ركب...
to get on (~ the bus)	rakib	ركب
to get off ...	nazil min	نزل من
stop (e.g., bus ~)	mawqif (m)	موقف
next stop	al maḥaṭṭa al qādima (f)	المحطة القادمة
terminus	āχir maḥaṭṭa (f)	آخر محطة
schedule	ӡadwal (m)	جدول
to wait (vt)	intaẓar	إنتظر
ticket	taðkira (f)	تذكرة
fare	uӡra (f)	أجرة
cashier (ticket seller)	ṣarrāf (m)	صرّاف
ticket inspection	taftīʃ taðkira (m)	تفتيش تذكرة
ticket inspector	mufattiʃ taðākir (m)	مفتّش تذاكر
to be late (for ...)	taʾaχχar	تأخّر
to miss (~ the train, etc.)	taʾaχχar	تأخّر
to be in a hurry	istaʿӡal	إستعجل
taxi, cab	taksi (m)	تاكسي
taxi driver	sāʾiq taksi (m)	سائق تاكسي
by taxi	bit taksi	بالتاكسي
taxi stand	mawqif taksi (m)	موقف تاكسي
to call a taxi	kallam tāksi	كلّم تاكسي
to take a taxi	aχað taksi	أخذ تاكسي
traffic	ḥarakat al murūr (f)	حركة المرور
traffic jam	zaḥmat al murūr (f)	زحمة المرور
rush hour	sāʿat að ðurwa (f)	ساعة الذروة
to park (vi)	awqaf	أوقف
to park (vt)	awqaf	أوقف
parking lot	mawqif as sayyārāt (m)	موقف السيارات
subway	mitru (m)	مترو
station	maḥaṭṭa (f)	محطة
to take the subway	rakib al mitru	ركب المترو
train	qiṭār (m)	قطار
train station	maḥaṭṭat qiṭār (f)	محطة قطار

82. Sightseeing

monument	timθāl (m)	تمثال
fortress	qal'a (f), ḥiṣn (m)	قلعة، حصن
palace	qaṣr (m)	قصر
castle	qal'a (f)	قلعة
tower	burʒ (m)	برج
mausoleum	ḍarīḥ (m)	ضريح
architecture	handasa mi'māriyya (f)	هندسة معماريّة
medieval (adj)	min al qurūn al wusṭa	من القرون الوسطى
ancient (adj)	qadīm	قديم
national (adj)	waṭaniy	وطنيّ
famous (monument, etc.)	maʃhūr	مشهور
tourist	sā'iḥ (m)	سائح
guide (person)	murʃid (m)	مرشد
excursion, sightseeing tour	ʒawla (f)	جولة
to show (vt)	'araḍ	عرض
to tell (vt)	ḥaddaθ	حدّث
to find (vt)	waʒad	وجد
to get lost (lose one's way)	ḍā'	ضاع
map (e.g., subway ~)	χarīṭa (f)	خريطة
map (e.g., city ~)	χarīṭa (f)	خريطة
souvenir, gift	tiðkār (m)	تذكار
gift shop	maḥall hadāya (m)	محلّ هدايا
to take pictures	ṣawwar	صوّر
to have one's picture taken	taṣawwar	تصوّر

83. Shopping

to buy (purchase)	iʃtara	إشترى
purchase	ʃay' (m)	شيء
to go shopping	iʃtara	إشترى
shopping	ʃubinɣ (m)	شوبينغ
to be open (ab. store)	maftūḥ	مفتوح
to be closed	muɣlaq	مغلق
footwear, shoes	aḥðiya (pl)	أحذية
clothes, clothing	malābis (pl)	ملابس
cosmetics	mawādd at taʒmīl (pl)	موادّ التجميل
food products	ma'kūlāt (pl)	مأكولات
gift, present	hadiyya (f)	هديّة
salesman	bā'i' (m)	بائع
saleswoman	bā'i'a (f)	بائعة

check out, cash desk	ṣundū' ad dafᶜ (m)	صندوق الدفع
mirror	mir'āt (f)	مرآة
counter (store ~)	minḍada (f)	منضدة
fitting room	ɣurfat al qiyās (f)	غرفة القياس

to try on	ʒarrab	جرّب
to fit (ab. dress, etc.)	nāsab	ناسب
to like (I like …)	aʿʒab	أعجب

price	siʿr (m)	سعر
price tag	tikit as siʿr (m)	تيكت السعر
to cost (vt)	kallaf	كلّف
How much?	bikam?	بكم؟
discount	xaṣm (m)	خصم

inexpensive (adj)	ɣayr ɣāli	غير غال
cheap (adj)	raxīṣ	رخيص
expensive (adj)	ɣāli	غال
It's expensive	haða ɣāli	هذا غال

rental (n)	istiʒār (m)	إستئجار
to rent (~ a tuxedo)	istaʒar	إستأجر
credit (trade credit)	iʾtimān (m)	إئتمان
on credit (adv)	bid dayn	بالدين

84. Money

money	nuqūd (pl)	نقود
currency exchange	taḥwīl ʿumla (m)	تحويل عملة
exchange rate	siʿr aṣ ṣarf (m)	سعر الصرف
ATM	ṣarrāf 'āliy (m)	صرّاف آليّ
coin	qiṭʿa naqdiyya (f)	قطعة نقديّة

| dollar | dulār (m) | دولار |
| euro | yuru (m) | يورو |

lira	lira iṭāliyya (f)	ليرة إيطالية
Deutschmark	mark almāniy (m)	مارك ألماني
franc	frank (m)	فرنك
pound sterling	ʒunayh istirlīniy (m)	جنيه استرلينيّ
yen	yīn (m)	ين

debt	dayn (m)	دين
debtor	mudīn (m)	مدين
to lend (money)	sallaf	سلّف
to borrow (vi, vt)	istalaf	إستلف

bank	bank (m)	بنك
account	ḥisāb (m)	حساب
to deposit (vt)	awdaʿ	أودع

to deposit into the account	awda' fil ḥisāb	أودع في الحساب
to withdraw (vt)	saḥab min al ḥisāb	سحب من الحساب
credit card	biṭāqat i'timān (f)	بطاقة إئتمان
cash	nuqūd (pl)	نقود
check	ʃīk (m)	شيك
to write a check	katab ʃīk	كتب شيكًا
checkbook	daftar ʃīkāt (m)	دفتر شيكات
wallet	maḥfaẓat ʒīb (f)	محفظة جيب
change purse	maḥfaẓat fakka (f)	محفظة فكّة
safe	χizāna (f)	خزانة
heir	wāris (m)	وارث
inheritance	wirāθa (f)	وراثة
fortune (wealth)	θarwa (f)	ثروة
lease	'īʒār (m)	إيجار
rent (money)	uʒrat as sakan (f)	أجرة السكن
to rent (sth from sb)	ista'ʒar	إستأجر
price	si'r (m)	سعر
cost	θaman (m)	ثمن
sum	mablaɣ (m)	مبلغ
to spend (vt)	ṣaraf	صرف
expenses	maṣārīf (pl)	مصاريف
to economize (vi, vt)	waffar	وفّر
economical	muwaffir	موفّر
to pay (vi, vt)	dafa'	دفع
payment	daf' (m)	دفع
change (give the ~)	al bāqi (m)	الباقي
tax	ḍarība (f)	ضريبة
fine	ɣarāma (f)	غرامة
to fine (vt)	faraḍ ɣarāma	فرض غرامة

85. Post. Postal service

post office	maktab al barīd (m)	مكتب البريد
mail (letters, etc.)	al barīd (m)	البريد
mailman	sā'i al barīd (m)	ساعي البريد
opening hours	awqāt al 'amal (pl)	أوقات العمل
letter	risāla (f)	رسالة
registered letter	risāla musaʒʒala (f)	رسالة مسجّلة
postcard	biṭāqa barīdiyya (f)	بطاقة بريديّة
telegram	barqiyya (f)	برقيّة
package (parcel)	ṭard (m)	طرد

money transfer	ḥawāla māliyya (f)	حوالة ماليّة
to receive (vt)	istalam	إستلم
to send (vt)	arsal	أرسل
sending	irsāl (m)	إرسال
address	'unwān (m)	عنوان
ZIP code	raqm al barīd (m)	رقم البريد
sender	mursil (m)	مرسل
receiver	mursal ilayh (m)	مرسل إليه
name (first name)	ism (m)	إسم
surname (last name)	ism al 'ā'ila (m)	إسم العائلة
postage rate	ta'rīfa (f)	تعريفة
standard (adj)	'ādiy	عاديً
economical (adj)	muwaffir	موفّر
weight	wazn (m)	وزن
to weigh (~ letters)	wazan	وزن
envelope	ẓarf (m)	ظرف
postage stamp	ṭābi' (m)	طابع
to stamp an envelope	alṣaq ṭābi'	ألصق طابعا

Dwelling. House. Home

86. House. Dwelling

house	bayt (m)	بيت
at home (adv)	fil bayt	في البيت
yard	finā' (m)	فناء
fence (iron ~)	sūr (m)	سور
brick (n)	ṭūb (m)	طوب
brick (as adj)	min aṭ ṭūb	من الطوب
stone (n)	ḥaʒar (m)	حجر
stone (as adj)	ḥaʒariy	حجري
concrete (n)	xarasāna (f)	خرسانة
concrete (as adj)	xarasāniy	خرساني
new (new-built)	ʒadīd	جديد
old (adj)	qadīm	قديم
decrepit (house)	'āyil lis suqūṭ	آيل للسقوط
modern (adj)	mu'āṣir	معاصر
multistory (adj)	muta'addid aṭ ṭawābiq	متعدد الطوابق
tall (~ building)	'āli	عال
floor, story	ṭābiq (m)	طابق
single-story (adj)	ðu ṭābiq wāḥid	ذو طابق واحد
1st floor	ṭābiq sufliy (m)	طابق سفلي
top floor	ṭābiq 'ulwiy (m)	طابق علوي
roof	saqf (m)	سقف
chimney	madxana (f)	مدخنة
roof tiles	qirmīd (m)	قرميد
tiled (adj)	min al qirmīd	من القرميد
attic (storage place)	'ullayya (f)	علّية
window	ʃubbāk (m)	شبّاك
glass	zuʒāʒ (m)	زجاج
window ledge	raff ʃubbāk (f)	رف شبّاك
shutters	darf ʃubbāk (m)	درف شبّاك
wall	ḥā'iṭ (m)	حائط
balcony	ʃurfa (f)	شرفة
downspout	masūrat at taṣrīf (f)	ماسورة التصريف
upstairs (to be ~)	fawq	فوق
to go upstairs	ṣa'ad	صعد
to come down (the stairs)	nazil	نزل
to move (to new premises)	intaqal	إنتقل

87. House. Entrance. Lift

entrance	madҳal (m)	مدخل
stairs (stairway)	sullam (m)	سلّم
steps	daraʒāt (pl)	درجات
banister	drabizīn (m)	درابزين
lobby (hotel ~)	ṣāla (f)	صالة

mailbox	ṣundūq al barīd (m)	صندوق البريد
garbage can	ṣundūq az zubāla (m)	صندوق الزبالة
trash chute	manfað að ðubāla (m)	منفذ الزبالة

elevator	miṣ'ad (m)	مصعد
freight elevator	miṣ'ad aʃʃahn (m)	مصعد الشحن
elevator cage	kabīna (f)	كابينة
to take the elevator	rakib al miṣ'ad	ركب المصعد

apartment	ʃaqqa (f)	شقّة
residents (~ of a building)	sukkān al 'imāra (pl)	سكّان العمارة
neighbor (masc.)	ʒār (m)	جار
neighbor (fem.)	ʒāra (f)	جارة
neighbors	ʒirān (pl)	جيران

88. House. Electricity

electricity	kahrabā' (m)	كهرباء
light bulb	lamba (f)	لمبة
switch	miftāḥ (m)	مفتاح
fuse (plug fuse)	fāṣima (f)	فاصمة

cable, wire (electric ~)	silk (m)	سلك
wiring	aslāk (pl)	أسلاك
electricity meter	'addād (m)	عدّاد
readings	qirā'a (f)	قراءة

89. House. Doors. Locks

door	bāb (m)	باب
gate (vehicle ~)	bawwāba (f)	بوّابة
handle, doorknob	qabḍat al bāb (f)	قبضة الباب
to unlock (unbolt)	fataḥ	فتح
to open (vt)	fataḥ	فتح
to close (vt)	aɣlaq	أغلق

key	miftāḥ (m)	مفتاح
bunch (of keys)	rabṭa (f)	ربطة
to creak (door, etc.)	ṣarr	صرّ

creak	ṣarīr (m)	صرير
hinge (door ~)	mufaṣṣala (f)	مفصّلة
doormat	siʒāda (f)	سجادة

door lock	qifl al bāb (m)	قفل الباب
keyhole	θaqb al bāb (m)	ثقب الباب
crossbar (sliding bar)	tirbās (m)	ترباس
door latch	mizlāʒ (m)	مزلاج
padlock	qifl (m)	قفل

to ring (~ the door bell)	rann	رنّ
ringing (sound)	ranīn (m)	رنين
doorbell	ʒaras (m)	جرس
doorbell button	zirr (m)	زرّ
knock (at the door)	ṭarq, daqq (m)	طرق، دقّ
to knock (vi)	daqq	دقّ

code	kūd (m)	كود
combination lock	kūd (m)	كود
intercom	ʒaras al bāb (m)	جرس الباب
number (on the door)	raqm (m)	رقم
doorplate	lawḥa (f)	لوحة
peephole	al ʿayn as siḥriyya (m)	العين السحريّة

90. Country house

village	qarya (f)	قرية
vegetable garden	bustān xuḍār (m)	بستان خضار
fence	sūr (m)	سور

| picket fence | sūr (m) | سور |
| wicket gate | bawwāba farʿiyya (f) | بوّابة فرعيّة |

| granary | ʃawna (f) | شونة |
| root cellar | sirdāb (m) | سرداب |

| shed (garden ~) | saqīfa (f) | سقيفة |
| well (water) | bi'r (m) | بئر |

| stove (wood-fired ~) | furn (m) | فرن |
| to stoke the stove | awqad | أوقد |

| firewood | ḥaṭab (m) | حطب |
| log (firewood) | qiṭ'at ḥaṭab (f) | قطعة حطب |

| veranda | virānda (f) | فيراندة |
| deck (terrace) | ʃurfa (f) | شرفة |

| stoop (front steps) | sullam (m) | سلّم |
| swing (hanging seat) | urʒūḥa (f) | أرجوحة |

91. Villa. Mansion

country house	bayt rīfiy (m)	بيت ريفيّ
villa (seaside ~)	villa (f)	فيلا
wing (~ of a building)	ʒanāḥ (m)	جناح
garden	ḥadīqa (f)	حديقة
park	ḥadīqa (f)	حديقة
tropical greenhouse	daffʼa (f)	دفيئة
to look after (garden, etc.)	ihtamm	إهتمّ
swimming pool	masbaḥ (m)	مسبح
gym (home gym)	qāʼat at tamrīnāt (f)	قاعة التمرينات
tennis court	malʻab tinis (m)	ملعب تنس
home theater (room)	sinima manziliyya (f)	سينما منزليّة
garage	qarāʒ (m)	جراج
private property	milkiyya χāṣṣa (f)	ملكيّة خاصّة
private land	arḍ χāṣṣa (m)	أرض خاصّة
warning (caution)	taḥðīr (m)	تحذير
warning sign	lāfitat taḥðīr (f)	لافتة تحذير
security	ḥirāsa (f)	حراسة
security guard	ḥāris amn (m)	حارس أمن
burglar alarm	ʒihāð inðār (m)	جهاز انذار

92. Castle. Palace

castle	qalʻa (f)	قلعة
palace	qaṣr (m)	قصر
fortress	qalʻa (f), ḥiṣn (m)	قلعة، حصن
wall (round castle)	sūr (m)	سور
tower	burʒ (m)	برج
keep, donjon	burʒ raʼīsiy (m)	برج رئيسيّ
portcullis	bāb mutaḥarrik (m)	باب متحرّك
underground passage	sirdāb (m)	سرداب
moat	χandaq māʼiy (m)	خندق مائيّ
chain	silsila (f)	سلسلة
arrow loop	mazɣal (m)	مزغل
magnificent (adj)	rāʼiʻ	رائع
majestic (adj)	muhīb	مهيب
impregnable (adj)	manīʻ	منيع
medieval (adj)	min al qurūn al wusṭa	من القرون الوسطى

93. Apartment

apartment	ʃaqqa (f)	شقّة
room	ɣurfa (f)	غرفة
bedroom	ɣurfat an nawm (f)	غرفة النوم
dining room	ɣurfat il akl (f)	غرفة الأكل
living room	ṣālat al istiqbāl (f)	صالة الإستقبال
study (home office)	maktab (m)	مكتب
entry room	madχal (m)	مدخل
bathroom (room with a bath or shower)	ḥammām (m)	حمّام
half bath	ḥammām (m)	حمّام
ceiling	saqf (m)	سقف
floor	arḍ (f)	أرض
corner	zāwiya (f)	زاوية

94. Apartment. Cleaning

to clean (vi, vt)	naẓẓaf	نظّف
to put away (to stow)	ʃāl	شال
dust	ɣubār (m)	غبار
dusty (adj)	muɣabbar	مغبّر
to dust (vt)	masaḥ al ɣubār	مسح الغبار
vacuum cleaner	miknasa kahrabā'iyya (f)	مكنسة كهربائيّة
to vacuum (vt)	naẓẓaf bi miknasa kahrabā'iyya	نظف بمكنسة كهربائيّة
to sweep (vi, vt)	kanas	كنس
sweepings	qumāma (f)	قمامة
order	niẓām (m)	نظام
disorder, mess	'adam an niẓām (m)	عدم النظام
mop	mimsaḥa ṭawīla (f)	ممسحة طويلة
dust cloth	mimsaḥa (f)	ممسحة
short broom	miqaʃʃa (f)	مقشّة
dustpan	ʒārūf (m)	جاروف

95. Furniture. Interior

furniture	aθāθ (m)	أثاث
table	maktab (m)	مكتب
chair	kursiy (m)	كرسيّ
bed	sarīr (m)	سرير
couch, sofa	kanaba (f)	كنبة
armchair	kursiy (m)	كرسيّ

| bookcase | χizānat kutub (f) | خزانة كتب |
| shelf | raff (m) | رفّ |

wardrobe	dūlāb (m)	دولاب
coat rack (wall-mounted ~)	ʃammā‘a (f)	شمّاعة
coat stand	ʃammā‘a (f)	شمّاعة

| bureau, dresser | dulāb adrāʒ (m) | دولاب أدراج |
| coffee table | ṭāwilat al qahwa (f) | طاولة القهوة |

mirror	mir'āt (f)	مرآة
carpet	siʒāda (f)	سجادة
rug, small carpet	siʒāda (f)	سجادة

fireplace	midfa'a ḥā'iṭiyya (f)	مدفأة حائطيّة
candle	ʃam‘a (f)	شمعة
candlestick	ʃam‘adān (m)	شمعدان

drapes	satā'ir (pl)	ستائر
wallpaper	waraq ḥī'ṭān (m)	ورق حيطان
blinds (jalousie)	haṣīrat ʃubbāk (f)	حصيرة شبّاك

table lamp	miṣbāḥ aṭ ṭāwila (m)	مصباح الطاولة
wall lamp (sconce)	miṣbāḥ al ḥā'iṭ (f)	مصباح الحائط
floor lamp	miṣbāḥ arḍiy (m)	مصباح أرضيّ
chandelier	naʒafa (f)	نجفة

leg (of chair, table)	riʒl (f)	رجل
armrest	masnad (m)	مسند
back (backrest)	masnad (m)	مسند
drawer	durʒ (m)	درج

96. Bedding

bedclothes	bayāḍāt as sarīr (pl)	بياضات السرير
pillow	wisāda (f)	وسادة
pillowcase	kīs al wisāda (m)	كيس الوسادة
duvet, comforter	baṭṭāniyya (f)	بطّانيّة
sheet	milāya (f)	ملاية
bedspread	ɣiṭā' as sarīr (m)	غطاء السرير

97. Kitchen

kitchen	maṭbaχ (m)	مطبخ
gas	ɣāz (m)	غاز
gas stove (range)	butuɣāz (m)	بوتوغاز
electric stove	furn kaharabā'iy (m)	فرن كهربائيّ
oven	furn (m)	فرن

microwave oven	furn al mikruwayv (m)	فرن الميكروويف
refrigerator	θallāʒa (f)	ثلاجة
freezer	frīzir (m)	فريزير
dishwasher	ɣassāla (f)	غسّالة
meat grinder	farrāmat laḥm (f)	فرّامة لحم
juicer	ʻaṣṣāra (f)	عصّارة
toaster	maḥmaṣat xubz (f)	محمصة خبز
mixer	xallāṭ (m)	خلّاط
coffee machine	mākinat ṣanʻ al qahwa (f)	ماكينة صنع القهوة
coffee pot	kanaka (f)	كنكة
coffee grinder	maṭḥanat qahwa (f)	مطحنة قهوة
kettle	barrād (m)	برّاد
teapot	barrād aʃ ʃāy (m)	برّاد الشاي
lid	ɣiṭāʼ (m)	غطاء
tea strainer	miṣfāt (f)	مصفاة
spoon	milʻaqa (f)	ملعقة
teaspoon	milʻaqat ʃāy (f)	ملعقة شاي
soup spoon	milʻaqa kabīra (f)	ملعقة كبيرة
fork	ʃawka (f)	شوكة
knife	sikkīn (m)	سكّين
tableware (dishes)	ṣuḥūn (pl)	صحون
plate (dinner ~)	ṭabaq (m)	طبق
saucer	ṭabaq finʒān (m)	طبق فنجان
shot glass	ka's (f)	كأس
glass (tumbler)	kubbāya (f)	كبّاية
cup	finʒān (m)	فنجان
sugar bowl	sukkariyya (f)	سكّريّة
salt shaker	mamlaḥa (f)	مملحة
pepper shaker	mabhara (f)	مبهرة
butter dish	ṣuḥn zubda (m)	صحن زبدة
stock pot (soup pot)	kassirūlla (f)	كاسرولة
frying pan (skillet)	ṭāsa (f)	طاسة
ladle	miɣrafa (f)	مغرفة
colander	miṣfāt (f)	مصفاة
tray (serving ~)	ṣīniyya (f)	صينيّة
bottle	zuʒāʒa (f)	زجاجة
jar (glass)	barṭamān (m)	برطمان
can	tanaka (f)	تنكة
bottle opener	fattāḥa (f)	فتّاحة
can opener	fattāḥa (f)	فتّاحة
corkscrew	barrīma (f)	بريمة
filter	filtir (m)	فلتر

to filter (vt)	ṣaffa	صفّى
trash, garbage (food waste, etc.)	zubāla (f)	زبالة
trash can (kitchen ~)	ṣundūq az zubāla (m)	صندوق الزبالة

98. Bathroom

bathroom	ḥammām (m)	حمّام
water	mā' (m)	ماء
faucet	ḥanafiyya (f)	حنفيّة
hot water	mā' sāxin (m)	ماء ساخن
cold water	mā' bārid (m)	ماء بارد

toothpaste	ma'ʒūn asnān (m)	معجون أسنان
to brush one's teeth	naẓẓaf al asnān	نظّف الأسنان
toothbrush	furʃat asnān (f)	فرشة أسنان

to shave (vi)	ḥalaq	حلق
shaving foam	raɣwa lil ḥilāqa (f)	رغوة للحلاقة
razor	mūs ḥilāqa (m)	موس حلاقة

to wash (one's hands, etc.)	ɣasal	غسل
to take a bath	istaḥamm	إستحمّ
shower	dūʃ (m)	دوش
to take a shower	axað ad duʃ	أخذ الدش

bathtub	ḥawḍ istiḥmām (m)	حوض استحمام
toilet (toilet bowl)	mirḥāḍ (m)	مرحاض
sink (washbasin)	ḥawḍ (m)	حوض

| soap | ṣābūn (m) | صابون |
| soap dish | ṣabbāna (f) | صبّانة |

sponge	līfa (f)	ليفة
shampoo	ʃāmbū (m)	شامبو
towel	fūṭa (f)	فوطة
bathrobe	θawb ḥammām (m)	ثوب حمّام

laundry (process)	ɣasīl (m)	غسيل
washing machine	ɣassāla (f)	غسّالة
to do the laundry	ɣasal al malābis	غسل الملابس
laundry detergent	mashūq ɣasīl (m)	مسحوق غسيل

99. Household appliances

TV set	tilivizyūn (m)	تليفزيون
tape recorder	ʒihāz tasʒīl (m)	جهاز تسجيل
VCR (video recorder)	ʒihāz tasʒīl vidiyu (m)	جهاز تسجيل فيديو

radio	ʒihāz radiyu (m)	جهاز راديو
player (CD, MP3, etc.)	blayir (m)	بليير
video projector	'āriḍ vidiyu (m)	عارض فيديو
home movie theater	sinima manziliyya (f)	سينما منزليّة
DVD player	di vi di (m)	دي في دي
amplifier	mukabbir aṣ ṣawt (m)	مكبّر الصوت
video game console	'atāri (m)	أتاري
video camera	kamira vidiyu (f)	كاميرا فيديو
camera (photo)	kamira (f)	كاميرا
digital camera	kamira diʒital (f)	كاميرا ديجيتال
vacuum cleaner	miknasa kahrabā'iyya (f)	مكنسة كهربائيّة
iron (e.g., steam ~)	makwāt (f)	مكواة
ironing board	lawḥat kayy (f)	لوحة كيّ
telephone	hātif (m)	هاتف
cell phone	hātif maḥmūl (m)	هاتف محمول
typewriter	'āla katiba (f)	آلة كاتبة
sewing machine	'ālat al xiyāṭa (f)	آلة الخياطة
microphone	mikrufūn (m)	ميكروفون
headphones	sammā'āt ra'siya (pl)	سمّاعات رأسيّة
remote control (TV)	rimuwt kuntrūl (m)	ريموت كنترول
CD, compact disc	si di (m)	سي دي
cassette, tape	ʃarīṭ (m)	شريط
vinyl record	usṭuwāna (f)	أسطوانة

100. Repairs. Renovation

renovations	taʒdīdāt (m)	تجديدات
to renovate (vt)	ʒaddad	جدّد
to repair, to fix (vt)	aṣlaḥ	أصلح
to put in order	naẓẓam	نظم
to redo (do again)	a'ād	أعاد
paint	dihān (m)	دهان
to paint (~ a wall)	dahan	دهن
house painter	dahhān (m)	دهّان
paintbrush	furʃat lit talwīn (f)	فرشة للتلوين
whitewash	maḥlūl mubayyiḍ (m)	محلول مبيّض
to whitewash (vt)	bayyaḍ	بيّض
wallpaper	waraq ḥīṭān (m)	ورق حيطان
to wallpaper (vt)	laṣaq waraq al ḥīṭān	لصق ورق الحيطان
varnish	warnīʃ (m)	ورنيش
to varnish (vt)	ṭala bil warnīʃ	طلى بالورنيش

101. Plumbing

water	mā' (m)	ماء
hot water	mā' sāχin (m)	ماء ساخن
cold water	mā' bārid (m)	ماء بارد
faucet	ḥanafiyya (f)	حنفية
drop (of water)	qaṭara (f)	قطرة
to drip (vi)	qaṭar	قطر
to leak (ab. pipe)	sarab	سرب
leak (pipe ~)	tasarrub (m)	تسرّب
puddle	birka (f)	بركة
pipe	māsūra (f)	ماسورة
valve (e.g., ball ~)	ṣimām (m)	صمام
to be clogged up	kān masdūdan	كان مسدودًا
tools	adawāt (pl)	أدوات
adjustable wrench	miftāḥ inʒlīziy (m)	مفتاح إنجليزيّ
to unscrew (lid, filter, etc.)	fataḥ	فتح
to screw (tighten)	aḥkam aʃ ʃadd	أحكم الشدّ
to unclog (vt)	sallak	سلّك
plumber	sabbāk (m)	سبّاك
basement	sirdāb (m)	سرداب
sewerage (system)	ʃabakit il maʒāry (f)	شبكة مياه المجاري

102. Fire. Conflagration

fire (accident)	ḥarīq (m)	حريق
flame	ʃuʻla (f)	شعلة
spark	ʃarāra (f)	شرارة
smoke (from fire)	duχān (m)	دخان
torch (flaming stick)	ʃuʻla (f)	شعلة
campfire	nār muχayyam (m)	نار مخيّم
gas, gasoline	banzīn (m)	بنزين
kerosene (type of fuel)	kirusīn (m)	كيروسين
flammable (adj)	qābil lil iḥtirāq	قابل للإحتراق
explosive (adj)	mutafaʒʒir	متفجّر
NO SMOKING	mamnūʻ at tadχīn	ممنوع التدخين
safety	amn (m)	أمن
danger	χaṭar (m)	خطر
dangerous (adj)	χaṭīr	خطير
to catch fire	iʃtaʻal	إشتعل
explosion	infiʒār (m)	إنفجار
to set fire	aʃʻal an nār	أشعل النار

arsonist	muʃʿil ħarīq (m)	مشعل حريق
arson	iħrāq (m)	إحراق
to blaze (vi)	talahhab	تلهّب
to burn (be on fire)	iħtaraq	إحترق
to burn down	iħtaraq	إحترق
to call the fire department	istadʿa qism al ħarīq	إستدعى قسم الحريق
firefighter, fireman	raʒul iṭfāʾ (m)	رجل إطفاء
fire truck	sayyārat iṭfāʾ (f)	سيّارة إطفاء
fire department	qism iṭfāʾ (m)	قسم إطفاء
fire truck ladder	sullam iṭfāʾ (m)	سلّم إطفاء
fire hose	xarṭūm al māʾ (m)	خرطوم الماء
fire extinguisher	miṭfaʾat ħarīq (f)	مطفأة حريق
helmet	xūða (f)	خوذة
siren	ṣaffārat inðār (f)	صفّارة إنذار
to cry (for help)	ṣarax	صرخ
to call for help	istaɣāθ	إستغاث
rescuer	munqið (m)	منقذ
to rescue (vt)	anqað	أنقذ
to arrive (vi)	waṣal	وصل
to extinguish (vt)	aṭfaʾ	أطفأ
water	māʾ (m)	ماء
sand	raml (m)	رمل
ruins (destruction)	ħiṭām (pl)	حطام
to collapse (building, etc.)	inhār	إنهار
to fall down (vi)	inhār	إنهار
to cave in (ceiling, floor)	inhār	إنهار
piece of debris	ħiṭma (f)	حطمة
ash	ramād (m)	رماد
to suffocate (die)	ixtanaq	إختنق
to be killed (perish)	halak	هلك

HUMAN ACTIVITIES

Job. Business. Part 1

103.   Office. Working in the office

office (company ~)	maktab (m)	مكتب
office (of director, etc.)	maktab (m)	مكتب
reception desk	istiqbāl (m)	إستقبال
secretary	sikirtīr (m)	سكرتير
director	mudīr (m)	مدير
manager	mudīr (m)	مدير
accountant	muḥāsib (m)	محاسب
employee	muwaẓẓaf (m)	موظّف
furniture	aθāθ (m)	أثاث
desk	maktab (m)	مكتب
desk chair	kursiy (m)	كرسيّ
drawer unit	waḥdat adrāʒ (f)	وحدة أدراج
coat stand	ʃammāʿa (f)	شمّاعة
computer	kumbyūtir (m)	كمبيوتر
printer	ṭābiʿa (f)	طابعة
fax machine	faks (m)	فاكس
photocopier	ʾālat nasχ (f)	آلة نسخ
paper	waraq (m)	ورق
office supplies	adawāt al kitāba (pl)	أدوات الكتابة
mouse pad	wisādat faʾra (f)	وسادة فأرة
sheet (of paper)	waraqa (f)	ورقة
binder	malaff (m)	ملفّ
catalog	fihris (m)	فهرس
phone directory	dalīl at tilifūn (m)	دليل التليفون
documentation	waθāʾiq (pl)	وثائق
brochure (e.g., 12 pages ~)	naʃra (f)	نشرة
leaflet (promotional ~)	manʃūr (m)	منشور
sample	namūðaʒ (m)	نموذج
training meeting	iʒtimāʿ tadrīb (m)	إجتماع تدريب
meeting (of managers)	iʒtimāʿ (m)	إجتماع
lunch time	fatrat al ɣadāʾ (f)	فترة الغذاء
to make a copy	ṣawwar	صوّر

to make multiple copies	şawwar	صوّر
to receive a fax	istalam faks	إستلم فاكس
to send a fax	arsal faks	أرسل فاكس
to call (by phone)	ittaşal	إتصل
to answer (vt)	radd	ردّ
to put through	waşşal	وصّل
to arrange, to set up	ḥaddad	حدّد
to demonstrate (vt)	ʼaraḍ	عرض
to be absent	ɣāb	غاب
absence	ɣiyāb (m)	غياب

104. Business processes. Part 1

occupation	ʃuɣl (m)	شغل
firm	ʃarika (f)	شركة
company	ʃarika (f)	شركة
corporation	muʼassasa tiʒāriyya (f)	مؤسسة تجارية
enterprise	ʃarika (f)	شركة
agency	wikāla (f)	وكالة
agreement (contract)	ittifāqiyya (f)	إتفاقيّة
contract	ʼaqd (m)	عقد
deal	şafqa (f)	صفقة
order (to place an ~)	ṭalab (m)	طلب
terms (of the contract)	ʃarṭ (m)	شرط
wholesale (adv)	bil ʒumla	بالجملة
wholesale (adj)	al ʒumla	الجملة
wholesale (n)	bayʼ bil ʒumla (m)	بيع بالجملة
retail (adj)	at taʒziʼa	التجزئة
retail (n)	bayʼ bit taʒziʼa (m)	بيع بالتجزئة
competitor	munāfis (m)	منافس
competition	munāfasa (f)	منافسة
to compete (vi)	nāfas	نافس
partner (associate)	ʃarīk (m)	شريك
partnership	ʃirāka (f)	شراكة
crisis	azma (f)	أزمة
bankruptcy	iflās (m)	إفلاس
to go bankrupt	aflas	أفلس
difficulty	şuʼūba (f)	صعوبة
problem	muʃkila (f)	مشكلة
catastrophe	kāriθa (f)	كارثة
economy	iqtişād (m)	إقتصاد
economic (~ growth)	iqtişādiy	إقتصاديّ

economic recession	rukūd iqtiṣādiy (m)	ركود إقتصاديّ
goal (aim)	hadaf (m)	هدف
task	muhimma (f)	مهمّة

to trade (vi)	tāʒir	تاجر
network (distribution ~)	ʃabaka (f)	شبكة
inventory (stock)	al maxzūn (m)	المخزون
range (assortment)	taʃkīla (f)	تشكيلة

leader (leading company)	qāʾid (m)	قائد
large (~ company)	kabīr	كبير
monopoly	iḥtikār (m)	إحتكار

theory	naẓariyya (f)	نظريَة
practice	mumārasa (f)	ممارسة
experience (in my ~)	xibra (f)	خبرة
trend (tendency)	ittiʒāh (m)	إتّجاه
development	tanmiya (f)	تنمية

105. Business processes. Part 2

| profit (foregone ~) | ribḥ (m) | ربح |
| profitable (~ deal) | murbiḥ | مربح |

delegation (group)	wafd (m)	وفد
salary	murattab (m)	مرتّب
to correct (an error)	ṣaḥḥaḥ	صحّح
business trip	riḥlat ʿamal (f)	رحلة عمل
commission	laʒna (f)	لجنة

to control (vt)	taḥakkam	تحكّم
conference	muʾtamar (m)	مؤتمر
license	ruxṣa (f)	رخصة
reliable (~ partner)	mawθūq	موثوق

initiative (undertaking)	mubādara (f)	مبادرة
norm (standard)	miʿyār (m)	معيار
circumstance	ẓarf (m)	ظرف
duty (of employee)	wāʒib (m)	واجب

organization (company)	munaẓẓama (f)	منظّمة
organization (process)	tanẓīm (m)	تنظيم
organized (adj)	munaẓẓam	منظّم
cancellation	ilɣāʾ (m)	إلغاء
to cancel (call off)	alɣa	ألغى
report (official ~)	taqrīr (m)	تقرير

patent	baraʾat al ixtirāʿ (f)	براءة الإختراع
to patent (obtain patent)	saʒʒal barāʾat al ixtirāʿ	سجّل براءة الإختراع
to plan (vt)	xaṭṭaṭ	خطّط

bonus (money)	'ilāwa (f)	علاوة
professional (adj)	mihaniy	مهني
procedure	iʒrā' (m)	إجراء
to examine (contract, etc.)	baḥaθ	بحث
calculation	ḥisāb (m)	حساب
reputation	sum'a (f)	سمعة
risk	muxāṭara (f)	مخاطرة
to manage, to run	adār	أدار
information	ma'lūmāt (pl)	معلومات
property	milkiyya (f)	ملكيّة
union	ittiḥād (m)	إتّحاد
life insurance	ta'mīn 'alal ḥayāt (m)	تأمين على الحياة
to insure (vt)	amman	أمّن
insurance	ta'mīn (m)	تأمين
auction (~ sale)	mazād (m)	مزاد
to notify (inform)	ablaɣ	أبلغ
management (process)	idāra (f)	إدارة
service (~ industry)	xidma (f)	خدمة
forum	nadwa (f)	ندوة
to function (vi)	adda waẓīfa	أدّى وظيفته
stage (phase)	marḥala (f)	مرحلة
legal (~ services)	qānūniy	قانونيّ
lawyer (legal advisor)	muḥāmi (m)	محام

106. Production. Works

plant	maṣna' (m)	مصنع
factory	maṣna' (m)	مصنع
workshop	warʃa (f)	ورشة
works, production site	maṣna' (m)	مصنع
industry (manufacturing)	ṣinā'a (f)	صناعة
industrial (adj)	ṣinā'iy	صناعيّ
heavy industry	ṣinā'a θaqīla (f)	صناعة ثقيلة
light industry	ṣinā'a xafīfa (f)	صناعة خفيفة
products	muntaʒāt (pl)	منتجات
to produce (vt)	antaʒ	أنتج
raw materials	mawādd xām (pl)	موادّ خام
foreman (construction ~)	ra'īs al 'ummāl (m)	رئيس العمّال
workers team (crew)	farīq al 'ummāl (m)	فريق العمّال
worker	'āmil (m)	عامل
working day	yawm 'amal (m)	يوم عمل
pause (rest break)	rāḥa (f)	راحة

| meeting | iʒtimāʻ (m) | إجتماع |
| to discuss (vt) | nāqaʃ | ناقش |

plan	xiṭṭa (f)	خطّة
to fulfill the plan	naffað al xuṭṭa	نفّذ الخطّة
rate of output	muʻaddal al intāʒ (m)	معدّل الإنتاج
quality	ʒawda (f)	جودة
control (checking)	taftīʃ (m)	تفتيش
quality control	ḍabṭ al ʒawda (m)	ضبط الجودة

workplace safety	salāmat makān al ʻamal (f)	سلامة مكان العمل
discipline	inḍibāṭ (m)	إنضباط
violation	muxālafa (f)	مخالفة
(of safety rules, etc.)		

| to violate (rules) | xālaf | خالف |

| strike | iḍrāb (m) | إضراب |
| striker | muḍrib (m) | مضرب |

| to be on strike | aḍrab | أضرب |
| labor union | ittiḥād al ʻummāl (m) | إتّحاد العمّال |

to invent (machine, etc.)	ixtaraʻ	إخترع
invention	ixtirāʻ (m)	إختراع
research	baḥθ (m)	بحث
to improve (make better)	ḥassan	حسّن

| technology | tiknulūʒiya (f) | تكنولوجيا |
| technical drawing | rasm taqniy (m) | رسم تقنيّ |

load, cargo	ʃaḥn (m)	شحن
loader (person)	ḥammāl (m)	حمّال
to load (vehicle, etc.)	ʃaḥan	شحن
loading (process)	taḥmīl (m)	تحميل

| to unload (vi, vt) | afraɣ | أفرغ |
| unloading | ifrāɣ (m) | إفراغ |

transportation	wasāʼil an naql (pl)	وسائل النقل
transportation company	ʃarikat naql (f)	شركة نقل
to transport (vt)	naqal	نقل

freight car	ʻarabat ʃaḥn (f)	عربة شحن
tank (e.g., oil ~)	xazzān (m)	خزّان
truck	ʃāḥina (f)	شاحنة

| machine tool | mākina (f) | ماكنة |
| mechanism | ʼāliyya (f) | آليّة |

industrial waste	muxallafāt ṣināʻiyya (pl)	مخلفّات صناعية
packing (process)	taʻbiʼa (f)	تعبئة
to pack (vt)	ʻabbaʼ	عبّأ

107. Contract. Agreement

contract	'aqd (m)	عقد
agreement	ittifāq (m)	إتَفاق
addendum	mulḥaq (m)	ملحق
to sign a contract	waqqa' 'ala 'aqd	وقَع على عقد
signature	tawqī' (m)	توقيع
to sign (vt)	waqqa'	وقَع
seal (stamp)	χatm (m)	ختم
subject of contract	mawḍū' al 'aqd (m)	موضوع العقد
clause	band (m)	بند
parties (in contract)	aṭrāf (pl)	أطراف
legal address	'unwān qānūniy (m)	عنوان قانوني
to violate the contract	χālaf al 'aqd	خالف العقد
commitment (obligation)	iltizām (m)	إلتزام
responsibility	mas'ūliyya (f)	مسؤولِيَة
force majeure	quwwa qāhira (m)	قوَة قاهرة
dispute	χilāf (m)	خلاف
penalties	'uqūbāt (pl)	عقوبات

108. Import & Export

import	istīrād (m)	إستيراد
importer	mustawrid (m)	مستورد
to import (vt)	istawrad	إستورد
import (as adj.)	wārid	وارد
export (exportation)	taṣdīr (m)	تصدير
exporter	muṣaddir (m)	مصدِر
to export (vi, vt)	ṣaddar	صدَر
export (as adj.)	ṣādir	صادر
goods (merchandise)	baḍā'i' (pl)	بضائع
consignment, lot	ʃaḥna (f)	شحنة
weight	wazn (m)	وزن
volume	ḥaʒm (m)	حجم
cubic meter	mitr muka''ab (m)	متر مكعَب
manufacturer	aʃ ʃarika al muṣni'a (f)	الشركة المصنعة
transportation company	ʃarikat naql (f)	شركة نقل
container	ḥāwiya (f)	حاوية
border	ḥadd (m)	حدّ
customs	ʒamārik (pl)	جمارك
customs duty	rasm ʒumrukiy (m)	رسم جمركيّ

customs officer	muwaẓẓaf al ʒamārik (m)	موظف الجمارك
smuggling	tahrīb (m)	تهريب
contraband (smuggled goods)	biḍā'a muharraba (pl)	بضاعة مهرّبة

109. Finances

stock (share)	sahm (m)	سهم
bond (certificate)	sanad (m)	سند
promissory note	kimbyāla (f)	كمبيالة
stock exchange	būrṣa (f)	بورصة
stock price	si'r as sahm (m)	سعر السهم
to go down (become cheaper)	raxuṣ	رخص
to go up (become more expensive)	ɣala	غلى
share	naṣīb (m)	نصيب
controlling interest	al maʒmū'a al musayṭara (f)	المجموعة المسيطرة
investment	istiθmār (pl)	إستثمار
to invest (vt)	istaθmar	إستثمر
percent	bil mi'a (m)	بالمئة
interest (on investment)	fa'ida (f)	فائدة
profit	ribḥ (m)	ربح
profitable (adj)	murbiḥ	مربح
tax	ḍarība (f)	ضريبة
currency (foreign ~)	'umla (f)	عملة
national (adj)	waṭaniy	وطنيّ
exchange (currency ~)	taḥwīl (m)	تحويل
accountant	muḥāsib (m)	محاسب
accounting	maḥasaba (f)	محاسبة
bankruptcy	iflās (m)	إفلاس
collapse, crash	inhiyār (m)	إنهيار
ruin	iflās (m)	إفلاس
to be ruined (financially)	aflas	أفلس
inflation	taḍaxxum māliy (m)	تضخّم ماليّ
devaluation	taxfīḍ qīmat 'umla (m)	تخفيض قيمة عملة
capital	ra's māl (m)	رأس مال
income	daxl (m)	دخل
turnover	dawrat ra's al māl (f)	دورة رأس المال
resources	mawārid (pl)	موارد
monetary resources	al mawārid an naqdiyya (pl)	الموارد النقديّة

| overhead | nafaqāt ʿāmma (pl) | نفقات عامّة |
| to reduce (expenses) | χaffaḍ | خفَض |

110. Marketing

marketing	taswīq (m)	تسويق
market	sūq (f)	سوق
market segment	qaṭāʿ as sūq (m)	قطاع السوق
product	muntaӡ (m)	منتج
goods (merchandise)	baḍāʾiʿ (pl)	بضائع

brand	mārka (f)	ماركة
trademark	mārka tiӡāriyya (f)	ماركة تجاريّة
logotype	ʃiʿār (m)	شعار
logo	ʃiʿār (m)	شعار

demand	ṭalab (m)	طلب
supply	maχzūn (m)	مخزون
need	ḥāӡa (f)	حاجة
consumer	mustahlik (m)	مستهلك

analysis	taḥlīl (m)	تحليل
to analyze (vt)	ḥallal	حلّل
positioning	waḍʿ (m)	وضع
to position (vt)	waḍaʿ	وضع

price	siʿr (m)	سعر
pricing policy	siyāsat al asʿār (f)	سياسة الأسعار
price formation	taʃkīl al asʿār (m)	تشكيل الأسعار

111. Advertising

advertising	iʿlān (m)	إعلان
to advertise (vt)	aʿlan	أعلن
budget	mīzāniyya (f)	ميزانيّة

ad, advertisement	iʿlān (m)	إعلان
TV advertising	iʿlān fit tiliviziyūn (m)	إعلان في التليفزيون
radio advertising	iʿlān fir rādiyu (m)	إعلان في الراديو
outdoor advertising	iʿlān ẓāhiriy (m)	إعلان ظاهريّ

mass media	wasāʾil al iʿlām (pl)	وسائل الإعلام
periodical (n)	ṣaḥifa dawriyya (f)	صحيفة دوريّة
image (public appearance)	imiӡ (m)	إيميج

slogan	ʃiʿār (m)	شعار
motto (maxim)	ʃiʿār (m)	شعار
campaign	ḥamla (f)	حملة

advertising campaign	ḥamla i'lāniyya (f)	حملة إعلانيّة
target group	maʒmū'a mustahdafa (f)	مجموعة مستهدفة
business card	biṭāqat al 'amal (f)	بطاقة العمل
leaflet (promotional ~)	manʃūr (m)	منشور
brochure	naʃra (f)	نشرة
(e.g., 12 pages ~)		
pamphlet	kutayyib (m)	كتيّب
newsletter	naʃra iχbāriyya (f)	نشرة إخبارية
signboard (store sign, etc.)	lāfita (f)	لافتة
poster	mulṣaq i'lāniy (m)	ملصق إعلانيّ
billboard	lawḥat i'lānāt (f)	لوحة إعلانات

112. Banking

bank	bank (m)	بنك
branch (of bank, etc.)	far' (m)	فرع
bank clerk, consultant	muwaẓẓaf bank (m)	موظّف بنك
manager (director)	mudīr (m)	مدير
bank account	ḥisāb (m)	حساب
account number	raqm al ḥisāb (m)	رقم الحساب
checking account	ḥisāb ʒāri (m)	حساب جار
savings account	ḥisāb tawfīr (m)	حساب توفير
to open an account	fataḥ ḥisāb	فتح حسابا
to close the account	aɣlaq ḥisāb	أغلق حسابا
to deposit into the account	awda' fil ḥisāb	أودع في الحساب
to withdraw (vt)	saḥab min al ḥisāb	سحب من الحساب
deposit	wadī'a (f)	وديعة
to make a deposit	awda'	أودع
wire transfer	ḥawāla (f)	حوالة
to wire, to transfer	ḥawwal	حوّل
sum	mablaɣ (m)	مبلغ
How much?	kam?	كم؟
signature	tawqī' (m)	توقيع
to sign (vt)	waqqa'	وقّع
credit card	biṭāqat i'timān (f)	بطاقة ائتمان
code (PIN code)	kūd (m)	كود
credit card number	raqm biṭāqat i'timān (m)	رقم بطاقة إئتمان
ATM	ṣarrāf 'āliy (m)	صرّاف آليّ
check	ʃīk (m)	شيك
to write a check	katab ʃīk	كتب شيكًا

checkbook	daftar ʃīkāt (m)	دفتر شيكات
loan (bank ~)	qarḍ (m)	قرض
to apply for a loan	qaddam ṭalab lil ḥuṣūl 'ala qarḍ	قدّم طلبا للحصول على قرض
to get a loan	ḥaṣal 'ala qarḍ	حصل على قرض
to give a loan	qaddam qarḍ	قدّم قرضا
guarantee	ḍamān (m)	ضمان

113. Telephone. Phone conversation

telephone	hātif (m)	هاتف
cell phone	hātif maḥmūl (m)	هاتف محمول
answering machine	muʒīb al hātif (m)	مجيب الهاتف
to call (by phone)	ittaṣal	إتّصل
phone call	mukālama tilifuniyya (f)	مكالمة تليفونية
to dial a number	ittaṣal bi raqm	إتّصل برقم
Hello!	alu!	ألو!
to ask (vt)	sa'al	سأل
to answer (vi, vt)	radd	ردّ
to hear (vt)	sami'	سمع
well (adv)	ʒayyidan	جيّدا
not well (adv)	sayyi'an	سيّئا
noises (interference)	taʃwīʃ (m)	تشويش
receiver	sammā'a (f)	سمّاعة
to pick up (~ the phone)	rafa' as sammā'a	رفع السمّاعة
to hang up (~ the phone)	qafal as sammā'a	قفل السمّاعة
busy (engaged)	maʃɣūl	مشغول
to ring (ab. phone)	rann	رنّ
telephone book	daḷīl at tilifūn (m)	دليل التليفون
local (adj)	maḥalliyya	ة محلّية
local call	mukālama hātifiyya maḥalliyya (f)	مكالمة هاتفيّة محلّية
long distance (~ call)	ba'īd al mada	بعيد المدى
long-distance call	mukālama ba'īdat al mada (f)	مكالمة بعيدة المدى
international (adj)	duwaliy	دوليّ
international call	mukālama duwaliyya (f)	مكالمة دوليّة

114. Cell phone

| cell phone | hātif maḥmūl (m) | هاتف محمول |
| display | ʒihāz 'arḍ (m) | جهاز عرض |

button	zirr (m)	زِرّ
SIM card	sim kart (m)	سيم كارت
battery	baṭṭāriyya (f)	بطّاريّة
to be dead (battery)	xalaṣat	خلصت
charger	ʃāḥin (m)	شاحن
menu	qā'ima (f)	قائمة
settings	awḍāʻ (pl)	أوضاع
tune (melody)	naɣma (f)	نغمة
to select (vt)	ixtār	إختار
calculator	'āla ḥāsiba (f)	آلة حاسبة
voice mail	barīd ṣawtiy (m)	بريد صوتيّ
alarm clock	munabbih (m)	منبّه
contacts	ʒihāt al ittiṣāl (pl)	جهات الإتّصال
SMS (text message)	risāla qaṣīra ɛsɛmɛs (f)	sms رسالة قصيرة
subscriber	muʃtarik (m)	مشترك

115. Stationery

ballpoint pen	qalam ʒāf (m)	قلم جاف
fountain pen	qalam rīʃa (m)	قلم ريشة
pencil	qalam ruṣāṣ (m)	قلم رصاص
highlighter	markir (m)	ماركر
felt-tip pen	qalam xaṭṭāṭ (m)	قلم خطّاط
notepad	muðakkira (f)	مذكّرة
agenda (diary)	ʒadwal al aʻmāl (m)	جدول الأعمال
ruler	masṭara (f)	مسطرة
calculator	'āla ḥāsiba (f)	آلة حاسبة
eraser	astīka (f)	استيكة
thumbtack	dabbūs (m)	دبّوس
paper clip	dabbūs waraq (m)	دبّوس ورق
glue	ṣamɣ (m)	صمغ
stapler	dabbāsa (f)	دبّاسة
hole punch	xarrāma (m)	خرّامة
pencil sharpener	mibrāt (f)	مبراة

116. Various kinds of documents

account (report)	taqrīr (m)	تقرير
agreement	ittifāq (m)	إتّفاق
application form	istimārat ṭalab (m)	إستمارة طلب

authentic (adj)	aṣliy	أَصْلِيّ
badge (identity tag)	ʃāra (f)	شارة
business card	biṭāqat al ʿamal (f)	بطاقة العمل
certificate (~ of quality)	ʃahāda (f)	شهادة
check (e.g., draw a ~)	ʃīk (m)	شيك
check (in restaurant)	ḥisāb (m)	حساب
constitution	dustūr (m)	دستور
contract (agreement)	ʿaqd (m)	عقد
copy	ṣūra (f)	صورة
copy (of contract, etc.)	nusxa (f)	نسخة
customs declaration	taṣrīḥ ʒumrukiy (m)	تصريح جمركيّ
document	waθīqa (f)	وثيقة
driver's license	ruxṣat al qiyāda (f)	رخصة قيادة
addendum	mulḥaq (m)	ملحق
form	istimāra (f)	إستمارة
ID card (e.g., FBI ~)	biṭāqat al huwiyya (f)	بطاقة الهويّة
inquiry (request)	istifsār (m)	إستفسار
invitation card	biṭāqat daʿwa (f)	بطاقة دعوة
invoice	fātūra (f)	فاتورة
law	qānūn (m)	قانون
letter (mail)	risāla (f)	رسالة
letterhead	tarwīsa (f)	ترويسة
list (of names, etc.)	qāʾima (f)	قائمة
manuscript	maxṭūṭa (f)	مخطوطة
newsletter	naʃra ixbāriyya (f)	نشرة إخبارية
note (short letter)	nūta (f)	نوتة
pass (for worker, visitor)	biṭāqat murūr (f)	بطاقة مرور
passport	ʒawāz as safar (m)	جواز السفر
permit	ruxṣa (f)	رخصة
résumé	sīra ðātiyya (f)	سيرة ذاتيّة
debt note, IOU	muðakkirat dayn (f)	مذكّرة دين
receipt (for purchase)	ʾīṣāl (m)	إيصال
sales slip, receipt	ʾīṣāl (m)	إيصال
report (mil.)	taqrīr (m)	تقرير
to show (ID, etc.)	qaddam	قدّم
to sign (vt)	waqqaʿ	وقّع
signature	tawqīʿ (m)	توقيع
seal (stamp)	xatm (m)	ختم
text	naṣṣ (m)	نص
ticket (for entry)	taðkira (f)	تذكرة
to cross out	ʃaṭab	شطب
to fill out (~ a form)	malaʾ	ملأ
waybill (shipping invoice)	bulīṣat ʃaḥn (f)	بوليصة شحن
will (testament)	waṣiyya (f)	وصبّة

117. Kinds of business

accounting services	χidamāt muḥasaba (pl)	خدمات محاسبة
advertising	i'lān (m)	إعلان
advertising agency	wikālat i'lān (f)	وكالة إعلان
air-conditioners	takyīf (m)	تكييف
airline	ʃarikat ṭayarān (f)	شركة طيران
alcoholic beverages	maʃrūbāt kuḥūliyya (pl)	مشروبات كحوليّة
antiques (antique dealers)	tuḥaf (pl)	تحف
art gallery (contemporary ~)	ma'raḍ fanniy (m)	معرض فنّيّ
audit services	tadqīq al ḥisābāt (pl)	تدقيق الحسابات
banking industry	al qiṭā' al maṣrafiy (m)	القطاع المصرفي
bar	bār (m)	بار
beauty parlor	ṣālūn taʒmīl (m)	صالون تجميل
bookstore	maḥall kutub (m)	محلّ كتب
brewery	maṣna' bīra (m)	مصنع بيرة
business center	markaz tiʒāriy (m)	مركز تجاريّ
business school	kulliyyat idārat al a'māl (f)	كلّيّة إدارة الأعمال
casino	kazinu (m)	كازينو
construction	binā' (m)	بناء
consulting	istiʃāra (f)	إستشارة
dental clinic	'iyādat asnān (f)	عيادة أسنان
design	taṣmīm (m)	تصميم
drugstore, pharmacy	ṣaydaliyya (f)	صيدليّة
dry cleaners	tanẓīf ʒāff (m)	تنظيف جافّ
employment agency	wikālat tawẓīf (f)	وكالة توظيف
financial services	χidamāt māliyya (pl)	خدمات ماليّة
food products	mawādd ɣiðā'iyya (pl)	موادّ غذائيّة
funeral home	bayt al ʒanāzāt (m)	بيت الجنازات
furniture (e.g., house ~)	aθāθ (m)	أثاث
clothing, garment	malābis (pl)	ملابس
hotel	funduq (m)	فندق
ice-cream	muθallaʒāt (pl)	مثلّجات
industry (manufacturing)	ṣinā'a (f)	صناعة
insurance	ta'mīn (m)	تأمين
Internet	intirnit (m)	إنترنت
investments (finance)	istiθmārāt (pl)	إستثمارات
jeweler	ṣā'iɣ (m)	صائغ
jewelry	muʒawharāt (pl)	مجوهرات
laundry (shop)	maɣsala (f)	مغسلة
legal advisor	χidamāt qānūniyya (pl)	خدمات قانونيّة
light industry	ṣinā'a χafīfa (f)	صناعة خفيفة
magazine	maʒalla (f)	مجلّة

mail-order selling	bayʻ bil barīd (m)	بيع بالبريد
medicine	ṭibb (m)	طبّ
movie theater	sinima (f)	سينما
museum	matḥaf (m)	متحف
news agency	wikālat anbāʼ (f)	وكالة أنباء
newspaper	ʒarīda (f)	جريدة
nightclub	malha layliy (m)	ملهى ليليّ
oil (petroleum)	nafṭ (m)	نفط
courier services	xidamāt aʃ ʃaḥn (pl)	خدمات الشحن
pharmaceutics	ṣaydala (f)	صيدلة
printing (industry)	ṭibāʻa (f)	طباعة
publishing house	dār aṭ ṭibāʻa wan naʃr (f)	دار الطباعة والنشر
radio (~ station)	iðāʻa (f)	إذاعة
real estate	ʻiqārāt (pl)	عقارات
restaurant	maṭʻam (m)	مطعم
security company	ʃarikat amn (f)	شركة أمن
sports	riyāḍa (f)	رياضة
stock exchange	būrṣa (f)	بورصة
store	maḥall (m)	محلّ
supermarket	subirmarkit (m)	سوبرماركت
swimming pool (public ~)	masbaḥ (m)	مسبح
tailor shop	ṣālūn (m)	صالون
television	tilivizyūn (m)	تليفزيون
theater	masraḥ (m)	مسرح
trade (commerce)	tiʒāra (f)	تجارة
transportation	wasāʼil an naql (pl)	وسائل النقل
travel	siyāḥa (f)	سياحة
veterinarian	ṭabīb bayṭariy (m)	طبيب بيطريّ
warehouse	mustawdaʻ (m)	مستودع
waste collection	ʒamʻ an nufāyāt (m)	جمع النفايات

Job. Business. Part 2

118. Show. Exhibition

exhibition, show	ma'raḍ (m)	معرض
trade show	ma'raḍ tiʒāriy (m)	معرض تجاريّ
participation	iʃtirāk (m)	إشتراك
to participate (vi)	iʃtarak	إشترك
participant (exhibitor)	muʃtarik (m)	مشترك
director	mudīr (m)	مدير
organizers' office	maktab al munaẓẓimīn (m)	مكتب المنظمين
organizer	munaẓẓim (m)	منظّم
to organize (vt)	naẓẓam	نظّم
participation form	istimārat al iʃtirāk (f)	إستمارة الإشتراك
to fill out (vt)	mala'	ملأ
details	tafāṣīl (pl)	تفاصيل
information	isti'lāmāt (pl)	إستعلامات
price (cost, rate)	si'r (m)	سعر
including	bima fīh	بما فيه
to include (vt)	taḍamman	تضمّن
to pay (vi, vt)	dafa'	دفع
registration fee	rusūm at tasʒīl (pl)	رسوم التسجيل
entrance	madχal (m)	مدخل
pavilion, hall	ʒanāh (m)	جناح
to register (vt)	saʒʒal	سجّل
badge (identity tag)	ʃāra (f)	شارة
booth, stand	kuʃk (m)	كشك
to reserve, to book	ḥaʒaz	حجز
display case	vatrīna (f)	فترينة
spotlight	miṣbāḥ (m)	مصباح
design	taṣmīm (m)	تصميم
to place (put, set)	waḍa'	وضع
distributor	muwazzi' (m)	موزّع
supplier	muwarrid (m)	مورّد
country	balad (m)	بلد
foreign (adj)	aʒnabiy	أجنبيّ
product	muntaʒ (m)	منتج

association	ӡamʻiyya (f)	جمعيّة
conference hall	qāʻat al muʻtamarāt (f)	قاعة المؤتمرات
congress	muʻtamar (m)	مؤتمر
contest (competition)	musābaqa (f)	مسابقة
visitor (attendee)	zāʼir (m)	زائر
to visit (attend)	ḥaḍar	حضر
customer	zubūn (m)	زبون

119. Mass Media

newspaper	ӡarīda (f)	جريدة
magazine	maӡalla (f)	مجلّة
press (printed media)	ṣiḥāfa (f)	صحافة
radio	iðāʻa (f)	إذاعة
radio station	maḥaṭṭat iðāʻa (f)	محطّة إذاعة
television	tilivizyūn (m)	تليفزيون
presenter, host	muʼaddim (m)	مقدّم
newscaster	muðīʻ (m)	مذيع
commentator	muʻalliq (m)	معلّق
journalist	ṣuḥufiy (m)	صحفيّ
correspondent (reporter)	murāsil (m)	مراسل
press photographer	muṣawwir ṣuḥufiy (m)	مصوّر صحفيّ
reporter	ṣuḥufiy (m)	صحفيّ
editor	muḥarrir (m)	محرّر
editor-in-chief	raʼīs taḥrīr (m)	رئيس تحرير
to subscribe (to ...)	iʃtarak	إشترك
subscription	iʃtirāk (m)	إشتراك
subscriber	muʃtarik (m)	مشترك
to read (vi, vt)	qaraʼ	قرأ
reader	qāriʼ (m)	قارئ
circulation (of newspaper)	tadāwul (m)	تداول
monthly (adj)	ʃahriy	شهريّ
weekly (adj)	usbūʻiy	أسبوعيّ
issue (edition)	ʻadad (m)	عدد
new (~ issue)	ӡadīd	جديد
headline	ʻunwān (m)	عنوان
short article	maqāla qaṣīra (f)	مقالة قصيرة
column (regular article)	ʻamūd (m)	عمود
article	maqāla (f)	مقالة
page	ṣafḥa (f)	صفحة
reportage, report	taqrīr (m)	تقرير
event (happening)	ḥadaθ (m)	حدث

sensation (news)	ḍaʒʒa (f)	ضِجّة
scandal	faḍīḥa (f)	فضيحة
scandalous (adj)	fāḍiḥ	فاضح
great (~ scandal)	ʃahīr	شهير
show (e.g., cooking ~)	barnāmaʒ (m)	برنامج
interview	muqābala (f)	مقابلة
live broadcast	iðāʿa mubāʃira (f)	إذاعة مباشرة
channel	qanāt (f)	قناة

120. Agriculture

agriculture	zirāʿa (f)	زراعة
peasant (masc.)	fallāḥ (m)	فلّاح
peasant (fem.)	fallāḥa (f)	فلّاحة
farmer	muzāriʿ (m)	مزارع
tractor (farm ~)	ʒarrār (m)	جرّار
combine, harvester	ḥaṣṣāda (f)	حصّادة
plow	miḥrāθ (m)	محراث
to plow (vi, vt)	ḥaraθ	حرث
plowland	ḥaql maḥrūθ (m)	حقل محروث
furrow (in field)	talam (m)	تلم
to sow (vi, vt)	baðar	بذر
seeder	baðð āra (f)	بذّارة
sowing (process)	zarʿ (m)	زرع
scythe	miḥaʃʃ (m)	محشّ
to mow, to scythe	ḥaʃʃ	حشّ
spade (tool)	karīk (m)	مجرفة
to till (vt)	ḥafar	حفر
hoe	miʿzaqa (f)	معزقة
to hoe, to weed	ista'ṣal nabātāt	إستأصل نباتات
weed (plant)	ḥaʃīʃa (m)	حشيشة
watering can	miraʃʃa al miyāh (f)	مرشّة المياه
to water (plants)	saqa	سقى
watering (act)	saqy (m)	سقي
pitchfork	maðrāt (f)	مذراة
rake	midamma (f)	مدمّة
fertilizer	samād (m)	سماد
to fertilize (vt)	sammad	سمّد
manure (fertilizer)	zibd (m)	زبل
field	ḥaql (m)	حقل

meadow	marӡ (m)	مرج
vegetable garden	bustān χuḍār (m)	بستان خضار
orchard (e.g., apple ~)	bustān (m)	بستان
to graze (vt)	ra'a	رعى
herder (herdsman)	rā'i (m)	راع
pasture	mar'a (m)	مرعى
cattle breeding	tarbiyat al mawāʃi (f)	تربية المواشي
sheep farming	tarbiyat aɣnām (f)	تربية أغنام
plantation	mazra'a (f)	مزرعة
row (garden bed ~s)	ḥawḍ (m)	حوض
hothouse	daff'a (f)	دفيئة
drought (lack of rain)	ӡafāf (m)	جفاف
dry (~ summer)	ӡāff	جافّ
grain	ḥubūb (pl)	حبوب
cereal crops	maḥāṣīl al ḥubūb (pl)	محاصيل الحبوب
to harvest, to gather	ḥaṣad	حصد
miller (person)	ṭaḥḥān (m)	طحّان
mill (e.g., gristmill)	ṭāḥūna (f)	طاحونة
to grind (grain)	ṭaḥan al ḥubūb	طحن الحبوب
flour	daqīq (m)	دقيق
straw	qaʃʃ (m)	قشّ

121. Building. Building process

construction site	arḍ binā' (f)	أرض بناء
to build (vt)	bana	بنى
construction worker	'āmil binā' (m)	عامل بناء
project	maʃrū' (m)	مشروع
architect	muhandis mi'māriy (m)	مهندس معماريّ
worker	'āmil (m)	عامل
foundation (of a building)	asās (m)	أساس
roof	saqf (m)	سقف
foundation pile	watad al asās (f)	وتد الأساس
wall	ḥā'iṭ (m)	حائط
reinforcing bars	ḥadīd taslīḥ (m)	حديد تسليح
scaffolding	saqāla (f)	سقالة
concrete	χarasāna (f)	خرسانة
granite	granīt (m)	جرانيت
stone	ḥaӡar (m)	حجر
brick	ṭūb (m)	طوب

sand	raml (m)	رمل
cement	ismant (m)	إسمنت
plaster (for walls)	qiṣāra (f)	قصارة
to plaster (vt)	ṭala bil ʒiṣṣ	طلى بالجصّ
paint	dihān (m)	دهان
to paint (~ a wall)	dahhan	دهّن
barrel	barmīl (m)	برميل

crane	rāfiʿa (f)	رافعة
to lift, to hoist (vt)	rafaʿ	رفع
to lower (vt)	anzal	أنزل

bulldozer	ʒarrāfa (f)	جرّافة
excavator	ḥaffāra (f)	حفّارة
scoop, bucket	dalw (m)	دلو
to dig (excavate)	ḥafar	حفر
hard hat	χūða (f)	خوذة

122. Science. Research. Scientists

science	ʿilm (m)	علم
scientific (adj)	ʿilmiy	علميّ
scientist	ʿālim (m)	عالم
theory	naẓariyya (f)	نظريّة

axiom	badīhiyya (f)	بديهيّة
analysis	taḥlīl (m)	تحليل
to analyze (vt)	ḥallal	حلّل
argument (strong ~)	burhān (m)	برهان
substance (matter)	mādda (f)	مادّة

hypothesis	farḍiyya (f)	فرضيّة
dilemma	muʿḍila (f)	معضلة
dissertation	risāla ʿilmiyya (f)	رسالة علميّة
dogma	ʿaqīda (f)	عقيدة

doctrine	maðhab (m)	مذهب
research	baḥθ (m)	بحث
to research (vt)	baḥaθ	بحث
tests (laboratory ~)	iχtibārāt (pl)	إختبارات
laboratory	muχtabar (m)	مختبر

method	manhaʒ (m)	منهج
molecule	ʒuzayʾ (m)	جزيء
monitoring	riqāba (f)	رقابة
discovery (act, event)	iktiʃāf (m)	إكتشاف

postulate	musallama (f)	مسلمة
principle	mabdaʾ (m)	مبدأ
forecast	tanabbuʾ (m)	تنبّؤ

to forecast (vt)	tanabba'	تنبأ
synthesis	tarkīb (m)	تركيب
trend (tendency)	ittiʒāh (m)	إتّجاه
theorem	naẓariyya (f)	نظريّة
teachings	ta'ālīm (pl)	تعاليم
fact	ḥaqīqa (f)	حقيقة
expedition	ba'θa (f)	بعثة
experiment	taʒriba (f)	تجربة
academician	akadīmiy (m)	أكاديميّ
bachelor (e.g., ~ of Arts)	bakalūriyūs (m)	بكالوريوس
doctor (PhD)	duktūr (m)	دكتور
Associate Professor	ustāð muʃārik (m)	أستاذ مشارك
Master (e.g., ~ of Arts)	maʒistīr (m)	ماجستير
professor	brufissūr (m)	بروفيسور

Professions and occupations

123. Job search. Dismissal

job	'amal (m)	عمل
staff (work force)	kawādir (pl)	كوادر
personnel	ṭāqim al 'āmilīn (m)	طاقم العاملين
career	masār mihniy (m)	مسار مهنيّ
prospects (chances)	'āfāq (pl)	آفاق
skills (mastery)	mahārāt (pl)	مهارات
selection (screening)	ixtiyār (m)	إختيار
employment agency	wikālat tawẓīf (f)	وكالة توظيف
résumé	sīra ðātiyya (f)	سيرة ذاتيّة
job interview	mu'ābalat 'amal (f)	مقابلة عمل
vacancy, opening	waẓīfa xāliya (f)	وظيفة خالية
salary, pay	murattab (m)	مرتّب
fixed salary	rātib θābit (m)	راتب ثابت
pay, compensation	uʒra (f)	أجرة
position (job)	manṣib (m)	منصب
duty (of employee)	wāʒib (m)	واجب
range of duties	maʒmū'a min al wāʒibāt (f)	مجموعة من الواجبات
busy (I'm ~)	maʃɣūl	مشغول
to fire (dismiss)	aqāl	أقال
dismissal	iqāla (m)	إقالة
unemployment	biṭāla (f)	بطالة
unemployed (n)	'āṭil (m)	عاطل
retirement	ma'āʃ (m)	معاش
to retire (from job)	uḥīl 'alal ma'āʃ	أحيل على المعاش

124. Business people

director	mudīr (m)	مدير
manager (director)	mudīr (m)	مدير
boss	mudīr (m), ra'īs (m)	مدير, رئيس
superior	ra'īs (m)	رئيس
superiors	ru'asā' (pl)	رؤساء
president	ra'īs (m)	رئيس

chairman	raʾīs (m)	رئيس
deputy (substitute)	nāʾib (m)	نائب
assistant	musāʿid (m)	مساعد
secretary	sikirtīr (m)	سكرتير
personal assistant	sikritīr ҳāṣṣ (m)	سكرتير خاصّ
businessman	raʒul aʿmāl (m)	رجل أعمال
entrepreneur	rāʾid aʿmāl (m)	رائد أعمال
founder	muʾassis (m)	مؤسّس
to found (vt)	assas	أسّس
incorporator	muʾassis (m)	مؤسّس
partner	ʃarīk (m)	شريك
stockholder	musāhim (m)	مساهم
millionaire	milyunīr (m)	مليونير
billionaire	milyardīr (m)	ملياردير
owner, proprietor	ṣāḥib (m)	صاحب
landowner	ṣāḥib al arḍ (m)	صاحب الأرض
client	ʿamīl (m)	عميل
regular client	ʿamīl dāʾim (m)	عميل دائم
buyer (customer)	muʃtari (m)	مشتر
visitor	zāʾir (m)	زائر
professional (n)	muhtarif (m)	محترف
expert	ҳabīr (m)	خبير
specialist	mutaҳaṣṣiṣ (m)	متخصّص
banker	ṣāḥib maṣraf (m)	صاحب مصرف
broker	simsār (m)	سمسار
cashier, teller	ṣarrāf (m)	صرّاف
accountant	muḥāsib (m)	محاسب
security guard	ḥāris amn (m)	حارس أمن
investor	mustaθmir (m)	مستثمر
debtor	mudīn (m)	مدين
creditor	dāʾin (m)	دائن
borrower	muqtariḍ (m)	مقترض
importer	mustawrid (m)	مستورد
exporter	muṣaddir (m)	مصدّر
manufacturer	aʃ ʃarika al muṣniʿa (f)	الشركة المصنعة
distributor	muwazziʿ (m)	موزّع
middleman	wasīṭ (m)	وسيط
consultant	mustaʃār (m)	مستشار
sales representative	mandūb mabiʿāt (m)	مندوب مبيعات
agent	wakīl (m)	وكيل
insurance agent	wakīl at taʾmīn (m)	وكيل التأمين

125. Service professions

cook	ṭabbāχ (m)	طبّاخ
chef (kitchen chef)	ʃāf (m)	شاف
baker	χabbāz (m)	خبّاز
bartender	bārman (m)	بارمان
waiter	nādil (m)	نادل
waitress	nādila (f)	نادلة
lawyer, attorney	muḥāmi (m)	محام
lawyer (legal expert)	muḥāmi (m)	محام
notary	muwaθθaq (m)	موثّق
electrician	kahrabā'iy (m)	كهربائيّ
plumber	sabbāk (m)	سبّاك
carpenter	naʒʒār (m)	نجّار
masseur	mudallik (m)	مدلك
masseuse	mudallika (f)	مدلكة
doctor	ṭabīb (m)	طبيب
taxi driver	sā'iq taksi (m)	سائق تاكسي
driver	sā'iq (m)	سائق
delivery man	sā'i (m)	ساع
chambermaid	ʿāmilat tanzīf χuraf (f)	عاملة تنظيف غرف
security guard	ḥāris amn (m)	حارس أمن
flight attendant (fem.)	muḍīfat ṭayarān (f)	مضيفة طيران
schoolteacher	mudarris madrasa (m)	مدرّس مدرسة
librarian	amīn maktaba (m)	أمين مكتبة
translator	mutarʒim (m)	مترجم
interpreter	mutarʒim fawriy (m)	مترجم فوريّ
guide	murʃid (m)	مرشد
hairdresser	ḥallāq (m)	حلّاق
mailman	sā'i al barīd (m)	سامي البريد
salesman (store staff)	bā'iʿ (m)	بائع
gardener	bustāniy (m)	بستانيّ
domestic servant	χādim (m)	خادم
maid (female servant)	χādima (f)	خادمة
cleaner (cleaning lady)	ʿāmilat tanzīf (f)	عاملة تنظيف

126. Military professions and ranks

private	ʒundiy (m)	جنديّ
sergeant	raqīb (m)	رقيب

| lieutenant | mulāzim (m) | ملازم |
| captain | naqīb (m) | نقيب |

major	rā'id (m)	رائد
colonel	'aqīd (m)	عقيد
general	ʒinirāl (m)	جنرال
marshal	mārʃāl (m)	مارشال
admiral	amirāl (m)	أميرال

military (n)	'askariy (m)	عسكريّ
soldier	ʒundiy (m)	جنديّ
officer	ḍābiṭ (m)	ضابط
commander	qā'id (m)	قائد

border guard	ḥāris ḥudūd (m)	حارس حدود
radio operator	'āmil lāsilkiy (m)	عامل لاسلكيّ
scout (searcher)	mustakʃif (m)	مستكشف
pioneer (sapper)	muhandis 'askariy (m)	مهندس عسكريّ
marksman	rāmi (m)	رام
navigator	mallāḥ (m)	ملّاح

127. Officials. Priests

| king | malik (m) | ملك |
| queen | malika (f) | ملكة |

| prince | amīr (m) | أمير |
| princess | amīra (f) | أميرة |

| czar | qayṣar (m) | قيصر |
| czarina | qayṣara (f) | قيصرة |

president	ra'īs (m)	رئيس
Secretary (minister)	wazīr (m)	وزير
prime minister	ra'īs wuzarā' (m)	رئيس وزراء
senator	'uḍw maʒlis aʃ ʃuyūχ (m)	عضو مجلس الشيوخ

diplomat	diblumāsiy (m)	دبلوماسيّ
consul	qunṣul (m)	قنصل
ambassador	safīr (m)	سفير
counsilor (diplomatic officer)	mustaʃār (m)	مستشار

| official, functionary
(civil servant) | muwaẓẓaf (m) | موظف |

prefect	ra'īs idārat al ḥayy (m)	رئيس إدارة الحيّ
mayor	ra'īs al baladiyya (m)	رئيس البلديّة
judge	qāḍi (m)	قاض
prosecutor (e.g., district attorney)	mudda'i (m)	مدّع

missionary	mubaʃʃir (m)	مبشّر
monk	rāhib (m)	راهب
abbot	raˈīs ad dayr (m)	رئيس الدير
rabbi	ḥāχām (m)	حاخام
vizier	wazīr (m)	وزير
shah	ʃāh (m)	شاه
sheikh	ʃɛyχ (m)	شيخ

128. Agricultural professions

beekeeper	naḥḥāl (m)	نحّال
herder, shepherd	rāˈi (m)	راع
agronomist	muhandis zirāˈiy (m)	مهندس زراعيّ
cattle breeder	murabbi al mawāʃi (m)	مربّي المواشي
veterinarian	ṭabīb bayṭariy (m)	طبيب بيطريّ
farmer	muzāriˈ (m)	مزارع
winemaker	ṣāniˈ an nabīð (m)	صانع النبيذ
zoologist	χabīr fi ˈilm al ḥayawān (m)	خبير في علم الحيوان
cowboy	rāˈi al baqar (m)	راعي البقر

129. Art professions

actor	mumaθθil (m)	ممثّل
actress	mumaθθila (f)	ممثّلة
singer (masc.)	muɣanni (m)	مغنّ
singer (fem.)	muɣanniya (f)	مغنّية
dancer (masc.)	rāqiṣ (m)	راقص
dancer (fem.)	rāqiṣa (f)	راقصة
performer (masc.)	fannān (m)	فنّان
performer (fem.)	fannāna (f)	فنّانة
musician	ˈāzif (m)	عازف
pianist	ˈāzif biyānu (m)	عازف بيانو
guitar player	ˈāzif gitār (m)	عازف جيتار
conductor (orchestra ~)	qāˈid urkistra (m)	قائد أركسترا
composer	mulaḥḥin (m)	ملحّن
impresario	mudīr firqa (m)	مدير فرقة
film director	muχriʒ (m)	مخرج
producer	muntiʒ (m)	منتج
scriptwriter	kātib sināriyu (m)	كاتب سيناريو
critic	nāqid (m)	ناقد

writer	kātib (m)	كاتب
poet	ʃāʿir (m)	شاعر
sculptor	naḥḥāt (m)	نحّات
artist (painter)	rassām (m)	رسّام

juggler	bahlawān (m)	بهلوان
clown	muharriʒ (m)	مهرّج
acrobat	bahlawān (m)	بهلوان
magician	sāḥir (m)	ساحر

130. Various professions

doctor	ṭabīb (m)	طبيب
nurse	mumarriḍa (f)	ممرّضة
psychiatrist	ṭabīb nafsiy (m)	طبيب نفسيّ
dentist	ṭabīb al asnān (m)	طبيب الأسنان
surgeon	ʒarrāḥ (m)	جرّاح

astronaut	rāʾid faḍāʾ (m)	رائد فضاء
astronomer	ʿālim falak (m)	عالم فلك
pilot	ṭayyār (m)	طيّار

driver (of taxi, etc.)	sāʾiq (m)	سائق
engineer (train driver)	sāʾiq (m)	سائق
mechanic	mikanīkiy (m)	ميكانيكيّ

miner	ʿāmil manʒam (m)	عامل منجم
worker	ʿāmil (m)	عامل
locksmith	qaffāl (m)	قفّال
joiner (carpenter)	naʒʒār (m)	نجّار
turner (lathe machine operator)	χarrāṭ (m)	خرّاط
construction worker	ʿāmil bināʾ (m)	عامل بناء
welder	laḥḥām (m)	لحّام

professor (title)	brufissūr (m)	بروفيسور
architect	muhandis miʿmāriy (m)	مهندس معماريّ
historian	muʾarriχ (m)	مؤرّخ
scientist	ʿālim (m)	عالم
physicist	fizyāʾiy (m)	فيزيائيّ
chemist (scientist)	kimyāʾiy (m)	كيميائيّ

archeologist	ʿālim ʾāθār (m)	عالم آثار
geologist	ʒiulūʒiy (m)	جيولوجيّ
researcher (scientist)	bāḥiθ (m)	باحث

babysitter	murabbiyat aṭfāl (f)	مربّية الأطفال
teacher, educator	muʿallim (m)	معلّم
editor	muḥarrir (m)	محرّر
editor-in-chief	raʾīs taḥrīr (m)	رئيس تحرير

| correspondent | murāsil (m) | مراسل |
| typist (fem.) | kāteba 'ala el 'āla el kāteba (f) | كاتبة على الآلة الكاتبة |

| designer | muṣammim (m) | مصمّم |
| computer expert | mutaxaṣṣiṣ bil kumbyūtir (m) | متخصص بالكمبيوتر |

| programmer | mubarmiʒ (m) | مبرمج |
| engineer (designer) | muhandis (m) | مهندس |

sailor	baḥḥār (m)	بحّار
seaman	baḥḥār (m)	بحّار
rescuer	munqið (m)	منقذ

fireman	raʒul iṭfā' (m)	رجل إطفاء
police officer	ʃurṭiy (m)	شرطيّ
watchman	ḥāris (m)	حارس
detective	muḥaqqiq (m)	محقّق

customs officer	muwaẓẓaf al ʒamārik (m)	موظّف الجمارك
bodyguard	ḥāris ʃaxṣiy (m)	حارس شخصيّ
prison guard	ḥāris siʒn (m)	حارس سجن
inspector	mufattiʃ (m)	مفتّش

sportsman	riyāḍiy (m)	رياضيّ
trainer, coach	mudarrib (m)	مدرّب
butcher	ʒazzār (m)	جزّار
cobbler (shoe repairer)	iskāfiy (m)	إسكافيّ
merchant	tāʒir (m)	تاجر
loader (person)	ḥammāl (m)	حمّال

| fashion designer | muṣammim azyā' (m) | مصمّم أزياء |
| model (fem.) | mudīl (f) | موديل |

131. Occupations. Social status

| schoolboy | tilmīð (m) | تلميذ |
| student (college ~) | ṭālib (m) | طالب |

philosopher	faylasūf (m)	فيلسوف
economist	iqtiṣādiy (m)	إقتصاديّ
inventor	muxtariʿ (m)	مخترع

unemployed (n)	'āṭil (m)	عاطل
retiree	mutaqāʿid (m)	متقاعد
spy, secret agent	ʒāsūs (m)	جاسوس

prisoner	saʒīn (m)	سجين
striker	muḍrib (m)	مضرب
bureaucrat	buruqrāṭiy (m)	بيوروقراطيّ

traveler (globetrotter)	raḥḥāla (m)	رحّالة
gay, homosexual (n)	miθliy ʒinsiyyan (m)	مثليّ جنسيًا
hacker	hākir (m)	ماكر
hippie	hippi (m)	هيبي
bandit	qāṭiʿ ṭarīq (m)	قاطع طريق
hit man, killer	qātil maʾʒūr (m)	قاتل مأجور
drug addict	mudmin muxaddirāt (m)	مدمن مخدّرات
drug dealer	tāʒir muxaddirāt (m)	تاجر مخدّرات
prostitute (fem.)	ʿāhira (f)	عاهرة
pimp	qawwād (m)	قوّاد
sorcerer	sāḥir (m)	ساحر
sorceress (evil ~)	sāḥira (f)	ساحرة
pirate	qurṣān (m)	قرصان
slave	ʿabd (m)	عبد
samurai	samurāy (m)	ساموراي
savage (primitive)	mutawaḥḥiʃ (m)	متوحّش

Sports

132.   Kinds of sports. Sportspersons

sportsman	riyāḍiy (m)	رياضيّ
kind of sports	naw' min ar riyāḍa (m)	نوع من الرياضة
basketball	kurat as salla (f)	كرة السلّة
basketball player	lā'ib kūrat as salla (m)	لاعب كرة السلّة
baseball	kurat al qā'ida (f)	كرة القاعدة
baseball player	lā'ib kurat al qā'ida (m)	لاعب كرة القاعدة
soccer	kurat al qadam (f)	كرة القدم
soccer player	lā'ib kurat al qadam (m)	لاعب كرة القدم
goalkeeper	ḥāris al marma (m)	حارس المرمى
hockey	huki (m)	هوكي
hockey player	lā'ib huki (m)	لاعب هوكي
volleyball	al kura aṭ ṭā'ira (m)	الكرة الطائرة
volleyball player	lā'ib al kura aṭ ṭā'ira (m)	لاعب الكرة الطائرة
boxing	mulākama (f)	ملاكمة
boxer	mulākim (m)	ملاكم
wrestling	muṣāra'a (f)	مصارعة
wrestler	muṣāri' (m)	مصارع
karate	karatī (m)	كاراتيه
karate fighter	lā'ib karatī (m)	لاعب كاراتيه
judo	ʒudu (m)	جودو
judo athlete	lā'ib ʒudu (m)	لاعب جودو
tennis	tinis (m)	تنس
tennis player	lā'ib tinnis (m)	لاعب تنس
swimming	sibāḥa (f)	سباحة
swimmer	sabbāḥ (m)	سبّاح
fencing	musāyafa (f)	مسايفة
fencer	mubāriz (m)	مبارز
chess	ʃaṭranʒ (m)	شطرنج
chess player	lā'ib ʃaṭranʒ (m)	لاعب شطرنج

| alpinism | tasalluq al ӡibāl (m) | تسلّق الجبال |
| alpinist | mutasalliq al ӡibāl (m) | متسلّق الجبال |

| running | ӡary (m) | جري |
| runner | 'addā' (m) | عدّاء |

| athletics | al'āb al qiwa (pl) | ألعاب القوى |
| athlete | lā'ib riyāḍiy (m) | لاعب رياضيّ |

| horseback riding | riyāḍat al furūsiyya (f) | رياضة الفروسيّة |
| horse rider | fāris (m) | فارس |

| figure skating | tazalluӡ fanniy 'alal ӡalīd (m) | تزلّج فنّيّ على الجليد |

| figure skater (masc.) | mutazalliӡ fanniy (m) | متزلّج فنّيّ |
| figure skater (fem.) | mutazalliӡa fanniyya (f) | متزلّجة فنّيّة |

| powerlifting | raf' al aθqāl (m) | رفع الأثقال |
| powerlifter | rāfi' al aθqāl (m) | رافع الأثقال |

| car racing | sibāq as sayyārāt (m) | سباق السيّارات |
| racing driver | sā'iq sibāq (m) | سائق سباق |

| cycling | sibāq ad darrāӡāt (m) | سباق الدرّاجات |
| cyclist | lā'ib ad darrāӡāt (m) | لاعب الدرّاجات |

broad jump	al qafz aṭ ṭawīl (m)	القفز الطويل
pole vault	al qafz biz zāna (m)	القفز بالزانة
jumper	qāfiz (m)	قافز

133. Kinds of sports. Miscellaneous

football	kurat al qadam (f)	كرة القدم
badminton	kurat ar rīʃa (f)	كرة الريشة
biathlon	al biatlūn (m)	البياثلون
billiards	bilyārdu (m)	بلياردو

bobsled	zallāӡa ӡama'iyya (f)	زلّاجة جماعيّة
bodybuilding	kamāl aӡsām (m)	كمال أجسام
water polo	kurat al mā' (f)	كرة الماء
handball	kurat al yad (f)	كرة اليد
golf	gūlf (m)	جولف

rowing, crew	taӡðīf (m)	تجذيف
scuba diving	al ɣaws taht al mā' (m)	الغوص تحت الماء
cross-country skiing	riyāḍat al iski (f)	رياضة الإسكي
table tennis (ping-pong)	kurat aṭ ṭāwila (f)	كرة الطاولة

| sailing | riyāḍa ibḥār al marākib (f) | رياضة إبحار المراكب |
| rally racing | sibāq as sayyārāt (m) | سباق السيّارات |

rugby	raɣbi (m)	رغبي
snowboarding	tazalluʒ 'laθ θuluʒ (m)	تزلج على الثلج
archery	rimāya (f)	رماية

134. Gym

| barbell | ḥadīda (f) | حديدة |
| dumbbells | dambilz (m) | دمبلز |

training machine	ʒihāz tadrīb (m)	جهاز تدريب
exercise bicycle	darrāʒat tadrīb (f)	دراجة تدريب
treadmill	ʒihāz al maʃy (m)	جهاز المشي

horizontal bar	'uqla (f)	عقلة
parallel bars	al mutawāzi (m)	المتوازي
vault (vaulting horse)	hisān al maqābiḍ (m)	حصان المقابض
mat (exercise ~)	ḥaṣīra (f)	حصيرة

jump rope	ḥabl an naṭṭ (m)	حبل النط
aerobics	at tamrīnāt al hiwā'iyya (pl)	التمرينات الهوائية
yoga	yūga (f)	يوجا

135. Hockey

hockey	huki (m)	هوكي
hockey player	lā'ib huki (m)	لاعب هوكي
to play hockey	la'ib al hūki	لعب الهوكي
ice	ʒalīd (m)	جليد

puck	qurṣ al huky (m)	قرص الهوكي
hockey stick	miḍrab al huki (m)	مضرب الهوكي
ice skates	zallāʒāt (pl)	زلاجات
board (ice hockey rink ~)	ʒānib (m)	جانب
shot	ramya (f)	رمية

goaltender	ḥāris al marma (m)	حارس المرمى
goal (score)	hadaf (m)	هدف
to score a goal	aṣāb al hadaf	أصاب الهدف
period	ʃawṭ (m)	شوط
second period	aʃ ʃawṭ aθ θāni (m)	الشوط الثاني
substitutes bench	dikkat al iḥṭiāṭy (f)	دكة الإحتياطي

136. Soccer

| soccer | kurat al qadam (f) | كرة القدم |
| soccer player | lā'ib kurat al qadam (m) | لاعب كرة القدم |

to play soccer	la'ib kurat al qadam	لعب كرة القدم
major league	ad dawriy al kibīr (m)	الدوريّ الكبير
soccer club	nādy kurat al qadam (m)	نادي كرة القدم
coach	mudarrib (m)	مدرّب
owner, proprietor	ṣāḥib (m)	صاحب
team	farīq (m)	فريق
team captain	kabtan al farīq (m)	كابتن الفريق
player	lā'ib (m)	لاعب
substitute	lā'ib iḥtiyāṭiy (m)	لاعب إحتياطيّ
forward	lā'ib huӡūm (m)	لاعب هجوم
center forward	wasaṭ al huӡūm (m)	وسط الهجوم
scorer	haddāf (m)	هدّاف
defender, back	mudāfi' (m)	مدافع
midfielder, halfback	lā'ib wasaṭ (m)	لاعب وسط
match	mubārāt (f)	مباراة
to meet (vi, vt)	qābal	قابل
final	mubarāt nihā'iyya (f)	مباراة نهائيّة
semi-final	dawr an niṣf an nihā'iy (m)	دور النصف النهائيّ
championship	buṭūla (f)	بطولة
period, half	ʃawṭ (m)	شوط
first period	aʃ ʃawṭ al awwal (m)	الشوط الأوّل
half-time	istirāḥa ma bayn aʃ ʃawṭayn (f)	إستراحة ما بين الشوطين
goal	marma (m)	مرمى
goalkeeper	ḥāris al marma (m)	حارس المرمى
goalpost	'ārida (f)	عارضة
crossbar	'ārida (f)	عارضة
net	ʃabaka (f)	شبكة
to concede a goal	samaḥ bi iṣābat al hadaf	سمح بإصابة الهدف
ball	kura (f)	كرة
pass	tamrīra (f)	تمريرة
kick	ḍarba (f)	ضربة
to kick (~ the ball)	ḍarab	ضرب
free kick (direct ~)	ḍarba ḥurra (f)	ضربة حرّة
corner kick	ḍarba zāwiya (f)	ضربة زاوية
attack	huӡūm (m)	هجوم
counterattack	haӡma muḍādda (f)	هجمة مضادّة
combination	tarkīb (m)	تركيب
referee	ḥakam (m)	حكم
to blow the whistle	ṣaffar	صفّر
whistle (sound)	ṣaffāra (f)	صفّارة
foul, misconduct	muxālafa (f)	مخالفة
to commit a foul	xālaf	خالف
to send off	ṭarad min al mal'ab	طرد من الملعب

yellow card	al kārt al aṣfar (m)	الكارت الأصفر
red card	al kart al aḥmar (m)	الكارت الأحمر
disqualification	ḥirmān (m)	حرمان
to disqualify (vt)	ḥaram	حرم
penalty kick	ḍarbat ʒazā' (f)	ضربة جزاء
wall	ḥā'iṭ (m)	حائط
to score (vi, vt)	aṣāb al hadaf	أصاب الهدف
goal (score)	hadaf (m)	هدف
to score a goal	aṣāb al hadaf	أصاب الهدف
substitution	tabdīl (m)	تبديل
to replace (a player)	baddal	بدّل
rules	qawā'id (pl)	قواعد
tactics	taktīk (m)	تكتيك
stadium	mal'ab (m)	ملعب
stand (bleachers)	mudarraʒ (m)	مدرّج
fan, supporter	muʃaʒʒi' (m)	مشجّع
to shout (vi)	ṣaraχ	صرخ
scoreboard	lawḥat an natīʒa (f)	لوحة النتيجة
score	natīʒa (f)	نتيجة
defeat	hazīma (f)	هزيمة
to lose (not win)	χasir	خسر
tie	ta'ādul (m)	تعادل
to tie (vi)	ta'ādal	تعادل
victory	fawz (m)	فوز
to win (vi, vt)	fāz	فاز
champion	baṭal (m)	بطل
best (adj)	aḥsan	أحسن
to congratulate (vt)	hanna'	هنّأ
commentator	mu'alliq (m)	معلق
to commentate (vt)	'allaq	علق
broadcast	iðā'a (f)	إذاعة

137. Alpine skiing

skis	zallāʒāt (pl)	زلاجات
to ski (vi)	tazallaʒ	تزلج
mountain-ski resort	muntaʒa' ʒabaliy lit tazalluʒ (m)	منتجع جبليّ للتزلّج
ski lift	miṣ'ad (m)	مصعد
ski poles	'aṣayān at tazalluʒ (pl)	عصيان التزلج
slope	munḥadar (m)	منحدر
slalom	slālum (m)	سلالوم

138. Tennis. Golf

golf	gūlf (m)	جولف
golf club	nādi gūlf (m)	نادي جولف
golfer	lā'ib gūlf (m)	لاعب جولف
hole	taʒwīf (m)	تجويف
club	miḍrab (m)	مضرب
golf trolley	'araba lil gūlf (f)	عربة للجولف
tennis	tinis (m)	تنس
tennis court	mal'ab tinis (m)	ملعب تنس
serve	munāwala (f)	مناولة
to serve (vt)	nāwil	ناول
racket	miḍrab (m)	مضرب
net	ʃabaka (f)	شبكة
ball	kura (f)	كرة

139. Chess

chess	ʃaṭranʒ (m)	شطرنج
chessmen	qita' aʃ ʃaṭranʒ (pl)	قطع الشطرنج
chess player	lā'ib ʃaṭranʒ (m)	لاعب شطرنج
chessboard	lawḥat aʃ ʃaṭranʒ (f)	لوحة الشطرنج
chessman	qiṭ'a (f)	قطعة
White (white pieces)	qiṭa' bayḍā' (pl)	قطع بيضاء
Black (black pieces)	qiṭa' sawdā' (pl)	قطع سوداء
pawn	baydaq (m)	بيدق
bishop	fīl (m)	فيل
knight	ḥiṣān (m)	حصان
rook	qal'a (f)	قلعة
queen	malika (f)	ملكة
king	malik (m)	ملك
move	xaṭwa (f)	خطوة
to move (vi, vt)	ḥarrak	حرّك
to sacrifice (vt)	ḍaḥḥa	ضحّى
castling	at tabyīt (m)	التبييت
check	kaʃʃ (m)	كشّ
checkmate	kaʃʃ māt (m)	كش مات
chess tournament	buṭūlat ʃaṭranʒ (f)	بطولة شطرنج
Grand Master	ustāð kabīr (m)	أستاذ كبير
combination	tarkīb (m)	تركيب
game (in chess)	dawr (m)	دور
checkers	dāma (f)	ضامة

140. Boxing

boxing	mulākama (f)	ملاكمة
fight (bout)	mulākama (f)	ملاكمة
boxing match	mubārāt mulākama (f)	مباراة ملاكمة
round (in boxing)	ʒawla (f)	جولة

ring	ḥalba (f)	حلبة
gong	nāqūs (m)	ناقوس

punch	ḍarba (f)	ضربة
knockdown	ḍarba ḥāsima (f)	ضربة حاسمة
knockout	ḍarba qāḍiya (f)	ضربة قاضية
to knock out	ḍarab ḍarba qāḍiya	ضرب ضربة قاضية

boxing glove	quffāz al mulākama (m)	قفّاز الملاكمة
referee	ḥakam (m)	حكم

lightweight	al wazn al xafīf (m)	الوزن الخفيف
middleweight	al wazn al mutawassiṭ (m)	الوزن المتوسّط
heavyweight	al wazn aθ θaqīl (m)	الوزن الثقيل

141. Sports. Miscellaneous

Olympic Games	al'āb ulumbiyya (pl)	ألعاب أولمبيّة
winner	fā'iz (m)	فائز
to be winning	fāz	فاز
to win (vi)	fāz	فاز

leader	za'īm (m)	زعيم
to lead (vi)	taqaddam	تقدّم

first place	al martaba al ūla (f)	المرتبة الأولى
second place	al martaba aθ θāniya (f)	المرتبة الثانية
third place	al martaba aθ θāliθa (f)	المرتبة الثالثة

medal	midāliyya (f)	ميداليّة
trophy	ʒā'iza (f)	جائزة
prize cup (trophy)	ka's (m)	كأس
prize (in game)	ʒā'iza (f)	جائزة
main prize	akbar ʒā'iza (f)	أكبر جائزة

record	raqm qiyāsiy (m)	رقم قياسيّ
to set a record	fāz bi raqm qiyāsiy	فاز برقم قياسيّ

final	mubarāt nihā'iyya (f)	مباراة نهائيّة
final (adj)	nihā'iy	نهائيّ
champion	baṭal (m)	بطل
championship	buṭūla (f)	بطولة

stadium	mal'ab (m)	ملعب
stand (bleachers)	mudarraʒ (m)	مدرّج
fan, supporter	muʃaʒʒi' (m)	مشجع
opponent, rival	'aduww (m)	عدوّ
start (start line)	χatt al bidāya (m)	خطّ البداية
finish line	χatt an nihāya (m)	خطّ النهاية
defeat	hazīma (f)	هزيمة
to lose (not win)	χasir	خسر
referee	ḥakam (m)	حكم
jury (judges)	hay'at al ḥukm (f)	هيئة الحكم
score	natīʒa (f)	نتيجة
tie	ta'ādul (m)	تعادل
to tie (vi)	ta'ādal	تعادل
point	nuqta (f)	نقطة
result (final score)	natīʒa nihā'iyya (f)	نتيجة نهائية
period	ʃawt (m)	شوط
half-time	istirāḥa ma bayn aʃ ʃawtayn (f)	إستراحة ما بين الشوطين
doping	munaʃʃitāt (pl)	منشّطات
to penalize (vt)	'āqab	عاقب
to disqualify (vt)	ḥaram	حرم
apparatus	ma'add riyāḍiy (f)	معدّ رياضيّ
javelin	rumḥ (m)	رمح
shot (metal ball)	ʒulla (f)	جلّة
ball (snooker, etc.)	kura (f)	كرة
aim (target)	hadaf (m)	هدف
target	hadaf (m)	هدف
to shoot (vi)	atlaq an nār	أطلق النار
accurate (~ shot)	maḍbūt	مضبوط
trainer, coach	mudarrib (m)	مدرّب
to train (sb)	darrab	درّب
to train (vi)	tadarrab	تدرّب
training	tadrīb (m)	تدريب
gym	markaz li liyāqa badaniyya (m)	مركز للياقة بدنيّة
exercise (physical)	tamrīn (m)	تمرين
warm-up (athlete ~)	tasχīn (m)	تسخين

Education

142. School

school	madrasa (f)	مدرسة
principal (headmaster)	mudīr madrasa (m)	مدير مدرسة
pupil (boy)	tilmīð (m)	تلميذ
pupil (girl)	tilmīða (f)	تلميذة
schoolboy	tilmīð (m)	تلميذ
schoolgirl	tilmīða (f)	تلميذة
to teach (sb)	'allam	علّم
to learn (language, etc.)	ta'allam	تعلّم
to learn by heart	ḥafaẓ	حفظ
to learn (~ to count, etc.)	ta'allam	تعلّم
to be in school	daras	درس
to go to school	ðahab ilal madrasa	ذهب إلى المدرسة
alphabet	alifbā' (m)	الفباء
subject (at school)	mādda (f)	مادّة
classroom	faṣl (m)	فصل
lesson	dars (m)	درس
recess	istirāḥa (f)	إستراحة
school bell	ʒaras al madrasa (m)	جرس المدرسة
school desk	taxta lil madrasa (m)	تخته للمدرسة
chalkboard	sabbūra (f)	سبّورة
grade	daraʒa (f)	درجة
good grade	daraʒa ʒayyida (f)	درجة جيّدة
bad grade	daraʒa ɣayr ʒayyida (f)	درجة غير جيّدة
to give a grade	a'ṭa daraʒa	أعطى درجة
mistake, error	xaṭa' (m)	خطأ
to make mistakes	axṭa'	أخطأ
to correct (an error)	ṣaḥḥaḥ	صحّح
cheat sheet	waraqat ɣaʃʃ (f)	ورقة غشّ
homework	wāʒib manziliy (m)	واجب منزليّ
exercise (in education)	tamrīn (m)	تمرين
to be present	ḥaḍar	حضر
to be absent	ɣāb	غاب
to miss school	taɣayyab 'an al madrasa	تغيّب عن المدرسة

to punish (vt)	ʿāqab	عاقب
punishment	ʿuqūba (f), ʿiqāb (m)	عقوبة, عقاب
conduct (behavior)	sulūk (m)	سلوك

report card	at taqrīr al madrasiy (m)	التقرير المدرسيّ
pencil	qalam ruṣāṣ (m)	قلم رصاص
eraser	astīka (f)	استيكة
chalk	ṭabāʃīr (m)	طباشير
pencil case	maqlama (f)	مقلمة

schoolbag	ʃanṭat al madrasa (f)	شنطة المدرسة
pen	qalam (m)	قلم
school notebook	daftar (m)	دفتر
textbook	kitāb taʿlīm (m)	كتاب تعليم
compasses	barʒal (m)	برجل

| to make technical drawings | rasam rasm taqniy | رسم رسمًا تقنيًا |
| technical drawing | rasm taqniy (m) | رسم تقنيّ |

poem	qaṣīda (f)	قصيدة
by heart (adv)	ʿan ẓahr qalb	عن ظهر قلب
to learn by heart	ḥafaẓ	حفظ

school vacation	ʿuṭla madrasiyya (f)	عطلة مدرسيّة
to be on vacation	ʿindahu ʿuṭla	عنده عطلة
to spend one's vacation	qaḍa al ʿuṭla	قضى العطلة

test (written math ~)	imtiḥān (m)	إمتحان
essay (composition)	inʃāʾ (m)	إنشاء
dictation	imlāʾ (m)	إملاء
exam (examination)	imtiḥān (m)	إمتحان
to take an exam	marr al imtiḥān	مرّ الإمتحان
experiment (e.g., chemistry ~)	taʒriba (f)	تجربة

143. College. University

academy	akadīmiyya (f)	أكاديميّة
university	ʒāmiʿa (f)	جامعة
faculty (e.g., ~ of Medicine)	kulliyya (f)	كليّة

student (masc.)	ṭālib (m)	طالب
student (fem.)	ṭāliba (f)	طالبة
lecturer (teacher)	muḥāḍir (m)	محاضر

lecture hall, room	mudarraʒ (m)	مدرّج
graduate	mutaxarriʒ (m)	متخرّج
diploma	diblūma (f)	دبلومة

dissertation	risāla 'ilmiyya (f)	رسالة علميّة
study (report)	dirāsa (f)	دراسة
laboratory	muxtabar (m)	مختبر
lecture	muḥāḍara (f)	محاضرة
coursemate	zamīl fiṣ ṣaff (m)	زميل في الصفّ
scholarship	minḥa dirāsiyya (f)	منحة دراسيّة
academic degree	daraʒa 'ilmiyya (f)	درجة علميّة

144. Sciences. Disciplines

mathematics	riyāḍīyyāt (pl)	رياضيّات
algebra	al ʒabr (m)	الجبر
geometry	handasa (f)	هندسة
astronomy	'ilm al falak (m)	علم الفلك
biology	'ilm al aḥyā' (m)	علم الأحياء
geography	ʒuɣrāfiya (f)	جغرافيا
geology	ʒiulūʒiya (f)	جيولوجيا
history	tarīx (m)	تاريخ
medicine	ṭibb (m)	طبّ
pedagogy	'ilm at tarbiya (f)	علم التربية
law	qānūn (m)	قانون
physics	fizyā' (f)	فيزياء
chemistry	kimyā' (f)	كيمياء
philosophy	falsafa (f)	فلسفة
psychology	'ilm an nafs (m)	علم النفس

145. Writing system. Orthography

grammar	an naḥw waṣ ṣarf (m)	النحو والصرف
vocabulary	mufradāt al luɣa (pl)	مفردات اللغة
phonetics	ṣawtīyyāt (pl)	صوتيّات
noun	ism (m)	إسم
adjective	ṣifa (f)	صفة
verb	fi'l (m)	فعل
adverb	ẓarf (m)	ظرف
pronoun	ḍamīr (m)	ضمير
interjection	ḥarf nidā' (m)	حرف نداء
preposition	ḥarf al ʒarr (m)	حرف الجرّ
root	ʒiðr al kalima (m)	جذر الكلمة
ending	nihāya (f)	نهاية
prefix	sābiqa (f)	سابقة

| syllable | maqtaʻ lafẓiy (m) | مقطع لفظيّ |
| suffix | lāḥiqa (f) | لاحقة |

| stress mark | nabra (f) | نبرة |
| apostrophe | ʻalāmat ḥaðf (f) | علامة حذف |

period, dot	nuqta (f)	نقطة
comma	fāṣila (f)	فاصلة
semicolon	nuqta wa fāṣila (f)	نقطة وفاصلة
colon	nuqtatān raʼsiyyatān (du)	نقطتان رأسيتان
ellipsis	θalāθ nuqat (pl)	ثلاث نقط

| question mark | ʻalāmat istifhām (f) | علامة إستفهام |
| exclamation point | ʻalāmat taʻaʒʒub (f) | علامة تعجّب |

quotation marks	ʻalāmāt al iqtibās (pl)	علامات الإقتباس
in quotation marks	bayn ʻalāmatay al iqtibās	بين علامتي الإقتباس
parenthesis	qawsān (du)	قوسان
in parenthesis	bayn al qawsayn	بين القوسين

hyphen	ʻalāmat waṣl (f)	علامة وصل
dash	ʃurṭa (f)	شرطة
space (between words)	farāɣ (m)	فراغ

| letter | ḥarf (m) | حرف |
| capital letter | ḥarf kabīr (m) | حرف كبير |

| vowel (n) | ḥarf ṣawtiy (m) | حرف صوتيّ |
| consonant (n) | ḥarf sākin (m) | حرف ساكن |

sentence	ʒumla (f)	جملة
subject	fāʻil (m)	فاعل
predicate	musnad (m)	مسند

line	saṭr (m)	سطر
on a new line	min bidāyat as saṭr	من بداية السطر
paragraph	fiqra (f)	فقرة

word	kalima (f)	كلمة
group of words	maʒmūʻa min al kalimāt (pl)	مجموعة من الكلمات
expression	ʻibāra (f)	عبارة
synonym	murādif (m)	مرادف
antonym	mutaḍādd luɣawiy (m)	متضادّ

rule	qāʻida (f)	قاعدة
exception	istiθnāʼ (m)	إستثناء
correct (adj)	ṣaḥīḥ	صحيح

conjugation	ṣarf (m)	صرف
declension	taṣrīf al asmāʼ (m)	تصريف الأسماء
nominal case	ḥāla ismiyya (f)	حالة إسميّة
question	suʼāl (m)	سؤال

| to underline (vt) | waḍaʿ xaṭṭ taḥt | وضع خطًا تحت |
| dotted line | xaṭṭ munaqqaṭ (m) | خط منقط |

146. Foreign languages

language	luɣa (f)	لغة
foreign (adj)	aʒnabiy	أجنبيّ
foreign language	luɣa aʒnabiyya (f)	لغة أجنبيّة
to study (vt)	daras	درس
to learn (language, etc.)	taʿallam	تعلّم

to read (vi, vt)	qaraʾ	قرأ
to speak (vi, vt)	takallam	تكلّم
to understand (vt)	fahim	فهم
to write (vt)	katab	كتب

fast (adv)	bi surʿa	بسرعة
slowly (adv)	bi buṭʾ	ببطء
fluently (adv)	bi ṭalāqa	بطلاقة

rules	qawāʿid (pl)	قواعد
grammar	an naḥw waṣ ṣarf (m)	النحو والصرف
vocabulary	mufradāt al luɣa (pl)	مفردات اللغة
phonetics	ṣawtīyyāt (pl)	صوتيّات

textbook	kitāb taʿlīm (m)	كتاب تعليم
dictionary	qāmūs (m)	قاموس
teach-yourself book	kitāb taʿlīm ðātiy (m)	كتاب تعليم ذاتيّ
phrasebook	kitāb lil ʿibārāt aʃ ʃāʾiʿa (m)	كتاب للعبارات الشائعة

cassette, tape	ʃarīṭ (m)	شريط
videotape	ʃarīṭ vidiyu (m)	شريط فيديو
CD, compact disc	si di (m)	سي دي
DVD	di vi di (m)	دي في دي

alphabet	alifbāʾ (m)	الفباء
to spell (vt)	tahaʒʒa	تهجّى
pronunciation	nuṭq (m)	نطق

accent	lukna (f)	لكنة
with an accent	bi lukna	بلكنة
without an accent	bi dūn lukna	بدون لكنة

| word | kalima (f) | كلمة |
| meaning | maʿna (m) | معنى |

course (e.g., a French ~)	dawra (f)	دورة
to sign up	saʒʒal ismahu	سجّل إسمه
teacher	mudarris (m)	مدرس
translation (process)	tarʒama (f)	ترجمة

translation (text, etc.)	tarʒama (f)	ترجمة
translator	mutarʒim (m)	مترجم
interpreter	mutarʒim fawriy (m)	مترجم فوريّ
polyglot	'alīm bi 'iddat luɣāt (m)	عليم بعدّة لغات
memory	ðākira (f)	ذاكرة

147. Fairy tale characters

Santa Claus	baba nuwīl (m)	بابا نويل
Cinderella	sindrīla	سيندريلا
mermaid	ḥūriyyat al baḥr (f)	حوريّة البحر
Neptune	nibtūn (m)	نبتون
magician, wizard	sāḥir (m)	ساحر
fairy	sāḥira (f)	ساحرة
magic (adj)	siḥriy	سحريّ
magic wand	'aṣa siḥriyya (f)	عصا سحريّة
fairy tale	ḥikāya χayāliyya (f)	حكاية خياليّة
miracle	mu'ʒiza (f)	معجزة
dwarf	qazam (m)	قزم
to turn into ...	taḥawwal ila ...	تحوّل إلى...
ghost	ʃabaḥ (m)	شبح
phantom	ʃabaḥ (m)	شبح
monster	waḥʃ (m)	وحش
dragon	tinnīn (m)	تنّين
giant	'imlāq (m)	عملاق

148. Zodiac Signs

Aries	burʒ al ḥamal (m)	برج الحمل
Taurus	burʒ aθ θawr (m)	برج الثور
Gemini	burʒ al ʒawzā' (m)	برج الجوزاء
Cancer	burʒ as saraṭān (m)	برج السرطان
Leo	burʒ al asad (m)	برج الأسد
Virgo	burʒ al 'aðrā' (m)	برج العذراء
Libra	burʒ al mīzān (m)	برج الميزان
Scorpio	burʒ al 'aqrab (m)	برج العقرب
Sagittarius	burʒ al qaws (m)	برج القوس
Capricorn	burʒ al ʒaday (m)	برج الجدي
Aquarius	burʒ ad dalw (m)	برج الدلو
Pisces	burʒ al ḥūt (m)	برج الحوت
character	ṭab' (m)	طبع
character traits	aṣ ṣifāt aʃ ʃaχṣiyya (pl)	الصفات الشخصيّة

behavior	sulūk (m)	سلوك
to tell fortunes	tanabba'	تنبّأ
fortune-teller	'arrāfa (f)	عرّافة
horoscope	tawaqqu'āt al abrāʒ (pl)	توقّعات الأبراج

Arts

149. Theater

theater	masraḥ (m)	مسرح
opera	ubra (f)	أوبرا
operetta	ubirīt (f)	أوبريت
ballet	balīh (m)	باليه
theater poster	mulṣaq (m)	ملصق
troupe (theatrical company)	firqa (f)	فرقة
tour	ʒawlat fannānīn (f)	جولة فنانين
to be on tour	taʒawwal	تجوّل
to rehearse (vi, vt)	aʒra bruvāt	أجرى بروفات
rehearsal	brūva (f)	بروفة
repertoire	barnāmaʒ al masraḥ (m)	برنامج المسرح
performance	adā' fanniy (m)	أداء فنّي
theatrical show	'arḍ masraḥiy (m)	عرض مسرحي
play	masraḥiyya (f)	مسرحية
ticket	taðkira (f)	تذكرة
box office (ticket booth)	ʃubbāk at taðākir (m)	شبّاك التذاكر
lobby, foyer	ṣāla (f)	صالة
coat check (cloakroom)	ɣurfat al ma'āṭif (f)	غرفة المعاطف
coat check tag	biṭāqat ʾīdā' al ma'āṭif (f)	بطاقة إيداع المعاطف
binoculars	minẓār (m)	منظار
usher	ḥāʒib (m)	حاجب
orchestra seats	karāsi al urkistra (pl)	كراسي الأوركسترا
balcony	balakūna (f)	بلكونة
dress circle	ʃurfa (f)	شرفة
box	lūʒ (m)	لوج
row	ṣaff (m)	صفّ
seat	maq'ad (m)	مقعد
audience	ʒumhūr (m)	جمهور
spectator	muʃāhid (m)	مشاهد
to clap (vi, vt)	ṣaffaq	صفّق
applause	taṣfīq (m)	تصفيق
ovation	taṣfīq ḥārr (m)	تصفيق حارّ
stage	xaʃabat al masraḥ (f)	خشبة المسرح
curtain	sitāra (f)	ستارة
scenery	dikūr (m)	ديكور

backstage	kawalīs (pl)	كواليس
scene (e.g., the last ~)	maʃhad (m)	مشهد
act	faṣl (m)	فصل
intermission	istirāḥa (f)	إستراحة

150. Cinema

| actor | mumaθθil (m) | ممثّل |
| actress | mumaθθila (f) | ممثّلة |

movies (industry)	sinima (f)	سينما
movie	film sinimā'iy (m)	فيلم سينمائيّ
episode	ʒuz' min al film (m)	جزء من الفيلم

detective movie	film bulīsiy (m)	فيلم بوليسيّ
action movie	film ḥaraka (m)	فيلم حركة
adventure movie	film muɣāmarāt (m)	فيلم مغامرات
science fiction movie	film xayāl 'ilmiy (m)	فيلم خيال علميّ
horror movie	film ru'b (m)	فيلم رعب

comedy movie	film kumīdiya (f)	فيلم كوميديا
melodrama	miludrāma (m)	ميلودراما
drama	drāma (f)	دراما

fictional movie	film fanniy (m)	فيلم فنّيّ
documentary	film waθā'iqiy (m)	فيلم وثائقيّ
cartoon	film kartūn (m)	فيلم كرتون
silent movies	sinima ṣāmita (f)	سينما صامتة

role (part)	dawr (m)	دور
leading role	dawr ra'īsi (m)	دور رئيسي
to play (vi, vt)	maθθal	مثّل

movie star	naʒm sinimā'iy (m)	نجم سينمائيّ
well-known (adj)	ma'rūf	معروف
famous (adj)	maʃhūr	مشهور
popular (adj)	maḥbūb	محبوب

script (screenplay)	sināriyu (m)	سيناريو
scriptwriter	kātib sināriyu (m)	كاتب سيناريو
movie director	muxriʒ (m)	مخرج
producer	muntiʒ (m)	منتج
assistant	musā'id (m)	مساعد
cameraman	muṣawwir (m)	مصوّر
stuntman	mu'addi maʃahid xaṭīra (m)	مؤدّي مشاهد خطيرة
double (stuntman)	mumaθθil badīl (m)	ممثّل بديل

to shoot a movie	ṣawwar film	صوّر فيلمًا
audition, screen test	taʒribat adā' (f)	تجربة أداء
shooting	taṣwīr (m)	تصوير

movie crew	ṭāqim al film (m)	طاقم الفيلم
movie set	mintaqat at taṣwīr (f)	منطقة التصوير
camera	kamira sinimā'iyya (f)	كاميرا سينمائية
movie theater	sinima (f)	سينما
screen (e.g., big ~)	ʃāʃa (f)	شاشة
to show a movie	'araḍ film	عرض فيلمًا
soundtrack	musīqa taṣwīriyya (f)	موسيقى تصويرية
special effects	mu'aθθirāt xāṣṣa (pl)	مؤثرات خاصّة
subtitles	tarʒamat al ḥiwār (f)	ترجمة الحوار
credits	ʃārat an nihāya (f)	شارة النهاية
translation	tarʒama (f)	ترجمة

151. Painting

art	fann (m)	فنّ
fine arts	funūn ʒamīla (pl)	فنون جميلة
art gallery	ma'raḍ fanniy (m)	معرض فنّي
art exhibition	ma'raḍ fanniy (m)	معرض فنّي
painting (art)	taṣwīr (m)	تصوير
graphic art	rusūmiyyāt (pl)	رسوميات
abstract art	fann taʒrīdiy (m)	فنّ تجريدي
impressionism	al intibā'iyya (f)	الإنطباعية
picture (painting)	lawḥa (f)	لوحة
drawing	rasm (m)	رسم
poster	mulṣaq i'lāniy (m)	ملصق إعلاني
illustration (picture)	rasm tawḍīḥiy (m)	رسم توضيحي
miniature	ṣūra muṣaɣɣara (f)	صورة مصغرة
copy (of painting, etc.)	nusxa (f)	نسخة
reproduction	nusxa ṭibq al aṣl (f)	نسخة طبق الأصل
mosaic	fusayfisā' (f)	فسيفساء
stained glass window	zuʒāʒ mu'aʃʃaq (m)	زجاج معشّق
fresco	taṣwīr ʒiṣṣiy (m)	تصوير جصّي
engraving	naqʃ (m)	نقش
bust (sculpture)	timθāl niṣfiy (m)	تمثال نصفي
sculpture	naḥt (m)	نحت
statue	timθāl (m)	تمثال
plaster of Paris	ʒībs (m)	جيبس
plaster (as adj)	min al ʒībs	من الجيبس
portrait	burtrī (m)	بورتريه
self-portrait	burtrīh ðātiy (m)	بورتريه ذاتي
landscape painting	lawḥat manẓar ṭabī'iy (f)	لوحة منظر طبيعي
still life	ṭabī'a ṣāmita (f)	طبيعة صامتة

| caricature | ṣūra karikaturiyya (f) | صورة كاريكاتوريّة |
| sketch | rasm tamhīdiy (m) | رسم تمهيدي |

paint	lawn (m)	لون
watercolor paint	alwān mā'iyya (m)	ألوان مائية
oil (paint)	zayt (m)	زيت
pencil	qalam ruṣāṣ (m)	قلم رصاص
India ink	ḥibr hindiy (m)	حبر هنديّ
charcoal	faḥm (m)	فحم

to draw (vi, vt)	rasam	رسم
to paint (vi, vt)	rasam	رسم
to pose (vi)	qaʿad	قعد
artist's model (masc.)	mudil ḥay (m)	موديل حيّ
artist's model (fem.)	mudil ḥay (m)	موديل حي

artist (painter)	rassām (m)	رسّام
work of art	ʿamal fanniy (m)	عمل فنّيّ
masterpiece	tuḥfa fanniyya (f)	تحفة فنيّة
studio (artist's workroom)	warʃa (f)	ورشة

canvas (cloth)	kanava (f)	كانفا
easel	musnad ar rasm (m)	مسند الرسم
palette	lawḥat al alwān (f)	لوحة الألوان

frame (picture ~, etc.)	iṭār (m)	إطار
restoration	tarmīm (m)	ترميم
to restore (vt)	rammam	رمّم

152. Literature & Poetry

literature	adab (m)	أدب
author (writer)	mu'allif (m)	مؤلّف
pseudonym	ism mustaʿār (m)	إسم مستعار

book	kitāb (m)	كتاب
volume	muʒallad (m)	مجلّد
table of contents	fihris (m)	فهرس
page	ṣafḥa (f)	صفحة
main character	aʃ ʃaxṣiyya ar raʾīsiyya (f)	الشخصيّة الرئيسيّة
autograph	tawqīʾ al mu'allif (m)	توقيع المؤلّف

short story	qiṣṣa qaṣīra (f)	قصّة قصيرة
story (novella)	qiṣṣa (f)	قصّة
novel	riwāya (f)	رواية
work (writing)	mu'allif (m)	مؤلّف
fable	ḥikāya (f)	حكاية
detective novel	riwāya būlīsiyya (f)	رواية بوليسيّة
poem (verse)	qaṣīda (f)	قصيدة
poetry	ʃiʿr (m)	شعر

poem (epic, ballad)	qaṣīda (f)	قصيدة
poet	ʃāʿir (m)	شاعر
fiction	adab ʒamīl (m)	أدب جميل
science fiction	xayāl ʿilmiy (m)	خيال علميّ
adventures	adab al muɣāmarāt (m)	أدب المغامرات
educational literature	adab tarbawiy (m)	أدب تربويّ
children's literature	adab al aṭfāl (m)	أدب الأطفال

153. Circus

circus	sirk (m)	سيرك
traveling circus	sirk mutanaqqil (m)	سيرك متنقّل
program	barnāmaʒ (m)	برنامج
performance	adā' fanniy (m)	أداء فنّيّ
act (circus ~)	dawr (m)	دور
circus ring	ḥalbat as sirk (f)	حلبة السيرك
pantomime (act)	ʿarḍ 'īmā'y (m)	عرض إيمائي
clown	muharriʒ (m)	مهرّج
acrobat	bahlawān (m)	بهلوان
acrobatics	alʿāb bahlawāniyya (f)	ألعاب بهلوانيّة
gymnast	lāʿib ʒumbāz (m)	لاعب جنباز
gymnastics	ʒumbāz (m)	جنباز
somersault	ʃaqlaba (f)	شقلبة
athlete (strongman)	lāʿib riyāḍiy (m)	لاعب رياضيّ
tamer (e.g., lion ~)	murawwiḍ (m)	مروّض
rider (circus horse ~)	fāris (m)	فارس
assistant	musāʿid (m)	مساعد
stunt	alʿāb bahlawāniyya (f)	ألعاب بهلوانيّة
magic trick	xidʿa siḥriyya (f)	خدعة سحريّة
conjurer, magician	sāḥir (m)	ساحر
juggler	bahlawān (m)	بهلوان
to juggle (vi, vt)	laʿib bi kurāt ʿadīda	لعب بكرات عديدة
animal trainer	mudarrib ḥayawānāt (m)	مدرّب حيوانات
animal training	tadrīb al ḥayawānāt (m)	تدريب الحيوانات
to train (animals)	darrab	درّب

154. Music. Pop music

music	musīqa (f)	موسيقى
musician	ʿāzif (m)	عازف
musical instrument	'āla musiqiyya (f)	آلة موسيقيّة

to play ...	'azaf ...	عزف...
guitar	gitār (m)	جيتار
violin	kamān (m)	كمان
cello	tʃīlu (m)	تشيلو
double bass	kamān aʒhar (m)	كمان أجهر
harp	qiθār (m)	قيثار
piano	biānu (m)	بيانو
grand piano	biānu kibīr (m)	بيانو كبير
organ	aryan (m)	أرغن
wind instruments	'ālāt nafχiyya (pl)	آلات نفخيّة
oboe	ubwa (m)	أوبوا
saxophone	saksufūn (m)	ساكسوفون
clarinet	klarnīt (m)	كلارنيت
flute	flut (m)	فلوت
trumpet	būq (m)	بوق
accordion	ukurdiūn (m)	أكورديون
drum	ṭabla (f)	طبلة
duo	θunā'iy (m)	ثنائيّ
trio	θulāθy (m)	ثلاثيّ
quartet	rubā'iy (m)	رباعيّ
choir	χūrus (m)	خورس
orchestra	urkistra (f)	أوركسترا
pop music	musīqa al bub (f)	موسيقى البوب
rock music	musīqa ar rūk (f)	موسيقى الروك
rock group	firqat ar rūk (f)	فرقة الروك
jazz	ʒāz (m)	جاز
idol	ma'būd (m)	معبود
admirer, fan	mu'ʒab (m)	معجب
concert	ḥafla mūsiqiyya (f)	حفلة موسيقيّة
symphony	simfūniyya (f)	سمفونيّة
composition	qiṭ'a mūsiqiyya (f)	قطعة موسيقيّة
to compose (write)	allaf	ألف
singing (n)	γinā' (m)	غناء
song	uγniyya (f)	أغنيّة
tune (melody)	laḥn (m)	لحن
rhythm	'īqā' (m)	إيقاع
blues	musīqa al blūz (f)	موسيقى البلوز
sheet music	nutāt (pl)	نوتات
baton	'aṣa al mayistru (m)	عصا المايسترو
bow	qaws (m)	قوس
string	watar (m)	وتر
case (e.g., guitar ~)	ʃanṭa (f)	شنطة

Rest. Entertainment. Travel

155. Trip. Travel

tourism, travel	siyāḥa (f)	سياحة
tourist	sā'iḥ (m)	سائح
trip, voyage	riḥla (f)	رحلة
adventure	muɣāmara (f)	مغامرة
trip, journey	riḥla (f)	رحلة
vacation	ʿuṭla (f)	عطلة
to be on vacation	ʿindahu ʿuṭla	عنده عطلة
rest	istirāḥa (f)	إستراحة
train	qiṭār (m)	قطار
by train	bil qiṭār	بالقطار
airplane	ṭā'ira (f)	طائرة
by airplane	biṭ ṭā'ira	بالطائرة
by car	bis sayyāra	بالسيّارة
by ship	bis safīna	بالسفينة
luggage	aʃ ʃunaṭ (pl)	الشنط
suitcase	ḥaqībat safar (f)	حقيبة سفر
luggage cart	ʿarabat ʃunaṭ (f)	عربة شنط
passport	ʒawāz as safar (m)	جواز السفر
visa	ta'ʃīra (f)	تأشيرة
ticket	taðkira (f)	تذكرة
air ticket	taðkirat ṭā'ira (f)	تذكرة طائرة
guidebook	dalīl (m)	دليل
map (tourist ~)	χarīṭa (f)	خريطة
area (rural ~)	mintaqa (f)	منطقة
place, site	makān (m)	مكان
exotica (n)	ɣarāba (f)	غرابة
exotic (adj)	ɣarīb	غريب
amazing (adj)	mudhiʃ	مدهش
group	maʒmūʿa (f)	مجموعة
excursion, sightseeing tour	ʒawla (f)	جولة
guide (person)	murʃid (m)	مرشد

156. Hotel

| hotel | funduq (m) | فندق |
| motel | mutīl (m) | موتيل |

three-star (~ hotel)	θalāθat nuʒūm	ثلاثة نجوم
five-star	xamsat nuʒūm	خمسة نجوم
to stay (in a hotel, etc.)	nazal	نزل

room	xurfa (f)	غرفة
single room	xurfa li faxṣ wāḥid (f)	غرفة لشخص واحد
double room	xurfa li faxṣayn (f)	غرفة لشخصين
to book a room	ḥaʒaz xurfa	حجز غرفة

| half board | waʒbitān fil yawm (du) | وجبتان في اليوم |
| full board | θalāθ waʒabāt fil yawm | ثلاث وجبات في اليوم |

with bath	bi ḥawḍ al istiḥmām	بحوض الإستحمام
with shower	bid duʃ	بالدوش
satellite television	tilivizyūn faḍā'iy (m)	تلفزيون فضائيّ
air-conditioner	takyīf (m)	تكييف
towel	fūṭa (f)	فوطة
key	miftāḥ (m)	مفتاح

administrator	mudīr (m)	مدير
chambermaid	'āmilat tanzīf xuraf (f)	عاملة تنظيف غرف
porter, bellboy	ḥammāl (m)	حمّال
doorman	bawwāb (m)	بوّاب

restaurant	maṭ'am (m)	مطعم
pub, bar	bār (m)	بار
breakfast	futūr (m)	فطور
dinner	'afā' (m)	عشاء
buffet	bufīh (m)	بوفيه

| lobby | radha (f) | ردهة |
| elevator | miṣ'ad (m) | مصعد |

| DO NOT DISTURB | ar raʒā' 'adam al iz'āʒ | الرجاء عدم الإزعاج |
| NO SMOKING | mamnū' at tadxīn | ممنوع التدخين |

157. Books. Reading

book	kitāb (m)	كتاب
author	mu'allif (m)	مؤلف
writer	kātib (m)	كاتب
to write (~ a book)	allaf	ألف
reader	qāri' (m)	قارئ
to read (vi, vt)	qara'	قرأ

reading (activity)	qirā'a (f)	قراءة
silently (to oneself)	sirran	سرًا
aloud (adv)	bi ṣawt 'āli	بصوت عال
to publish (vt)	naʃar	نشر
publishing (process)	naʃr (m)	نشر
publisher	nāʃir (m)	ناشر
publishing house	dār aṭ ṭibā'a wan naʃr (f)	دار الطباعة والنشر
to come out (be released)	ṣadar	صدر
release (of a book)	ṣudūr (m)	صدور
print run	'adad an nusaχ (m)	عدد النسخ
bookstore	maḥall kutub (m)	محلّ كتب
library	maktaba (f)	مكتبة
story (novella)	qiṣṣa (f)	قصّة
short story	qiṣṣa qaṣīra (f)	قصّة قصيرة
novel	riwāya (f)	رواية
detective novel	riwāya bulīsiyya (f)	رواية بوليسيّة
memoirs	muðakkirāt (pl)	مذكّرات
legend	usṭūra (f)	أسطورة
myth	χurāfa (f)	خرافة
poetry, poems	ʃi'r (m)	شعر
autobiography	sīrat ḥayāt (f)	سيرة حياة
selected works	muχtārāt (pl)	مختارات
science fiction	χayāl 'ilmiy (m)	خيال علميّ
title	'unwān (m)	عنوان
introduction	muqaddima (f)	مقدّمة
title page	ṣafḥat al 'unwān (f)	صفحة العنوان
chapter	faṣl (m)	فصل
extract	qiṭ'a (f)	قطعة
episode	maʃhad (m)	مشهد
plot (storyline)	mawdū' (m)	موضوع
contents	muḥtawayāt (pl)	محتويات
table of contents	fihris (m)	فهرس
main character	aʃ ʃaχṣiyya ar ra'īsiyya (f)	الشخصيّة الرئيسيّة
volume	muʒallad (m)	مجلّد
cover	ɣilāf (m)	غلاف
binding	taʒlīd (m)	تجليد
bookmark	ʃarīṭ (m)	شريط
page	ṣafḥa (f)	صفحة
to page through	qallab aṣ ṣafaḥāt	قلب الصفحات
margins	hāmiʃ (m)	هامش
annotation (marginal note, etc.)	mulāḥaza (f)	ملاحظة

footnote	mulāḥaza (f)	ملاحظة
text	naṣṣ (m)	نصّ
type, font	nawʿ al ẖaṭṭ (m)	نوع الخطّ
misprint, typo	ẖaṭaʾ maṭbaʿiy (m)	خطأ مطبعيّ

translation	tarʒama (f)	ترجمة
to translate (vt)	tarʒam	ترجم
original (n)	aṣliy (m)	أصليّ

famous (adj)	maʃhūr	مشهور
unknown (not famous)	ɣayr maʿrūf	غير معروف
interesting (adj)	mumtiʿ	ممتع
bestseller	akθar mabīʿan (m)	أكثر مبيعًا

dictionary	qāmūs (m)	قاموس
textbook	kitāb taʿlīm (m)	كتاب تعليم
encyclopedia	mawsūʿa (f)	موسوعة

158. Hunting. Fishing

hunting	ṣayd (m)	صيد
to hunt (vi, vt)	iṣṭād	إصطاد
hunter	ṣayyād (m)	صيّاد

to shoot (vi)	aṭlaq an nār	أطلق النار
rifle	bunduqiyya (f)	بندقيّة
bullet (shell)	ruṣāṣa (f)	رصاصة
shot (lead balls)	raʃʃ (m)	رشّ

steel trap	maṣyada (f)	مصيدة
snare (for birds, etc.)	faẖẖ (m)	فخّ
to fall into the steel trap	waqaʿ fi faẖẖ	وقع في فخّ
to lay a steel trap	naṣab faẖẖ	نصب فخّا

poacher	sāriq aṣ ṣayd (m)	سارق الصيد
game (in hunting)	ṣayd (m)	صيد
hound dog	kalb ṣayd (m)	كلب صيد
safari	safāri (m)	سفاري
mounted animal	ḥayawān muḥannaṭ (m)	حيوان محنّط

fisherman, angler	ṣayyād as samak (m)	صيّاد السمك
fishing (angling)	ṣayd as samak (m)	صيد السمك
to fish (vi)	iṣṭād as samak	إصطاد السمك

fishing rod	ṣannāra (f)	صنّارة
fishing line	ẖayṭ (m)	خيط
hook	ʃaṣṣ aṣ ṣayd (m)	شصّ الصيد
float, bobber	ʿawwāma (f)	عوّامة
bait	ṭuʿm (m)	طعم
to cast a line	ṭaraḥ aṣ ṣinnāra	طرح الصنّارة

to bite (ab. fish)	'aḍḍ	عضّ
catch (of fish)	as samak al muṣṭād (m)	السمك المصطاد
ice-hole	fatḥa fil ʒalīd (f)	فتحة في الجليد
fishing net	ʃabakat aṣ ṣayd (f)	شبكة الصيد
boat	markab (m)	مركب
to net (to fish with a net)	iṣṭād biʃ ʃabaka	إصطاد بالشبكة
to cast[throw] the net	rama ʃabaka	رمى شبكة
to haul the net in	aҳraʒ ʃabaka	أخرج شبكة
to fall into the net	waqa' fi ʃabaka	وقع في شبكة
whaler (person)	ṣayyād al ḥūt (m)	صيّاد الحوت
whaleboat	safīnat ṣayd al ḥītān (f)	سفينة صيد الحيتان
harpoon	ḥarba (f)	حربة

159. Games. Billiards

billiards	bilyārdu (m)	بلياردو
billiard room, hall	qā'at bilyārdu (m)	قاعة بلياردو
ball (snooker, etc.)	kura (f)	كرة
to pocket a ball	aṣqaṭ kura	أصقط كرة
cue	'aṣa bilyardu (f)	عصا بلياردو
pocket	ʒayb bilyārdu (m)	جيب بلياردو

160. Games. Playing cards

diamonds	ad dināriy (m)	الديناريّ
spades	al bastūniy (m)	البستونيّ
hearts	al kūba (f)	الكوبة
clubs	as sibātiy (m)	السباتيّ
ace	'ās (m)	آس
king	malik (m)	ملك
queen	malika (f)	ملكة
jack, knave	walad (m)	ولد
playing card	waraqa (f)	ورقة
cards	waraq (m)	ورق
trump	waraqa rābiḥa (f)	ورقة رابحة
deck of cards	dasta waraq al la'b (f)	دستة ورق اللعب
point	nuqṭa (f)	نقطة
to deal (vi, vt)	farraq	فرّق
to shuffle (cards)	ҳallaṭ	خلط
lead, turn (n)	dawr (m)	دور
cardsharp	muḥtāl fil qimār (m)	محتال في القمار

161. Casino. Roulette

casino	kazinu (m)	كازينو
roulette (game)	rulīt (m)	روليت
bet	rihān (m)	رهان
to place bets	waḍa' ar rihān	وضع الرهان
red	aḥmar (m)	أحمر
black	aswad (m)	أسود
to bet on red	wada' ar rihān 'alal aḥmar	وضع الرهان على الأحمر
to bet on black	wada' ar rihān 'alal aswad	وضع الرهان على الأسود
croupier (dealer)	muwaẓẓaf nādi al qimār (m)	موظف نادى القمار
to spin the wheel	dawwar al 'aẓala	دوِّر العجلة
rules (of game)	qawā'id (pl)	قواعد
chip	fīʃa (f)	فيشة
to win (vi, vt)	kasab	كسب
win (winnings)	ribḥ (m)	ربح
to lose (~ 100 dollars)	χasir	خسر
loss (losses)	χisāra (f)	خسارة
player	lā'ib (m)	لاعب
blackjack (card game)	blɛkdʒɛk (m)	بلاك جاك
craps (dice game)	lu'bat an nard (f)	لعبة النرد
dice (a pair of ~)	zahr an nard (m)	زهر النرد
slot machine	'ālat qumār (f)	آلة قمار

162. Rest. Games. Miscellaneous

to stroll (vi, vt)	tanazzah	تنزّه
stroll (leisurely walk)	tanazzuh (m)	تنزّه
car ride	ʒawla bis sayyāra (f)	جولة بالسيّارة
adventure	muɣāmara (f)	مغامرة
picnic	nuzha (f)	نزهة
game (chess, etc.)	lu'ba (f)	لعبة
player	lā'ib (m)	لاعب
game (one ~ of chess)	dawr (m)	دور
collector (e.g., philatelist)	ʒāmi' (m)	جامع
to collect (stamps, etc.)	ʒama'	جمع
collection	maʒmū'a (f)	مجموعة
crossword puzzle	kalimāt mutaqāṭi'a (pl)	كلمات متقاطعة
racetrack (horse racing venue)	ḥalbat sibāq al χuyūl (f)	حلبة سباق الخيول
disco (discotheque)	disku (m)	ديسكو

sauna	sāuna (f)	ساونا
lottery	yanaṣīb (m)	يانصيب
camping trip	riḥlat taxyīm (f)	رحلة تخييم
camp	muxayyam (m)	مخيّم
tent (for camping)	xayma (f)	خيمة
compass	būṣila (f)	بوصلة
camper	muxayyim (m)	مخيّم
to watch (movie, etc.)	ʃāhid	شاهد
viewer	muʃāhid (m)	مشاهد
TV show (TV program)	barnāmaʒ tiliviziyūniy (m)	برنامج تلیفزیونيّ

163. Photography

camera (photo)	kamira (f)	كاميرا
photo, picture	ṣūra (f)	صورة
photographer	muṣawwir (m)	مصوّر
photo studio	istūdiyu taṣwīr (m)	إستوديو تصوير
photo album	albūm aṣ ṣuwar (m)	ألبوم الصور
camera lens	'adasa (f)	عدسة
telephoto lens	'adasa tiliskūpiyya (f)	عدسة تلسكويّة
filter	filtir (m)	فلتر
lens	'adasa (f)	عدسة
optics (high-quality ~)	aʒhiza baṣariyya (pl)	أجهزة بصريّة
diaphragm (aperture)	bu'ra (f)	بؤرة
exposure time (shutter speed)	muddat at ta'rīḍ (f)	مدّة التعريض
viewfinder	al 'ayn al fāḥiṣa (f)	العين الفاحصة
digital camera	kamira raqmiyya (f)	كاميرا رقميّة
tripod	ḥāmil θulāθiy (m)	حامل ثلاثيّ
flash	flāʃ (m)	فلاش
to photograph (vt)	ṣawwar	صوّر
to take pictures	ṣawwar	صوّر
to have one's picture taken	taṣawwar	تصوّر
focus	bu'rat al 'adasa (f)	بؤرة العدسة
to focus	rakkaz	ركّز
sharp, in focus (adj)	wāḍiḥ	واضح
sharpness	wuḍūḥ (m)	وضوح
contrast	tabāyun (m)	تباين
contrast (as adj)	mutabāyin	متباين
picture (photo)	ṣūra (f)	صورة
negative (n)	ṣūra sāliba (f)	صورة سالبة

film (a roll of ~)	film (m)	فيلم
frame (still)	iṭār (m)	إطار
to print (photos)	ṭaba'	طبع

164. Beach. Swimming

beach	ʃāṭi' (m)	شاطئ
sand	raml (m)	رمل
deserted (beach)	mahʒūr	مهجور
suntan	sumrat al baʃara (f)	سمرة البشرة
to get a tan	taʃammas	تشمّس
tan (adj)	asmar	أسمر
sunscreen	krīm wāqi aʃ ʃams (m)	كريم واقي الشمس
bikini	bikini (m)	بكيني
bathing suit	libās sibāḥa (m)	لباس سباحة
swim trunks	libās sibāḥa riʒāliy (m)	لباس سباحة رجاليّ
swimming pool	masbaḥ (m)	مسبح
to swim (vi)	sabaḥ	سبح
shower	dūʃ (m)	دوش
to change (one's clothes)	ɣayyar libāsuh	غيّر لباسه
towel	fūṭa (f)	فوطة
boat	markab (m)	مركب
motorboat	lanʃ (m)	لنش
water ski	tazalluʒ 'alal mā' (m)	تزلج على الماء
paddle boat	'aʒala mā'iyya (f)	عجلة مائيّة
surfing	rukūb al amwāʒ (m)	ركوب الأمواج
surfer	rākib al amwāʒ (m)	راكب الأمواج
scuba set	ʒihāz at tanaffus (m)	جهاز التنفس
flippers (swim fins)	za'ānif as sibāḥa (pl)	زعانف السباحة
mask (diving ~)	kimāma (f)	كمامة
diver	ɣawwāṣ (m)	غوّاص
to dive (vi)	ɣāṣ	غاص
underwater (adv)	taḥt al mā'	تحت الماء
beach umbrella	ʃamsiyya (f)	شمسيّة
sunbed (lounger)	kursiy blāʒ (m)	كرسيّ بلاج
sunglasses	naẓẓārat ʃams (f)	نظّارة شمس
air mattress	martaba hawā'iyya (f)	مرتبة هوائيّة
to play (amuse oneself)	la'ib	لعب
to go for a swim	sabaḥ	سبح
beach ball	kura (f)	كرة
to inflate (vt)	nafaχ	نفخ

inflatable, air (adj)	qābil lin nafχ	قابل للنفخ
wave	mawʒa (f)	موجة
buoy (line of ~s)	ʃamandūra (f)	شمندورة
to drown (ab. person)	ɣariq	غرق
to save, to rescue	anqað	أنقذ
life vest	sutrat naʒāt (f)	سترة نجاة
to observe, to watch	rāqab	راقب
lifeguard	ḥāris ʃāṭi' (m)	حارس شاطئ

TECHNICAL EQUIPMENT. TRANSPORTATION

Technical equipment

165. Computer

computer	kumbyūtir (m)	كمبيوتر
notebook, laptop	kumbyūtir maḥmūl (m)	كمبيوتر محمول
to turn on	ʃayyal	شغّل
to turn off	aylaq	أغلق
keyboard	lawḥat al mafātīḥ (f)	لوحة المفاتيح
key	miftāḥ (m)	مفتاح
mouse	fa'ra (f)	فأرة
mouse pad	wisādat fa'ra (f)	وسادة فأرة
button	zirr (m)	زرّ
cursor	mu'aʃʃir (m)	مؤشّر
monitor	ʃāʃa (f)	شاشة
screen	ʃāʃa (f)	شاشة
hard disk	qurṣ ṣalib (m)	قرص صلب
hard disk capacity	si'at taχzīn (f)	سعة تخزين
memory	ðākira (f)	ذاكرة
random access memory	ðākirat al wuṣūl al 'aʃwā'iy (f)	ذاكرة الوصول العشوائيّ
file	malaff (m)	ملفّ
folder	ḥāfiẓa (m)	حافظة
to open (vt)	fataḥ	فتح
to close (vt)	aylaq	أغلق
to save (vt)	ḥafaẓ	حفظ
to delete (vt)	masaḥ	مسح
to copy (vt)	nasaχ	نسخ
to sort (vt)	ṣannaf	صنّف
to transfer (copy)	naqal	نقل
program	barnāmaз (m)	برنامج
software	barāmiз kumbyūtir (pl)	برامج كمبيوتر
programmer	mubarmiз (m)	مبرمج
to program (vt)	barmaз	برمج
hacker	hākir (m)	هاكر

password	kalimat as sirr (f)	كلمة السرّ
virus	virūs (m)	فيروس
to find, to detect	waӡad	وجد
byte	bayt (m)	بايت
megabyte	miӡabāyt (m)	ميجابايت
data	bayānāt (pl)	بيانات
database	qa'idat bayānāt (f)	قاعدة بيانات
cable (USB, etc.)	kābil (m)	كابل
to disconnect (vt)	faṣal	فصل
to connect (sth to sth)	waṣṣal	وصّل

166. Internet. E-mail

Internet	intirnit (m)	إنترنت
browser	mutaṣaffiḥ (m)	متصفح
search engine	muḥarrik baḥθ (m)	محرّك بحث
provider	ʃarikat al intirnīt (f)	شركة الإنترنيت
webmaster	mudīr al mawqi' (m)	مدير الموقع
website	mawqi' iliktrūniy (m)	موقع إلكتروني
webpage	ṣafḥat wīb (f)	صفحة ويب
address (e-mail ~)	'unwān (m)	عنوان
address book	daftar al 'anāwīn (m)	دفتر العناوين
mailbox	ṣundūq al barīd (m)	صندوق البريد
mail	barīd (m)	بريد
full (adj)	mumtali'	ممتلىء
message	risāla iliktrūniyya (f)	رسالة إلكترونيّة
incoming messages	rasa'il wārida (pl)	رسائل واردة
outgoing messages	rasa'il ṣādira (pl)	رسائل صادرة
sender	mursil (m)	مرسل
to send (vt)	arsal	أرسل
sending (of mail)	irsāl (m)	إرسال
receiver	mursal ilayh (m)	مرسل إليه
to receive (vt)	istalam	إستلم
correspondence	murāsala (f)	مراسلة
to correspond (vi)	tarāsal	تراسل
file	malaff (m)	ملفّ
to download (vt)	ḥammal	حمّل
to create (vt)	anʃa'	أنشأ
to delete (vt)	masaḥ	مسح
deleted (adj)	mamsūḥ	ممسوح

connection (ADSL, etc.)	ittiṣāl (m)	إتّصال
speed	surʿa (f)	سرعة
modem	mudim (m)	مودم
access	wuṣūl (m)	وصول
port (e.g., input ~)	maxraʒ (m)	مخرج

| connection (make a ~) | ittiṣāl (m) | إتّصال |
| to connect to ... (vi) | ittaṣal | إتّصل |

| to select (vt) | ixtār | إختار |
| to search (for ...) | baḥaθ | بحث |

167. Electricity

electricity	kahrabā' (m)	كهرباء
electric, electrical (adj)	kahrabā'iy	كهربائيّ
electric power plant	maḥaṭṭa kahrabā'iyya (f)	محطّة كهربائيّة
energy	ṭāqa (f)	طاقة
electric power	ṭāqa kahrabā'iyya (f)	طاقة كهربائيّة

light bulb	lamba (f)	لمبة
flashlight	kaʃʃāf an nūr (m)	كشّاف النور
street light	ʿamūd an nūr (m)	عمود النور

light	nūr (m)	نور
to turn on	fataḥ, ʃaɣɣal	فتح، شغّل
to turn off	ṭaffa	طفّى
to turn off the light	ṭaffa n nūr	طفّى النور

| to burn out (vi) | intafa' | إنطفأ |
| short circuit | da'ira kahrabā'iyya qaṣīra (f) | دائرة كهربائية قصيرة |

| broken wire | silk maqṭūʿ (m) | سلك مقطوع |
| contact (electrical ~) | talāmus (m) | تلامس |

light switch	miftāḥ an nūr (m)	مفتاح النور
wall socket	barizat al kahrabā' (f)	بريزة الكهرباء
plug	fīʃat al kahrabā' (f)	فيشة الكهرباء
extension cord	silk tawṣīl (m)	سلك توصيل

fuse	fāṣima (f)	فاصمة
cable, wire	silk (m)	سلك
wiring	aslāk (pl)	أسلاك

ampere	ambīr (m)	أمبير
amperage	ʃiddat at tayyār al kahrabā'iy (f)	شدّة التيّار الكهربائيّ
volt	vūlt (m)	فولت
voltage	ʒuhd kahrabā'iy (m)	جهد كهربائيّ
electrical device	ʒihāz kahrabā'iy (m)	جهاز كهربائيّ

indicator	mu'aʃʃir (m)	مؤشِّر
electrician	kahrabā'iy (m)	كهربائيّ
to solder (vt)	laḥam	لحم
soldering iron	adāt laḥm (f)	أداة لحم
electric current	tayyār kahrabā'iy (m)	تيّار كهربائيّ

168. Tools

tool, instrument	adāt (f)	أداة
tools	adawāt (pl)	أدوات
equipment (factory ~)	mu'addāt (pl)	معدّات

hammer	miṭraqa (f)	مطرقة
screwdriver	mifakk (m)	مفكّ
ax	fa's (m)	فأس

saw	minʃār (m)	منشار
to saw (vt)	naʃar	نشر
plane (tool)	masḥāʒ (m)	مسحج
to plane (vt)	saḥaʒ	سحج
soldering iron	adāt laḥm (f)	أداة لحم
to solder (vt)	laḥam	لحم

file (tool)	mibrad (m)	مبرد
carpenter pincers	kammāʃa (f)	كمّاشة
lineman's pliers	zardiyya (f)	زرديّة
chisel	izmīl (m)	إزميل

drill bit	luqmat θaqb (m)	لقمة ثقب
electric drill	miθqab (m)	مثقب
to drill (vi, vt)	θaqab	ثقب

knife	sikkīn (m)	سكّين
pocket knife	sikkīn ʒayb (m)	سكّين جيب
blade	ʃafra (f)	شفرة

sharp (blade, etc.)	ḥādd	حادّ
dull, blunt (adj)	θālim	ثالم
to get blunt (dull)	taθallam	تثلّم
to sharpen (vt)	ʃaḥaθ	شحذ

bolt	mismār qalāwūz (m)	مسمار قلاووظ
nut	ṣamūla (f)	صامولة
thread (of a screw)	naẓm (m)	نظم
wood screw	qalāwūz (m)	قلاووظ

nail	mismār (m)	مسمار
nailhead	ra's al mismār (m)	رأس المسمار
ruler (for measuring)	masṭara (f)	مسطرة
tape measure	ʃarīʈ al qiyās (m)	شريط القياس

spirit level	mīzān al mā' (m)	ميزان الماء
magnifying glass	'adasa mukabbira (f)	عدسة مكبّرة
measuring instrument	ʒihāz qiyās (m)	جهاز قياس
to measure (vt)	qās	قاس
scale	miqyās (m)	مقياس
(of thermometer, etc.)		
readings	qirā'a (f)	قراءة
compressor	ḍāɣiṭ al ɣāz (m)	ضاغط الغاز
microscope	mikruskūb (m)	ميكروسكوب
pump (e.g., water ~)	ṭulumba (f)	طلمبة
robot	rūbut (m)	روبوت
laser	layzir (m)	ليزر
wrench	miftāḥ aṣ ṣawāmīl (m)	مفتاح الصواميل
adhesive tape	lazq (m)	لزق
glue	ṣamɣ (m)	صمغ
sandpaper	waraq ṣanfara (m)	ورق صنفرة
spring	sūsta (f)	سوستة
magnet	miɣnaṭīs (m)	مغنطيس
gloves	quffāz (m)	قفّاز
rope	ḥabl (m)	حبل
cord	ḥabl (m)	حبل
wire (e.g., telephone ~)	silk (m)	سلك
cable	kābil (m)	كابل
sledgehammer	mirzaba (f)	مرزبة
prybar	'atala (f)	عتلة
ladder	sullam (m)	سلّم
stepladder	sullam (m)	سلّم
to screw (tighten)	aḥkam aʃ ʃadd	أحكم الشدّ
to unscrew (lid, filter, etc.)	fataḥ	فتح
to tighten	kamaʃ	كمش
(e.g., with a clamp)		
to glue, to stick	alṣaq	ألصق
to cut (vt)	qaṭa'	قطع
malfunction (fault)	ta'aṭṭul (m)	تعطّل
repair (mending)	iṣlāḥ (m)	إصلاح
to repair, to fix (vt)	aṣlaḥ	أصلح
to adjust (machine, etc.)	ḍabaṭ	ضبط
to check (to examine)	iχtabar	إختبر
checking	faḥṣ (m)	فحص
readings	qirā'a (f)	قراءة
reliable, solid (machine)	matīn	متين
complex (adj)	murakkab	مركّب

to rust (get rusted)	ṣadi'	صدئ
rusty, rusted (adj)	ṣadi'	صديء
rust	ṣada' (m)	صدأ

Transportation

169. Airplane

airplane	ṭā'ira (f)	طائرة
air ticket	taðkirat ṭā'ira (f)	تذكرة طائرة
airline	ʃarikat ṭayarān (f)	شركة طيران
airport	maṭār (m)	مطار
supersonic (adj)	xāriq liṣ ṣawt	خارق للصوت
captain	qā'id aṭ ṭā'ira (m)	قائد الطائرة
crew	ṭāqim (m)	طاقم
pilot	ṭayyār (m)	طيّار
flight attendant (fem.)	muḍīfat ṭayarān (f)	مضيفة طيران
navigator	mallāḥ (m)	مَلّاح
wings	aʒniḥa (pl)	أجنحة
tail	ðayl (m)	ذيل
cockpit	kabīna (f)	كابينة
engine	mutūr (m)	موتور
undercarriage (landing gear)	'aʒalāt al hubūṭ (pl)	عجلات الهبوط
turbine	turbīna (f)	تربينة
propeller	mirwaḥa (f)	مروحة
black box	musaʒʒil aṭ ṭayarān (m)	مسجّل الطيران
yoke (control column)	'aʒalat qiyāda (f)	عجلة قيادة
fuel	wuqūd (m)	وقود
safety card	biṭāqat as salāma (f)	بطاقة السلامة
oxygen mask	qinā' uksiʒīn (m)	قناع أوكسيجين
uniform	libās muwaḥḥad (m)	لباس موحّد
life vest	sutrat naʒāt (f)	سترة نجاة
parachute	miẓallat hubūṭ (f)	مظلّة هبوط
takeoff	iqlā' (m)	إقلاع
to take off (vi)	aqla'at	أقلعت
runway	madraʒ aṭ ṭā'irāt (m)	مدرج الطائرات
visibility	ru'ya (f)	رؤية
flight (act of flying)	ṭayarān (m)	طيران
altitude	irtifā' (m)	إرتفاع
air pocket	ʒayb hawā'iy (m)	جيب هوائيّ
seat	maq'ad (m)	مقعد
headphones	sammā'āt ra'siya (pl)	سمّاعات رأسيّة

folding tray (tray table)	sīniyya qābila liṭ ṭayy (f)	صينية قابلة للطيّ
airplane window	ʃubbāk aṭ ṭā'ira (m)	شبّاك الطائرة
aisle	mamarr (m)	ممرّ

170. Train

train	qiṭār (m)	قطار
commuter train	qiṭār (m)	قطار
express train	qiṭār sarī' (m)	قطار سريع
diesel locomotive	qāṭirat dīzil (f)	قاطرة ديزل
steam locomotive	qāṭira buxāriyya (f)	قاطرة بخاريّة
passenger car	'araba (f)	عربة
dining car	'arabat al maṭ'am (f)	عربة المطعم
rails	quḍubān (pl)	قضبان
railroad	sikka ḥadīdiyya (f)	سكّة حديديّة
railway tie	'āriḍa (f)	عارضة
platform (railway ~)	raṣīf (m)	رصيف
track (~ 1, 2, etc.)	xaṭṭ (m)	خطّ
semaphore	simafūr (m)	سيمافور
station	maḥaṭṭa (f)	محطّة
engineer (train driver)	sā'iq (m)	سائق
porter (of luggage)	ḥammāl (m)	حمّال
car attendant	mas'ūl 'arabat al qiṭār (m)	مسؤول عربة القطار
passenger	rākib (m)	راكب
conductor	kamsariy (m)	كمسريّ
(ticket inspector)		
corridor (in train)	mamarr (m)	ممرّ
emergency brake	farāmil aṭ ṭawāri' (pl)	فرامل الطوارئ
compartment	yurfa (f)	غرفة
berth	sarīr (m)	سرير
upper berth	sarīr 'ulwiy (m)	سرير علويّ
lower berth	sarīr sufliy (m)	سرير سفليّ
bed linen, bedding	ayṭiyat as sarīr (pl)	أغطية السرير
ticket	taðkira (f)	تذكرة
schedule	ʒadwal (m)	جدول
information display	lawḥat ma'lūmāt (f)	لوحة معلومات
to leave, to depart	yādar	غادر
departure (of train)	muyādara (f)	مغادرة
to arrive (ab. train)	waṣal	وصل
arrival	wuṣūl (m)	وصول
to arrive by train	waṣal bil qiṭār	وصل بالقطار
to get on the train	rakib al qiṭār	ركب القطار

to get off the train	nazil min al qiṭār	نزل من القطار
train wreck	ḥiṭām qiṭār (m)	حطام قطار
to derail (vi)	xaraʒ 'an xaṭṭ sayrih	خرج عن خطّ سيره
steam locomotive	qāṭira buxāriyya (f)	قاطرة بخاريّة
stoker, fireman	'ataʃʒiy (m)	عطشجي
firebox	furn al muḥarrik (m)	فرن المُحرّك
coal	faḥm (m)	فحم

171. Ship

ship	safīna (f)	سفينة
vessel	safīna (f)	سفينة
steamship	bāxira (f)	باخرة
riverboat	bāxira nahriyya (f)	باخرة نهريّة
cruise ship	bāxira siyaḥiyya (f)	باخرة سياحيّة
cruiser	ṭarrād (m)	طرّاد
yacht	yaxt (m)	يخت
tugboat	qāṭira (f)	قاطرة
barge	ṣandal (m)	صندل
ferry	'abbāra (f)	عبّارة
sailing ship	safīna ʃirā'iyya (m)	سفينة شراعيّة
brigantine	markab ʃirā'iy (m)	مركب شراعيّ
ice breaker	muḥaṭṭimat ʒalīd (f)	محطّمة جليد
submarine	ɣawwāṣa (f)	غوّاصة
boat (flat-bottomed ~)	markab (m)	مركب
dinghy	zawraq (m)	زورق
lifeboat	qārib naʒāt (m)	قارب نجاة
motorboat	lanʃ (m)	لنش
captain	qubṭān (m)	قبطان
seaman	baḥḥār (m)	بحّار
sailor	baḥḥār (m)	بحّار
crew	ṭāqim (m)	طاقم
boatswain	ra'īs al baḥḥāra (m)	رئيس البحّارة
ship's boy	ṣabiy as safīna (m)	صبي السفينة
cook	ṭabbāx (m)	طبّاخ
ship's doctor	ṭabīb as safīna (m)	طبيب السفينة
deck	saṭḥ as safīna (m)	سطح السفينة
mast	sāriya (f)	سارية
sail	ʃirā' (m)	شراع
hold	'ambar (m)	عنبر
bow (prow)	muqaddama (m)	مقدّمة

stern	mu'axirat as safina (f)	مؤخّرة السفينة
oar	miӡðāf (m)	مجذاف
screw propeller	mirwaḥa (f)	مروحة
cabin	kabīna (f)	كابينة
wardroom	yurfat al istirāḥa (f)	غرفة الإستراحة
engine room	qism al 'ālāt (m)	قسم الآلات
bridge	burӡ al qiyāda (m)	برج القيادة
radio room	yurfat al lāsilkiy (f)	غرفة اللاسلكيّ
wave (radio)	mawӡa (f)	موجة
logbook	siӡil as safina (m)	سجل السفينة
spyglass	minẓār (m)	منظار
bell	ӡaras (m)	جرس
flag	'alam (m)	علم
hawser (mooring ~)	ḥabl (m)	حبل
knot (bowline, etc.)	'uqda (f)	عقدة
deckrails	drabizīn (m)	درابزين
gangway	sullam (m)	سلّم
anchor	mirsāt (f)	مرساة
to weigh anchor	rafa' mirsāt	رفع مرساة
to drop anchor	rasa	رسا
anchor chain	silsilat mirsāt (f)	سلسلة مرساة
port (harbor)	mīnā' (m)	ميناء
quay, wharf	marsa (m)	مرسى
to berth (moor)	rasa	رسا
to cast off	aqla'	أقلع
trip, voyage	riḥla (f)	رحلة
cruise (sea trip)	riḥla baḥriyya (f)	رحلة بحرية
course (route)	masār (m)	مسار
route (itinerary)	ṭarīq (m)	طريق
fairway (safe water channel)	maӡra milāḥiy (m)	مجرى ملاحيّ
shallows	miyāh ḍaḥla (f)	مياه ضحلة
to run aground	ӡanaḥ	جنح
storm	'āṣifa (f)	عاصفة
signal	iʃāra (f)	إشارة
to sink (vi)	yariq	غرق
Man overboard!	saqaṭ raӡul min as safina!	سقط رجل من السفينة!
SOS (distress signal)	nidā' iyāθa (m)	نداء إغاثة
ring buoy	ṭawq naӡāt (m)	طوق نجاة

172. Airport

airport	maṭār (m)	مطار
airplane	ṭā'ira (f)	طائرة
airline	ʃarikat ṭayarān (f)	شركة طيران
air traffic controller	marāqib al ḥaraka al ʒawwiyya (pl)	مراقب الحركة الجويّة
departure	muɣādara (f)	مغادرة
arrival	wuṣūl (m)	وصول
to arrive (by plane)	waṣal	وصل
departure time	waqt al muɣādara (m)	وقت المغادرة
arrival time	waqt al wuṣūl (m)	وقت الوصول
to be delayed	ta'aχχar	تأخّر
flight delay	ta'aχχur ar riḥla (m)	تأخّر الرحلة
information board	lawḥat al maʕlūmāt (f)	لوحة المعلومات
information	isti'lāmāt (pl)	إستعلامات
to announce (vt)	a'lan	أعلن
flight (e.g., next ~)	riḥla (f)	رحلة
customs	ʒamārik (pl)	جمارك
customs officer	muwaẓẓaf al ʒamārik (m)	موظّف الجمارك
customs declaration	taṣrīḥ ʒumrukiy (m)	تصريح جمركيّ
to fill out (vt)	mala'	ملأ
to fill out the declaration	mala' at taṣrīḥ	ملأ التصريح
passport control	taftīʃ al ʒawāzāt (m)	تفتيش الجوازات
luggage	aʃ ʃunaṭ (pl)	الشنط
hand luggage	ʃunaṭ al yad (pl)	شنط اليد
luggage cart	'arabat ʃunaṭ (f)	عربة شنط
landing	hubūṭ (m)	هبوط
landing strip	mamarr al hubūṭ (m)	ممرّ الهبوط
to land (vi)	habaṭ	هبط
airstairs	sullam aṭ ṭā'ira (m)	سلّم الطائرة
check-in	tasʒīl (m)	تسجيل
check-in counter	makān at tasʒīl (m)	مكان التسجيل
to check-in (vi)	saʒʒal	سجّل
boarding pass	biṭāqat ṣuʕūd (f)	بطاقة صعود
departure gate	bawwābat al muɣādara (f)	بوّابة المغادرة
transit	tranzīt (m)	ترانزيت
to wait (vt)	intazar	إنتظر
departure lounge	qā'at al muɣādara (f)	قاعة المغادرة
to see off	wadda'	ودّع
to say goodbye	wadda'	ودّع

173. Bicycle. Motorcycle

bicycle	darrā3a (f)	درّاجة
scooter	skutir (m)	سكوتر
motorcycle, bike	darrā3a nāriyya (f)	درّاجة نارية
to go by bicycle	rakib ad darrā3a	ركب الدرّاجة
handlebars	miqwad (m)	مقود
pedal	dawwāsa (f)	دوّاسة
brakes	farāmil (pl)	فرامل
bicycle seat (saddle)	maq'ad (m)	مقعد
pump	ṭulumba (f)	طلمبة
luggage rack	raff al amti'a (m)	رفّ الأمتعة
front lamp	miṣbāḥ (m)	مصباح
helmet	xūða (f)	خوذة
wheel	'a3ala (f)	عجلة
fender	rafraf (m)	رفرف
rim	iṭār (m)	إطار
spoke	barmaq al 'a3ala (m)	برمق العجلة

Cars

174. Types of cars

automobile, car	sayyāra (f)	سيّارة
sports car	sayyāra riyāḍiyya (f)	سيّارة رياضيّة
limousine	limuzīn (m)	ليموزين
off-road vehicle	sayyārat ṭuruq waʿra (f)	سيارة طرق وعرة
convertible (n)	kabriulīh (m)	كابريوليه
minibus	mikrubāṣ (m)	ميكروباص
ambulance	isʿāf (m)	إسعاف
snowplow	ʒarrāfat θalʒ (f)	جرّافة ثلج
truck	ʃāḥina (f)	شاحنة
tanker truck	nāqilat bitrūl (f)	ناقلة بترول
van (small truck)	ʿarabat naql (f)	عربة نقل
road tractor (trailer truck)	ʒarrār (m)	جرّار
trailer	maqṭūra (f)	مقطورة
comfortable (adj)	murīḥ	مريح
used (adj)	mustaʿmal	مستعمل

175. Cars. Bodywork

hood	kabbūt (m)	كبّوت
fender	rafraf (m)	رفرف
roof	saqf (m)	سقف
windshield	zuʒāʒ amāmiy (m)	زجاج أماميّ
rear-view mirror	mirʾāt dāxiliyya (f)	مرآة داخليّة
windshield washer	munaẓẓif az zuʒāʒ (m)	منظّف الزجاج
windshield wipers	massāḥāt (pl)	مسّاحات
side window	zuʒāʒ ʒānibiy (m)	زجاج جانبيّ
window lift (power window)	mākina zuʒāʒ (f)	ماكينة زجاج
antenna	hawāʾiy (m)	هوائيّ
sunroof	nāfiðat as saqf (f)	نافذة السقف
bumper	miṣadd as sayyāra (m)	مصدّ السيارة
trunk	ṣundūq as sayyāra (m)	صندوق السيّارة
roof luggage rack	raff saqf as sayyāra (m)	رفّ سقف السيّارة
door	bāb (m)	باب

door handle	ukrat al bāb (f)	أوكرة الباب
door lock	qifl al bāb (m)	قفل الباب
license plate	lawḥat raqm as sayyāra (f)	لوحة رقم السيارة
muffler	kātim aṣ ṣawt (m)	كاتم الصوت
gas tank	χazzān al banzīn (m)	خزّان البنزين
tailpipe	umbūb al 'ādim (m)	أنبوب العادم
gas, accelerator	ɣāz (m)	غاز
pedal	dawwāsa (f)	دوّاسة
gas pedal	dawwāsat al wuqūd (f)	دوّاسة الوقود
brake	farāmil (pl)	فرامل
brake pedal	dawwāsat al farāmil (m)	دوّاسة الفرامل
to brake (use the brake)	farmal	فرمل
parking brake	farmalat al yad (f)	فرملة اليد
clutch	ta'ʃīq (m)	تعشيق
clutch pedal	dawwāsat at ta'ʃīq (f)	دوّاسة التعشيق
clutch disc	qurṣ at ta'ʃīq (m)	قرص التعشيق
shock absorber	mumtaṣṣ liṣ ṣadamāt (m)	ممتصّ الصدمات
wheel	'aʒala (f)	عجلة
spare tire	'aʒala iḥtiyāṭiyya (f)	عجلة احتياطيّة
tire	iṭār (m)	إطار
hubcap	ɣiṭā' miḥwar al 'aʒala (m)	غطاء محور العجلة
driving wheels	'aʒalāt al qiyāda (pl)	عجلات القيادة
front-wheel drive (as adj)	daf' amāmiy (m)	دفع أماميّ
rear-wheel drive (as adj)	daf' χalfiy (m)	دفع خلفيّ
all-wheel drive (as adj)	daf' rubā'iy (m)	دفع رباعيّ
gearbox	ṣundūq at turūs (m)	صندوق التروس
automatic (adj)	utumatīkiy	أوتوماتيكيّ
mechanical (adj)	yadawiy	يدويّ
gear shift	nāqil as sur'a (m)	ناقل السرعة
headlight	al miṣbāḥ al amāmiy (m)	المصباح الأماميّ
headlights	al maṣābīḥ al amāmiyya (pl)	المصابيح الأماميّة
low beam	al anwār al munχafiḍa (pl)	الأنوار المنخفضة
high beam	al anwār al 'āliya (m)	الأنوار العالية
brake light	ḍū' al farāmil (m)	ضوء الفرامل
parking lights	aḍwā' ʒānibiyya (pl)	أضواء جانبيّة
hazard lights	aḍwā' at taḥḏīr (pl)	أضواء التحذير
fog lights	aḍwā' aḍ ḍabāb (pl)	أضواء الضباب
turn signal	iʃārat al in'iṭāf (f)	إشارة الإنعطاف
back-up light	miṣbāḥ ar ruʒū' lil χalf (m)	مصباح الرجوع للخلف

176. Cars. Passenger compartment

car inside (interior)	ṣālūn as sayyāra (m)	صالون السيّارة
leather (as adj)	min al ʒild	من الجلد
velour (as adj)	min al muxmal	من المخمل
upholstery	tanʒīd (m)	تنجيد
instrument (gage)	ʒihāz (m)	جهاز
dashboard	lawḥat at taḥakkum (f)	لوحة التحكم
speedometer	'addād sur'a (m)	عدّاد سرعة
needle (pointer)	mu'aʃʃir (m)	مؤشّر
odometer	'addād al masāfāt (m)	عدّاد المسافات
indicator (sensor)	'addād (m)	عدّاد
level	mustawa (m)	مستوى
warning light	lammbat inðār (f)	لمبة إنذار
steering wheel	miqwad (m)	مقود
horn	zāmūr (m)	زامور
button	zirr (m)	زرّ
switch	nāqil, miftāḥ (m)	ناقل، مفتاح
seat	maq'ad (m)	مقعد
backrest	misnad aẓ ẓahr (m)	مسند الظهر
headrest	masnad ar ra's (m)	مسند الرأس
seat belt	ḥizām al amn (m)	حزام الأمن
to fasten the belt	rabaṭ al ḥizām	ربط الحزام
adjustment (of seats)	ḍabṭ (m)	ضبط
airbag	wisāda hawā'iyya (f)	وسادة هوائيّة
air-conditioner	takyīf (m)	تكييف
radio	iðā'a (f)	إذاعة
CD player	muʃaɣɣil sidi (m)	مشغّل سي دي
to turn on	fataḥ, ʃaɣɣal	فتح، شغّل
antenna	hawā'iy (m)	هوائي
glove box	durʒ (m)	درج
ashtray	ṭaqṭūqa (f)	طقطوقة

177. Cars. Engine

engine	muḥarrik (m)	محرّك
motor	mutūr (m)	موتور
diesel (as adj)	dīzil	ديزل
gasoline (as adj)	'alal banzīn	على البنزين
engine volume	si'at al muḥarrik (f)	سعة المحرّك
power	qudra (f)	قدرة
horsepower	ḥiṣān (m)	حصان

piston	mikbas (m)	مكبس
cylinder	usṭuwāna (f)	أسطوانة
valve	ṣimām (m)	صمام

injector	ʒihāz baxxāx (f)	جهاز بخّاخ
generator (alternator)	muwallid (m)	مولّد
carburetor	karburātir (m)	كاربراتير
motor oil	zayt al muḥarrik (m)	زيت المحرّك

radiator	mubarrid al muḥarrik (m)	مبرّد المحرّك
coolant	mādda mubarrida (f)	مادّة مبرّدة
cooling fan	mirwaḥa (f)	مروحة

battery (accumulator)	baṭṭāriyya (f)	بطّاريّة
starter	miftāḥ at tafʃīl (m)	مفتاح التشغيل
ignition	niẓām tafʃīl (m)	نظام تشغيل
spark plug	ʃamʿat al iḥtirāq (f)	شمعة الاحتراق

terminal (of battery)	ṭaraf tawṣīl (m)	طرف توصيل
positive terminal	ṭaraf mūʒab (m)	طرف موجب
negative terminal	ṭaraf sālib (m)	طرف سالب
fuse	fāṣima (f)	فاصمة

air filter	miṣfāt al hawā' (f)	مصفاة الهواء
oil filter	miṣfāt az zayt (f)	مصفاة الزيت
fuel filter	miṣfāt al banzīn (f)	مصفاة البنزين

178. Cars. Crash. Repair

car crash	ḥādiθ sayyāra (f)	حادث سيّارة
traffic accident	ḥādiθ murūriy (m)	حادث مروريّ
to crash (into the wall, etc.)	iṣṭadam	إصطدم

to get smashed up	taḥaṭṭam	تحطّم
damage	xasāra (f)	خسارة
intact (unscathed)	salīm	سليم

| to break down (vi) | taʿaṭṭal | تعطّل |
| towrope | ḥabl as saḥb (m) | حبل السحب |

puncture	θuqb (m)	ثقب
to be flat	faʃʃ	فشّ
to pump up	nafax	نفخ
pressure	ḍaɣṭ (m)	ضغط
to check (to examine)	ixtabar	إختبر

repair	iṣlāḥ (m)	إصلاح
auto repair shop	warʃat iṣlāḥ as sayyārāt (f)	ورشة إصلاح السيّارات
spare part	qiṭʿat ɣiyār (f)	قطعة غيار
part	qiṭʿa (f)	قطعة

bolt (with nut)	mismār qalāwūz (m)	مسمار قلاووظ
screw (fastener)	burɣiy (m)	برغي
nut	ṣamūla (f)	صامولة
washer	ḥalqa (f)	حلقة
bearing	maḥmal (m)	محمل

tube	umbūba (f)	أنبوبة
gasket (head ~)	'azaqa (f)	عزقة
cable, wire	silk (m)	سلك

jack	rāfi'at sayyāra (f)	رافعة سيّارة
wrench	miftāḥ aṣ ṣawāmīl (m)	مفتاح الصواميل
hammer	miṭraqa (f)	مطرقة
pump	ṭulumba (f)	طلمبة
screwdriver	mifakk (m)	مفكّ

| fire extinguisher | miṭfa'at ḥarīq (f) | مطفأة حريق |
| warning triangle | muθallaθ taḥðīr (m) | مثلث تحذير |

to stall (vi)	tawaqqaf	توقف
stall (n)	tawaqquf (m)	توقف
to be broken	kān maksūran	كان مكسورًا

to overheat (vi)	saxan bi ʃidda	سخن بشدّة
to be clogged up	kān masdūdan	كان مسدودًا
to freeze up (pipes, etc.)	taʒammad	تجمّد
to burst (vi, ab. tube)	infaʒar	إنفجر

pressure	ḍaɣṭ (m)	ضغط
level	mustawa (m)	مستوى
slack (~ belt)	ḍa'īf	ضعيف

dent	ba'ʒa (f)	بعجة
knocking noise (engine)	daqq (m)	دقّ
crack	ʃaqq (m)	شقّ
scratch	xadʃ (m)	خدش

179. Cars. Road

road	ṭarīq (m)	طريق
highway	ṭarīq sarī' (m)	طريق سريع
freeway	ṭarīq sarī' (m)	طريق سريع
direction (way)	ittiʒāh (m)	إتجاه
distance	masāfa (f)	مسافة

bridge	ʒisr (m)	جسر
parking lot	mawqif as sayyārāt (m)	موقف السيّارات
square	maydān (m)	ميدان
interchange	taqāṭu' ṭuruq (m)	تقاطع طرق
tunnel	nafaq (m)	نفق

gas station	maḥaṭṭat banzīn (f)	محطة بنزين
parking lot	mawqif as sayyārāt (m)	موقف السيّارات
gas pump (fuel dispenser)	miḍaxxat banzīn (f)	مضخة بنزين
auto repair shop	warʃat iṣlāḥ as sayyārāt (f)	ورشة إصلاح السيّارات
to get gas (to fill up)	mala' bil wuqūd	ملأ بالوقود
fuel	wuqūd (m)	وقود
jerrycan	ʒirikan (m)	جركن

asphalt	asfalt (m)	أسفلت
road markings	ʿalāmāt aṭ ṭarīq (pl)	علامات الطريق
curb	ḥāffat ar raṣīf (f)	حافة الرصيف
guardrail	sūr (m)	سور
ditch	qanāt (f)	قناة
roadside (shoulder)	ḥāffat aṭ ṭarīq (f)	حافة الطريق
lamppost	ʿamūd nūr (m)	عمود نور

to drive (a car)	sāq	ساق
to turn (e.g., ~ left)	inʿaṭaf	إنعطف
to make a U-turn	istadār lil xalf	إستدار للخلف
reverse (~ gear)	ḥaraka ilal warā' (f)	حركة إلى الوراء

to honk (vi)	zammar	زمّر
honk (sound)	ṣawṭ az zāmūr (m)	صوت الزامور
to get stuck (in the mud, etc.)	waḥil	وحل
to spin the wheels	dawwar al ʿaʒala	دوّر العجلة
to cut, to turn off (vt)	awqaf	أوقف

speed	surʿa (f)	سرعة
to exceed the speed limit	taʒāwaz as surʿa al quṣwa	تجاوز السرعة القصوى
to give a ticket	faraḍ ɣarāma	فرض غرامة
traffic lights	iʃārāt al murūr (pl)	إشارات المرور
driver's license	ruxṣat al qiyāda (f)	رخصة قيادة

grade crossing	maʿbar (m)	معبر
intersection	taqāṭuʿ (m)	تقاطع
crosswalk	maʿbar al muʃāt (m)	معبر المشاة
bend, curve	munʿaṭif (m)	منعطف
pedestrian zone	makān muxaṣṣaṣ lil muʃāt (f)	مكان مخصّص للمشاة

180. Traffic signs

rules of the road	qawāʿid al murūr (pl)	قواعد المرور
road sign (traffic sign)	ʿalāma (f)	علامة
passing (overtaking)	taʒāwuz (m)	تجاوز
curve	munʿaṭif (m)	منعطف
U-turn	dawarān lil xalf (m)	دوران للخلف
traffic circle	dawarān murūriy (m)	دوران مروري
No entry	mamnūʿ ad duxūl	ممنوع الدخول

No vehicles allowed	mamnūʿ murūr as sayyārāt	ممنوع مرور السيارات
No passing	mamnūʿ at taʒāwuz	ممنوع التجاوز
No parking	mamnūʿ al wuqūf	ممنوع الوقوف
No stopping	mamnūʿ al wuqūf	ممنوع الوقوف
dangerous bend	munʿaṭaf χaṭir (m)	منعطف خطر
steep descent	munḥadar χaṭar (m)	منحدر خطر
one-way traffic	ṭarīq ittiʒāh wāḥid (m)	طريق إتجاه واحد
crosswalk	maʿbar al muʃāt (m)	معبر المشاة
slippery road	ṭarīq zaliq (m)	طريق زلق
YIELD	iʃārat waḍʿiyyat tark al awlawiyya	إشارة وضعيّة ترك الأولويّة

PEOPLE. LIFE EVENTS

Life events

181. Holidays. Event

celebration, holiday	ʿīd (m)	عيد
national day	ʿīd waṭaniy (m)	عيد وطنيّ
public holiday	yawm al ʿuṭla ar rasmiyya (m)	يوم العطلة الرسمية
to commemorate (vt)	iḥtafal	إحتفل
event (happening)	ḥadaθ (m)	حدث
event (organized activity)	munasaba (f)	مناسبة
banquet (party)	walīma (f)	وليمة
reception (formal party)	ḥaflat istiqbāl (f)	حفلة إستقبال
feast	walīma (f)	وليمة
anniversary	ðikra sanawiyya (f)	ذكرى سنويّة
jubilee	yubīl (m)	يوبيل
to celebrate (vt)	iḥtafal	إحتفل
New Year	ra's as sana (m)	رأس السنة
Happy New Year!	kull sana wa anta ṭayyib!	كلّ سنة وأنت طيّب!
Santa Claus	baba nuwīl (m)	بابا نويل
Christmas	ʿīd al mīlād (m)	عيد الميلاد
Merry Christmas!	ʿīd mīlād saʿīd!	عيد ميلاد سعيد!
Christmas tree	ʃaʒarat ra's as sana (f)	شجرة رأس السنة
fireworks (fireworks show)	alʿāb nāriyya (pl)	ألعاب ناريّة
wedding	zifāf (m)	زفاف
groom	ʿarīs (m)	عريس
bride	ʿarūsa (f)	عروسة
to invite (vt)	daʿa	دعا
invitation card	biṭāqat daʿwa (f)	بطاقة دعوة
guest	ḍayf (m)	ضيف
to visit (~ your parents, etc.)	zār	زار
to meet the guests	istaqbal aḍ ḍuyūf	إستقبل الضيوف
gift, present	hadiyya (f)	هديّة
to give (sth as present)	qaddam	قدّم

| to receive gifts | istalam al hadāya | إستلم الهدايا |
| bouquet (of flowers) | bāqat zuhūr (f) | باقة زهور |

| congratulations | tahnī'a (f) | تهنئة |
| to congratulate (vt) | hanna' | هنّأ |

greeting card	biṭāqat tahnī'a (f)	بطاقة تهنئة
to send a postcard	arsal biṭāqat tahni'a	أرسل بطاقة تهنئة
to get a postcard	istalam biṭāqat tahnī'a	إستلم بطاقة تهنئة

toast	naχb (m)	نخب
to offer (a drink, etc.)	ḍayyaf	ضيّف
champagne	ʃambāniya (f)	شمبانيا

to enjoy oneself	istamta'	إستمتع
merriment (gaiety)	farah (m)	فرح
joy (emotion)	sa'āda (f)	سعادة

| dance | rāqiṣa (f) | رقصة |
| to dance (vi, vt) | raqaṣ | رقص |

| waltz | vāls (m) | فالس |
| tango | tāngu (m) | تانجو |

182. Funerals. Burial

cemetery	maqbara (f)	مقبرة
grave, tomb	qabr (m)	قبر
cross	ṣalīb (m)	صليب
gravestone	ʃāhid al qabr (m)	شاهد القبر
fence	sūr (m)	سور
chapel	kanīsa saɣīra (f)	كنيسة صغيرة

death	mawt (m)	موت
to die (vi)	māt	مات
the deceased	al mutawaffi (m)	المتوفّي
mourning	hidād (m)	حداد

to bury (vt)	dafan	دفن
funeral home	bayt al ʒanāzāt (m)	بيت الجنازات
funeral	ʒanāza (f)	جنازة

wreath	iklīl (m)	إكليل
casket, coffin	tābūt (m)	تابوت
hearse	sayyārat naql al mawta (f)	سيّارة نقل الموتى
shroud	kafan (m)	كفن

| funeral procession | ʒanāza (f) | جنازة |
| funerary urn | qārūra li hifẓ ramād al mawta (f) | قارورة لحفظ رماد الموتى |

crematory	maḥraqat ʒuθaθ al mawta (f)	محرقة جثث الموتى
obituary	naʿiy (m)	نعي
to cry (weep)	baka	بكى
to sob (vi)	naḥab	نحب

183. War. Soldiers

platoon	faṣīla (f)	فصيلة
company	sariyya (f)	سرية
regiment	fawʒ (m)	فوج
army	ʒayʃ (m)	جيش
division	firqa (f)	فرقة
section, squad	waḥda (f)	وحدة
host (army)	ʒayʃ (m)	جيش
soldier	ʒundiy (m)	جندي
officer	ḍābiṭ (m)	ضابط
private	ʒundiy (m)	جندي
sergeant	raqīb (m)	رقيب
lieutenant	mulāzim (m)	ملازم
captain	naqīb (m)	نقيب
major	rā'id (m)	رائد
colonel	ʿaqīd (m)	عقيد
general	ʒinirāl (m)	جنرال
sailor	baḥḥār (m)	بحار
captain	qubṭān (m)	قبطان
boatswain	raʾīs al baḥḥāra (m)	رئيس البحارة
artilleryman	madfaʿiy (m)	مدفعي
paratrooper	ʒundiy al maẓallāt (m)	جندي المظلات
pilot	ṭayyār (m)	طيار
navigator	mallāḥ (m)	ملاح
mechanic	mikanīkiy (m)	ميكانيكي
pioneer (sapper)	muhandis ʿaskariy (m)	مهندس عسكري
parachutist	miẓalliy (m)	مظلي
reconnaissance scout	mustakʃif (m)	مستكشف
sniper	qannāṣ (m)	قناص
patrol (group)	dawriyya (f)	دورية
to patrol (vt)	qām bi dawriyya	قام بدورية
sentry, guard	ḥāris (m)	حارس
warrior	muḥārib (m)	محارب
patriot	waṭaniy (m)	وطني
hero	baṭal (m)	بطل

heroine	baṭala (f)	بطلة
traitor	χā'in (m)	خائن
to betray (vt)	χān	خان
deserter	hārib min al ʒayʃ (m)	هارب من الجيش
to desert (vi)	harab min al ʒayʃ	هرب من الجيش
mercenary	ma'ʒūr (m)	مأجور
recruit	ʒundiy ʒadīd (m)	جندي جديد
volunteer	mutaṭawwi' (m)	متطوع
dead (n)	qatīl (m)	قتيل
wounded (n)	ʒarīḥ (m)	جريح
prisoner of war	asīr (m)	أسير

184. War. Military actions. Part 1

war	ḥarb (f)	حرب
to be at war	ḥārab	حارب
civil war	ḥarb ahliyya (f)	حرب أهلية
treacherously (adv)	γadran	غدراً
declaration of war	i'lān ḥarb (m)	إعلان حرب
to declare (~ war)	a'lan	أعلن
aggression	'udwān (m)	عدوان
to attack (invade)	haʒam	هجم
to invade (vt)	iḥtall	إحتلّ
invader	muḥtall (m)	محتلّ
conqueror	fātiḥ (m)	فاتح
defense	difā' (m)	دفاع
to defend (a country, etc.)	dāfa'	دافع
to defend (against ...)	dāfa' 'an nafsih	دافع عن نفسه
enemy	'aduww (m)	عدوّ
foe, adversary	χaṣm (m)	خصم
enemy (as adj)	'aduww	عدوّ
strategy	istratiʒiyya (f)	إستراتيجية
tactics	taktīk (m)	تكتيك
order	amr (m)	أمر
command (order)	amr (m)	أمر
to order (vt)	amar	أمر
mission	muhimma (f)	مهمة
secret (adj)	sirriy	سرّي
battle	ma'raka (f)	معركة
combat	qitāl (m)	قتال
attack	huʒūm (m)	هجوم

charge (assault)	inqiḍāḍ (m)	إنقضاض
to storm (vt)	inqaḍḍ	إنقضّ
siege (to be under ~)	ḥiṣār (m)	حصار
offensive (n)	huᴣūm (m)	هجوم
to go on the offensive	haᴣam	هجم
retreat	insiḥāb (m)	إنسحاب
to retreat (vi)	insaḥab	إنسحب
encirclement	iḥāṭa (f)	إحاطة
to encircle (vt)	aḥāṭ	أحاط
bombing (by aircraft)	qaṣf (m)	قصف
to drop a bomb	asqaṭ qumbula	أسقط قنبلة
to bomb (vt)	qaṣaf	قصف
explosion	infiᴣār (m)	إنفجار
shot	ṭalaqa (f)	طلقة
to fire (~ a shot)	aṭlaq an nār	أطلق النار
firing (burst of ~)	iṭlāq an nār (m)	إطلاق النار
to aim (to point a weapon)	ṣawwab	صوّب
to point (a gun)	ṣawwab	صوّب
to hit (the target)	aṣāb al hadaf	أصاب الهدف
to sink (~ a ship)	aɣraq	أغرق
hole (in a ship)	θuqb (m)	ثقب
to founder, to sink (vi)	ɣariq	غرق
front (war ~)	ᴣabha (f)	جبهة
evacuation	iχlā' aṭ ṭawāri' (m)	إخلاء الطوارئ
to evacuate (vt)	aχla	أخلى
trench	χandaq (m)	خندق
barbwire	aslāk ʃā'ika (pl)	أسلاك شائكة
barrier (anti tank ~)	ḥāᴣiz (m)	حاجز
watchtower	burᴣ muraqaba (m)	برج مراقبة
military hospital	mustaʃfa 'askariy (m)	مستشفى عسكريّ
to wound (vt)	ᴣaraḥ	جرح
wound	ᴣurḥ (m)	جرح
wounded (n)	ᴣarīḥ (m)	جريح
to be wounded	uṣīb bil ᴣirāḥ	أصيب بالجراح
serious (wound)	χaṭīr	خطير

185. War. Military actions. Part 2

| captivity | asr (m) | أسر |
| to take captive | asar | أسر |

to be held captive	kān asīran	كان أسيرًا
to be taken captive	waqaʿ fil asr	وقع في الأسر
concentration camp	muʿaskar iʿtiqāl (m)	معسكر إعتقال
prisoner of war	asīr (m)	أسير
to escape (vi)	harab	هرب
to betray (vt)	χān	خان
betrayer	χāʾin (m)	خائن
betrayal	χiyāna (f)	خيانة
to execute (by firing squad)	aʿdam ramyan bir raṣāṣ	أعدم رميًا بالرصاص
execution (by firing squad)	iʿdām ramyan bir raṣāṣ (m)	إعدام رميًا بالرصاص
equipment (military gear)	al ʿitād al ʿaskariy (m)	العتاد العسكريّ
shoulder board	katāfa (f)	كتافة
gas mask	qināʿ al ɣāz (m)	قناع الغاز
field radio	ʒihāz lāsilkiy (m)	جهاز لاسلكيّ
cipher, code	ʃifra (f)	شفرة
secrecy	sirriyya (f)	سرّيّة
password	kalimat al murūr (f)	كلمة مرور
land mine	laɣm (m)	لغم
to mine (road, etc.)	laɣɣam	لغّم
minefield	ḥaql alɣām (m)	حقل ألغام
air-raid warning	inðār ʒawwiy (m)	إنذار جوّيّ
alarm (alert signal)	inðār (m)	إنذار
signal	iʃāra (f)	إشارة
signal flare	iʃāra muḍīʾa (f)	إشارة مضيئة
headquarters	maqarr (m)	مقرّ
reconnaissance	kaʃʃāfat al istiṭlāʿ (f)	كشّافة الإستطلاع
situation	waḍʿ (m)	وضع
report	taqrīr (m)	تقرير
ambush	kamīn (m)	كمين
reinforcement (of army)	imdādāt ʿaskariyya (pl)	إمدادات عسكرية
target	hadaf (m)	هدف
proving ground	ḥaql taʒārib (m)	حقل تجارب
military exercise	munāwarāt ʿaskariyya (pl)	مناورات عسكرية
panic	ðuʿr (m)	ذعر
devastation	damār (m)	دمار
destruction, ruins	ḥiṭām (pl)	حطام
to destroy (vt)	dammar	دمّر
to survive (vi, vt)	naʒa	نجا
to disarm (vt)	ʒarrad min as silāḥ	جرّد من السلاح
to handle (~ a gun)	istaʿmal	إستعمل

| Attention! | intibāh! | إنتباه! |
| At ease! | istariḥ! | إسترح! |

act of courage	ma'θara (f)	مأثرة
oath (vow)	qasam (m)	قسم
to swear (an oath)	aqsam	أقسم

decoration (medal, etc.)	wisām (m)	وسام
to award (give medal to)	manaḥ	منح
medal	midāliyya (f)	ميداليّة
order (e.g., ~ of Merit)	wisām 'askariy (m)	وسام عسكريّ

victory	intiṣār - fawz (m)	إنتصار، فوز
defeat	hazīma (f)	هزيمة
armistice	hudna (f)	هدنة

standard (battle flag)	rāyat al ma'raka (f)	راية المعركة
glory (honor, fame)	maʒd (m)	مجد
parade	isti'rāḍ 'askariy (m)	إستعراض عسكريّ
to march (on parade)	sār	سار

186. Weapons

weapons	asliḥa (pl)	أسلحة
firearms	asliḥa nāriyya (pl)	أسلحة ناريّة
cold weapons (knives, etc.)	asliḥa bayḍā' (pl)	أسلحة بيضاء

chemical weapons	asliḥa kīmyā'iyya (pl)	أسلحة كيميائيّة
nuclear (adj)	nawawiy	نوويّ
nuclear weapons	asliḥa nawawiyya (pl)	أسلحة نوويّة

| bomb | qumbula (f) | قنبلة |
| atomic bomb | qumbula nawawiyya (f) | قنبلة نوويّة |

pistol (gun)	musaddas (m)	مسدّس
rifle	bunduqiyya (f)	بندقيّة
submachine gun	bunduqiyya huʒūmiyya (f)	بندقيّة هجوميّة
machine gun	raʃʃāʃ (m)	رشّاش

muzzle	fūha (f)	فوهة
barrel	sabṭāna (f)	سبطانة
caliber	'iyār (m)	عيار

trigger	zinād (m)	زناد
sight (aiming device)	muṣawwib (m)	مصوّب
magazine	maxzan (m)	مخزن
butt (shoulder stock)	'aqab al bunduqiyya (m)	عقب البندقيّة
hand grenade	qumbula yadawiyya (f)	قنبلة يدويّة
explosive	mawādd mutafaʒʒira (pl)	موادّ متفجّرة

bullet	ruṣāṣa (f)	رصاصة
cartridge	χarṭūʃa (f)	خرطوشة
charge	haʃwa (f)	حشوة
ammunition	ðaχāʾir (pl)	ذخائر

bomber (aircraft)	qāðifat qanābil (f)	قاذفة قنابل
fighter	ṭāʾira muqātila (f)	طائرة مقاتلة
helicopter	hiliukūbtir (m)	هليكوبتر

anti-aircraft gun	madfaθ muḍādd liṭ ṭaʾirāṭ (m)	مدفع مضادّ للطائرات
tank	dabbāba (f)	دبّابة
tank gun	madfaʿ ad dabbāba (m)	مدفع الدبّابة

artillery	madfaʿiyya (f)	مدفعيّة
gun (cannon, howitzer)	madfaʿ (m)	مدفع
to lay (a gun)	ṣawwab	صوّب

shell (projectile)	qaðīfa (f)	قذيفة
mortar bomb	qumbula hāwun (f)	قنبلة هاون
mortar	hāwun (m)	هاون
splinter (shell fragment)	ʃaẓiyya (f)	شظيّة

submarine	ɣawwāṣa (f)	غوّاصة
torpedo	ṭurbīd (m)	طوربيد
missile	ṣārūχ (m)	صاروخ

to load (gun)	haʃa	حشا
to shoot (vi)	aṭlaq an nār	أطلق النار
to point at (the cannon)	ṣawwab	صوّب
bayonet	harba (f)	حربة

rapier	ʃiʃ (m)	شيش
saber (e.g., cavalry ~)	sayf munhani (m)	سيف منحن
spear (weapon)	rumḥ (m)	رمح
bow	qaws (m)	قوس
arrow	sahm (m)	سهم
musket	muskīt (m)	مسكيت
crossbow	qaws mustaʿraḍ (m)	قوس مستعرض

187. Ancient people

primitive (prehistoric)	bidāʾiy	بدائيّ
prehistoric (adj)	ma qabl at tarīχ	ما قبل التاريخ
ancient (~ civilization)	qadīm	قديم

Stone Age	al ʿaṣr al haǧariy (m)	العصر الحجريّ
Bronze Age	al ʿaṣr al brunziy (m)	العصر البرونزيّ
Ice Age	al ʿaṣr al ǧalīdiy (m)	العصر الجليديّ
tribe	qabīla (f)	قبيلة

cannibal	'ākil laḥm al baʃar (m)	آكل لحم البشر
hunter	ṣayyād (m)	صيّاد
to hunt (vi, vt)	iṣṭād	إصطاد
mammoth	mamūθ (m)	ماموث

cave	kahf (m)	كهف
fire	nār (f)	نار
campfire	nār muxayyam (m)	نار مخيّم
cave painting	rasm fil kahf (m)	رسم في الكهف

tool (e.g., stone ax)	adāt (f)	أداة
spear	rumḥ (m)	رمح
stone ax	fa's haʒariy (m)	فأس حجريّ
to be at war	ḥārab	حارب
to domesticate (vt)	daʒʒan	دجّن

idol	ṣanam (m)	صنم
to worship (vt)	'abad	عبد
superstition	xurāfa (f)	خرافة
rite	mansak (m)	منسك

evolution	taṭawwur (m)	تطوّر
development	numuww (m)	نمو
disappearance (extinction)	ixtifā' (m)	إختفاء
to adapt oneself	takayyaf	تكيّف

archeology	'ilm al 'āθār (m)	علم الآثار
archeologist	'ālim'āθār (m)	عالم آثار
archeological (adj)	aθariy	أثريّ

excavation site	mawqi' ḥafr (m)	موقع حفر
excavations	tanqīb (m)	تنقيب
find (object)	iktiʃāf (m)	إكتشاف
fragment	qiṭ'a (f)	قطعة

188. Middle Ages

people (ethnic group)	ʃa'b (m)	شعب
peoples	ʃu'ūb (pl)	شعوب
tribe	qabīla (f)	قبيلة
tribes	qabā'il (pl)	قبائل

barbarians	al barābira (pl)	البرابرة
Gauls	al ɣalyūn (pl)	الغاليون
Goths	al qūṭiyyūn (pl)	القوطيّون
Slavs	as silāf (pl)	السلاف
Vikings	al vaykinɣ (pl)	الفايكينغ

| Romans | ar rūmān (pl) | الرومان |
| Roman (adj) | rumāniy | رومانيّ |

Byzantines	bizantiyyūn (pl)	بيزنطيون
Byzantium	bīzanṭa (f)	بيزنطة
Byzantine (adj)	bizanṭiy	بيزنطيّ
emperor	imbiraṭūr (m)	إمبراطور
leader, chief (tribal ~)	zaʿīm (m)	زعيم
powerful (~ king)	qawiy	قويّ
king	malik (m)	ملك
ruler (sovereign)	ḥākim (m)	حاكم
knight	fāris (m)	فارس
feudal lord	iqṭāʿiy (m)	إقطاعيّ
feudal (adj)	iqṭāʿiy	إقطاعيّ
vassal	muqṭaʿ (m)	مقطع
duke	dūq (m)	دوق
earl	īrl (m)	إيرل
baron	barūn (m)	بارون
bishop	usquf (m)	أسقف
armor	dirʿ (m)	درع
shield	turs (m)	ترس
sword	sayf (m)	سيف
visor	ḥāffa amāmiyya lil ẖūða (f)	حافّة أماميّة للخوذة
chainmail	dirʿ az zarad (m)	درع الزرد
Crusade	ḥamla ṣalībiyya (f)	حملة صليبيّة
crusader	ṣalībiy (m)	صليبيّ
territory	arḍ (f)	أرض
to attack (invade)	haǧam	هجم
to conquer (vt)	fataḥ	فتح
to occupy (invade)	iḥtall	إحتلّ
siege (to be under ~)	ḥiṣār (m)	حصار
besieged (adj)	muḥāṣar	محاصر
to besiege (vt)	ḥāṣar	حاصر
inquisition	maḥākim at taftīʃ (pl)	محاكم التفتيش
inquisitor	mufattiʃ (m)	مفتّش
torture	taʿðīb (m)	تعذيب
cruel (adj)	qās	قاس
heretic	harṭūqiy (m)	هرطوقيّ
heresy	harṭaqa (f)	هرطقة
seafaring	as safar bil baḥr (m)	السفر بالبحر
pirate	qurṣān (m)	قرصان
piracy	qarṣana (f)	قرصنة
boarding (attack)	muhāǧmat safina (f)	مهاجمة سفينة
loot, booty	ɣanīma (f)	غنيمة
treasures	kunūz (pl)	كنوز
discovery	iktiʃāf (m)	إكتشاف

to discover (new land, etc.)	iktaʃaf	إكتشف
expedition	baʿθa (f)	بعثة
musketeer	fāris (m)	فارس
cardinal	kardināl (m)	كاردينال
heraldry	ʃiʿārāt an nabāla (pl)	شعارات النبالة
heraldic (adj)	χāṣṣ bi ʃiʿārāt an nabāla	خاصّ بشعارات النبالة

189. Leader. Chief. Authorities

king	malik (m)	ملك
queen	malika (f)	ملكة
royal (adj)	malakiy	ملكيّ
kingdom	mamlaka (f)	مملكة
prince	amīr (m)	أمير
princess	amīra (f)	أميرة
president	raʾīs (m)	رئيس
vice-president	nāʾib ar raʾīs (m)	نائب الرئيس
senator	ʿuḍw maʒlis aʃ ʃuyūχ (m)	عضو مجلس الشيوخ
monarch	ʿāhil (m)	عاهل
ruler (sovereign)	ḥākim (m)	حاكم
dictator	diktatūr (m)	ديكتاتور
tyrant	ṭāɣiya (f)	طاغية
magnate	ra'smāliy kabīr (m)	رأسمالي كبير
director	mudīr (m)	مدير
chief	raʾīs (m)	رئيس
manager (director)	mudīr (m)	مدير
boss	raʾīs (m), mudīr (m)	رئيس, مدير
owner	ṣāḥib (m)	صاحب
leader	zaʿīm (m)	زعيم
head (~ of delegation)	raʾīs (m)	رئيس
authorities	sulutāt (pl)	سلطات
superiors	ru'asā' (pl)	رؤساء
governor	muḥāfiẓ (m)	محافظ
consul	qunṣul (m)	قنصل
diplomat	diblumāsiy (m)	دبلوماسيّ
mayor	raʾīs al baladiyya (m)	رئيس البلديّة
sheriff	ʃarīf (m)	شريف
emperor	imbiraṭūr (m)	إمبراطور
tsar, czar	qayṣar (m)	قيصر
pharaoh	firʿawn (m)	فرعون
khan	χān (m)	خان

190. Road. Way. Directions

road	ṭarīq (m)	طريق
way (direction)	ṭarīq (m)	طريق
freeway	ṭarīq sarīʿ (m)	طريق سريع
highway	ṭarīq sarīʿ (m)	طريق سريع
interstate	ṭarīq waṭaniy (m)	طريق وطني
main road	ṭarīq raʾīsiy (m)	طريق رئيسيّ
dirt road	ṭarīq turābiy (m)	طريق ترابي
pathway	mamarr (m)	ممرّ
footpath (troddenpath)	mamarr (m)	ممرّ
Where?	ayna?	أين؟
Where (to)?	ila ayna?	إلى أين؟
From where?	min ayna?	من أين؟
direction (way)	ittiʒāh (m)	إتّجاه
to point (~ the way)	aʃār	أشار
to the left	ilaʃ ʃimāl	إلى الشمال
to the right	ilal yamīn	إلى اليمين
straight ahead (adv)	ilal amām	إلى الأمام
back (e.g., to turn ~)	ilal warāʾ	إلى الوراء
bend, curve	munʿaṭif (m)	منعطف
to turn (e.g., ~ left)	inʿaṭaf	إنعطف
to make a U-turn	istadār lil χalf	إستدار للخلف
to be visible (mountains, castle, etc.)	ẓahar	ظهر
to appear (come into view)	ẓahar	ظهر
stop, halt (e.g., during a trip)	istirāḥa (f)	إستراحة
to rest, to pause (vi)	istarāḥ	إستراح
rest (pause)	istirāḥa (f)	إستراحة
to lose one's way	tāh	تاه
to lead to ... (ab. road)	adda ila ...	أدّى إلى...
to come out (e.g., on the highway)	waṣal ila ...	وصل إلى...
stretch (of road)	imtidād (m)	إمتداد
asphalt	asfalt (m)	اسفلت
curb	ḥāffat ar raṣīf (f)	حافة الرصيف
ditch	χandaq (m)	خندق
manhole	fatḥat ad duχūl (f)	فتحة الدخول
roadside (shoulder)	ḥāffat aṭ ṭarīq (f)	حافة الطريق

pit, pothole	ḥufra (f)	حفرة
to go (on foot)	maʃa	مشى
to pass (overtake)	laḥiq bi	لحق بـ
step (footstep)	xaṭwa (f)	خطوة
on foot (adv)	māʃiyan	ماشيًا
to block (road)	sadd	سدّ
boom gate	ḥāǧiz ṭarīq (m)	حاجز طريق
dead end	ṭarīq masdūd (m)	طريق مسدود

191. Breaking the law. Criminals. Part 1

bandit	qāṭi' ṭarīq (m)	قاطع طريق
crime	ʒarīma (f)	جريمة
criminal (person)	muʒrim (m)	مجرم
thief	sāriq (m)	سارق
to steal (vi, vt)	saraq	سرق
stealing, theft	sirqa (f)	سرقة
to kidnap (vt)	xaṭaf	خطف
kidnapping	xaṭf (m)	خطف
kidnapper	xāṭif (m)	خاطف
ransom	fidya (f)	فدية
to demand ransom	ṭalab fidya	طلب فدية
to rob (vt)	nahab	نهب
robbery	nahb (m)	نهب
robber	nahhāb (m)	نهّاب
to extort (vt)	balṭaʒ	بلطج
extortionist	balṭaʒiy (m)	بلطجيّ
extortion	balṭaʒa (f)	بلطجة
to murder, to kill	qatal	قتل
murder	qatl (m)	قتل
murderer	qātil (m)	قاتل
gunshot	ṭalaqat nār (f)	طلقة نار
to fire (~ a shot)	aṭlaq an nār	أطلق النار
to shoot to death	qatal bir ruṣāṣ	قتل بالرصاص
to shoot (vi)	aṭlaq an nār	أطلق النار
shooting	iṭlāq an nār (m)	إطلاق النار
incident (fight, etc.)	ḥādiθ (m)	حادث
fight, brawl	'irāk (m)	عراك
Help!	sā'idni	ساعدني!
victim	ḍaḥiyya (f)	ضحيّة

to damage (vt)	atlaf	أتلف
damage	χasāra (f)	خسارة
dead body, corpse	ʒuθθa (f)	جثّة
grave (~ crime)	'anīf	عنيف
to attack (vt)	haʒam	هجم
to beat (to hit)	ḍarab	ضرب
to beat up	ḍarab	ضرب
to take (rob of sth)	salab	سلب
to stab to death	ṭa'an ḥatta al mawt	طعن حتّى الموت
to maim (vt)	ʃawwah	شوّه
to wound (vt)	ʒaraḥ	جرح
blackmail	balṭaʒa (f)	بلطجة
to blackmail (vt)	ibtazz	إبتزّ
blackmailer	mubtazz (m)	مبتزّ
protection racket	naṣb (m)	نصب
racketeer	naṣṣāb (m)	نصّاب
gangster	raʒul 'iṣāba (m)	رجل عصابة
mafia, Mob	māfia (f)	مافيا
pickpocket	naʃʃāl (m)	نشّال
burglar	liṣṣ buyūt (m)	لصّ بيوت
smuggling	tahrīb (m)	تهريب
smuggler	muharrib (m)	مهرّب
forgery	tazwīr (m)	تزوير
to forge (counterfeit)	zawwar	زوّر
fake (forged)	muzawwar	مزوّر

192. Breaking the law. Criminals. Part 2

rape	iɣtiṣāb (m)	إغتصاب
to rape (vt)	iɣtaṣab	إغتصب
rapist	muɣtaṣib (m)	مغتصب
maniac	mahwūs (m)	مهووس
prostitute (fem.)	'āhira (f)	عاهرة
prostitution	da'āra (f)	دعارة
pimp	qawwād (m)	قوّاد
drug addict	mudmin muχaddarāt (m)	مدمن مخدّرات
drug dealer	tāʒir muχaddarāt (m)	تاجر مخدّرات
to blow up (bomb)	faʒʒar	فجّر
explosion	infiʒār (m)	إنفجار
to set fire	aʃ'al an nār	أشعل النار
arsonist	muʃ'il ḥarīq (m)	مشعل حريق
terrorism	irhāb (m)	إرهاب

| terrorist | irhābiy (m) | إرهابيّ |
| hostage | rahīna (m) | رهينة |

to swindle (deceive)	iḥtāl	إحتال
swindle, deception	iḥtiyāl (m)	إحتيال
swindler	muḥtāl (m)	محتال

to bribe (vt)	raʃa	رشا
bribery	irtiʃā' (m)	إرتشاء
bribe	raʃwa (f)	رشوة

poison	samm (m)	سمّ
to poison (vt)	sammam	سمّم
to poison oneself	sammam nafsahu	سمّم نفسه

| suicide (act) | intiḥār (m) | إنتحار |
| suicide (person) | muntaḥir (m) | منتحر |

to threaten (vt)	haddad	هدّد
threat	tahdīd (m)	تهديد
to make an attempt	ḥāwal iɣtiyāl	حاول الإغتيال
attempt (attack)	muḥāwalat iɣtiyāl (f)	محاولة إغتيال

| to steal (a car) | saraq | سرق |
| to hijack (a plane) | iɣtataf | إختطف |

| revenge | intiqām (m) | إنتقام |
| to avenge (get revenge) | intaqam | إنتقم |

to torture (vt)	ʿaððab	عذّب
torture	taʿðīb (m)	تعذيب
to torment (vt)	ʿaððab	عذّب

pirate	qurṣān (m)	قرصان
hooligan	wabaʃ (m)	وبش
armed (adj)	musallaḥ	مسلح
violence	ʿunf (m)	عنف
illegal (unlawful)	ɣayr qānūniy	غير قانونيّ

| spying (espionage) | taʒassas (m) | تجسّس |
| to spy (vi) | taʒassas | تجسّس |

193. Police. Law. Part 1

| justice | qaḍā' (m) | قضاء |
| court (see you in ~) | maḥkama (f) | محكمة |

judge	qāḍi (m)	قاض
jurors	muḥallafūn (pl)	محلّفون
jury trial	qaḍā' al muḥallafīn (m)	قضاء المحلّفين

to judge (vt)	ḥakam	حكم
lawyer, attorney	muḥāmi (m)	محام
defendant	mudda'a 'alayh (m)	مدّعى عليه
dock	qafṣ al ittihām (m)	قفص الإتهام
charge	ittihām (m)	إتهام
accused	muttaham (m)	متّهم
sentence	ḥukm (m)	حكم
to sentence (vt)	ḥakam	حكم
guilty (culprit)	muðnib (m)	مذنب
to punish (vt)	'āqab	عاقب
punishment	'uqūba (f), 'iqāb (m)	عقوبة، عقاب
fine (penalty)	ɣarāma (f)	غرامة
life imprisonment	siʒn mada al ḥayāt (m)	سجن مدى الحياة
death penalty	'uqūbat 'i'dām (f)	عقوبة إعدام
electric chair	kursiy kaharabā'iy (m)	كرسيّ كهربائيّ
gallows	maʃnaqa (f)	مشنقة
to execute (vt)	a'dam	أعدم
execution	i'dām (m)	إعدام
prison, jail	siʒn (m)	سجن
cell	zinzāna (f)	زنزانة
escort	ḥirāsa (f)	حراسة
prison guard	ḥāris siʒn (m)	حارس سجن
prisoner	saʒīn (m)	سجين
handcuffs	aṣfād (pl)	أصفاد
to handcuff (vt)	ṣaffad	صفّد
prison break	hurūb min as siʒn (m)	هروب من السجن
to break out (vi)	harab	هرب
to disappear (vi)	iχtafa	إختفى
to release (from prison)	aχla sabīl	أخلى سبيل
amnesty	'afw 'āmm (m)	عفو عامّ
police	ʃurṭa (f)	شرطة
police officer	ʃurṭiy (m)	شرطيّ
police station	qism ʃurṭa (m)	قسم شرطة
billy club	hirāwat aʃ ʃurṭiy (f)	هراوة الشرطيّ
bullhorn	būq (m)	بوق
patrol car	sayyārat dawrīyyāt (f)	سيّارة دوريّات
siren	ṣaffārat inðār (f)	صفّارة إنذار
to turn on the siren	aṭlaq sirīna	أطلق سرينة
siren call	ṣawt sirīna (m)	صوت سرينة
crime scene	masraḥ al ʒarīma (m)	مسرح الجريمة
witness	ʃāhid (m)	شاهد

freedom	ḥurriyya (f)	حرّية
accomplice	ʃarīk fil ʒarīma (m)	شريك في الجريمة
to flee (vi)	harab	هرب
trace (to leave a ~)	aθar (m)	أثر

194. Police. Law. Part 2

search (investigation)	baḥθ (m)	بحث
to look for ...	baḥaθ	بحث
suspicion	ʃubha (f)	شبهة
suspicious (e.g., ~ vehicle)	maʃbūh	مشبوه
to stop (cause to halt)	awqaf	أوقف
to detain (keep in custody)	iʿtaqal	إعتقل

case (lawsuit)	qaḍiyya (f)	قضيّة
investigation	taḥqīq (m)	تحقيق
detective	muḥaqqiq (m)	محقّق
investigator	mufattiʃ (m)	مفتّش
hypothesis	riwāya (f)	رواية

motive	dāfiʿ (m)	دافع
interrogation	istiʒwāb (m)	إستجواب
to interrogate (vt)	istaʒwab	إستجوب
to question (~ neighbors, etc.)	istanṭaq	إستنطق
check (identity ~)	faḥṣ (m)	فحص

round-up	ʒamʿ (m)	جمع
search (~ warrant)	taftīʃ (m)	تفتيش
chase (pursuit)	muṭārada (f)	مطاردة
to pursue, to chase	ṭārad	طارد
to track (a criminal)	tābaʿ	تابع

arrest	iʿtiqāl (m)	إعتقال
to arrest (sb)	iʿtaqal	إعتقل
to catch (thief, etc.)	qabaḍ	قبض
capture	qabḍ (m)	قبض

document	waθīqa (f)	وثيقة
proof (evidence)	dalīl (m)	دليل
to prove (vt)	aθbat	أثبت
footprint	baṣma (f)	بصمة
fingerprints	baṣamāt al aṣābiʿ (pl)	بصمات الأصابع
piece of evidence	dalīl (m)	دليل

alibi	dafʿ bil ɣayba (f)	دفع بالغيبة
innocent (not guilty)	barīʾ	بريء
injustice	ẓulm (m)	ظلم
unjust, unfair (adj)	ɣayr ʿādil	غير عادل
criminal (adj)	iʒrāmiy	إجراميّ

to confiscate (vt)	ṣādar	صادر
drug (illegal substance)	muxaddirāt (pl)	مخدّرات
weapon, gun	silāḥ (m)	سلاح
to disarm (vt)	ʒarrad min as silāḥ	جرّد من السلاح
to order (command)	amar	أمر
to disappear (vi)	ixtafa	إختفى
law	qānūn (m)	قانون
legal, lawful (adj)	qānūniy, ʃarʿiy	قانونيّ، شرعيّ
illegal, illicit (adj)	ɣayr qanūny, ɣayr ʃarʿi	غير قانونيّ، غير شرعيّ
responsibility (blame)	mas'ūliyya (f)	مسؤوليّة
responsible (adj)	mas'ūl (m)	مسؤول

NATURE

The Earth. Part 1

195. Outer space

space	faḍā' (m)	فضاء
space (as adj)	faḍā'iy	فضائيّ
outer space	faḍā' (m)	فضاء
world	'ālam (m)	عالم
universe	al kawn (m)	الكون
galaxy	al maʒarra (f)	المجرّة
star	naʒm (m)	نجم
constellation	burʒ (m)	برج
planet	kawkab (m)	كوكب
satellite	qamar ṣinā'iy (m)	قمر صناعيّ
meteorite	haʒar nayzakiy (m)	حجر نيزكيّ
comet	muðannab (m)	مذنّب
asteroid	kuwaykib (m)	كويكب
orbit	madār (m)	مدار
to revolve (~ around the Earth)	dār	دار
atmosphere	al ɣilāf al ʒawwiy (m)	الغلاف الجوّيّ
the Sun	aʃʃams (f)	الشمس
solar system	al maʒmū'a aʃ ʃamsiyya (f)	المجموعة الشمسيّة
solar eclipse	kusūf aʃ ʃams (m)	كسوف الشمس
the Earth	al arḍ (f)	الأرض
the Moon	al qamar (m)	القمر
Mars	al mirrīχ (m)	المرّيخ
Venus	az zahra (f)	الزهرة
Jupiter	al muʃtari (m)	المشتري
Saturn	zuḥal (m)	زحل
Mercury	'aṭārid (m)	عطارد
Uranus	urānus (m)	اورانوس
Neptune	nibtūn (m)	نبتون
Pluto	blūtu (m)	بلوتو
Milky Way	darb at tabbāna (m)	درب التبّانة
Great Bear (Ursa Major)	ad dubb al akbar (m)	الدبّ الأكبر

North Star	naʒm al ʼquṭb (m)	نجم القطب
Martian	sākin al mirrīχ (m)	ساكن المرّيخ
extraterrestrial (n)	faḍāʼiy (m)	فضائيّ
alien	faḍāʼiy (m)	فضائيّ
flying saucer	ṭabaq ṭāʼir (m)	طبق طائر

spaceship	markaba faḍāʼiyya (f)	مركبة فضائيّة
space station	maḥaṭṭat faḍāʼ (f)	محطّة فضاء
blast-off	inṭilāq (m)	إنطلاق

engine	mutūr (m)	موتور
nozzle	manfaθ (m)	منفث
fuel	wuqūd (m)	وقود

cockpit, flight deck	kabīna (f)	كابينة
antenna	hawāʼiy (m)	هوائيّ
porthole	kuwwa mustadīra (f)	كوّة مستديرة
solar panel	lawḥ ʃamsiy (m)	لوح شمسيّ
spacesuit	baðlat al faḍāʼ (f)	بذلة الفضاء

| weightlessness | inʻidām al wazn (m) | إنعدام الوزن |
| oxygen | uksiʒīn (m) | أكسجين |

| docking (in space) | rasw (m) | رسو |
| to dock (vi, vt) | rasa | رسا |

observatory	marṣad (m)	مرصد
telescope	tiliskūp (m)	تلسكوب
to observe (vt)	rāqab	راقب
to explore (vt)	istakʃaf	إستكشف

196. The Earth

the Earth	al arḍ (f)	الأرض
the globe (the Earth)	al kura al arḍiyya (f)	الكرة الأرضيّة
planet	kawkab (m)	كوكب

atmosphere	al χilāf al ʒawwiy (m)	الغلاف الجوّيَ
geography	ʒuγrāfiya (f)	جغرافيا
nature	ṭabīʻa (f)	طبيعة

| globe (table ~) | namūðaʒ lil kura al arḍiyya (m) | نموذج للكرة الأرضيّة |

| map | χarīṭa (f) | خريطة |
| atlas | aṭlas (m) | أطلس |

Europe	urūbba (f)	أوروبّا
Asia	ʼāsiya (f)	آسيا
Africa	afrīqiya (f)	أفريقيا
Australia	usturāliya (f)	أستراليا

America	amrīka (f)	أمريكا
North America	amrīka aʃʃimāliyya (f)	أمريكا الشماليّة
South America	amrīka al ʒanūbiyya (f)	أمريكا الجنوبيّة
Antarctica	al quṭb ʒanūbiy (m)	القطب الجنوبيّ
the Arctic	al quṭb aʃʃimāliy (m)	القطب الشماليّ

197. Cardinal directions

north	ʃimāl (m)	شمال
to the north	ilaʃʃimāl	إلى الشمال
in the north	fiʃʃimāl	في الشمال
northern (adj)	ʃimāliy	شماليّ
south	ʒanūb (m)	جنوب
to the south	ilal ʒanūb	إلى الجنوب
in the south	fil ʒanūb	في الجنوب
southern (adj)	ʒanūbiy	جنوبيّ
west	ɣarb (m)	غرب
to the west	ilal ɣarb	إلى الغرب
in the west	fil ɣarb	في الغرب
western (adj)	ɣarbiy	غربيّ
east	ʃarq (m)	شرق
to the east	ilaʃʃarq	إلى الشرق
in the east	fiʃʃarq	في الشرق
eastern (adj)	ʃarqiy	شرقيّ

198. Sea. Ocean

sea	baḥr (m)	بحر
ocean	muḥīṭ (m)	محيط
gulf (bay)	xalīʒ (m)	خليج
straits	maḍīq (m)	مضيق
land (solid ground)	barr (m)	برّ
continent (mainland)	qārra (f)	قارّة
island	ʒazīra (f)	جزيرة
peninsula	ʃibh ʒazīra (f)	شبه جزيرة
archipelago	maʒmūʕat ʒuzur (f)	مجموعة جزر
bay, cove	xalīʒ (m)	خليج
harbor	mīnāʾ (m)	ميناء
lagoon	buḥayra ʃāṭiʾa (f)	بحيرة شاطئة
cape	raʾs (m)	رأس
atoll	ʒazīra marʒāniyya istiwāʾiyya (f)	جزيرة مرجانيّة إستوائيّة

reef	ʃiʻāb (pl)	شعاب
coral	murʒān (m)	مرجان
coral reef	ʃiʻāb marʒāniyya (pl)	شعاب مرجانيّة

deep (adj)	ʻamīq	عميق
depth (deep water)	ʻumq (m)	عمق
abyss	mahwāt (f)	مهواة
trench (e.g., Mariana ~)	χandaq (m)	خندق

| current (Ocean ~) | tayyār (m) | تيّار |
| to surround (bathe) | aḥāṭ | أحاط |

| shore | sāḥil (m) | ساحل |
| coast | sāḥil (m) | ساحل |

flow (flood tide)	madd (m)	مدّ
ebb (ebb tide)	ʒazr (m)	جزر
shoal	miyāh ḍaḥla (f)	مياه ضحلة
bottom (~ of the sea)	qāʻ (m)	قاع
wave	mawʒa (f)	موجة
crest (~ of a wave)	qimmat mawʒa (f)	قمة موجة
spume (sea foam)	zabad al baḥr (m)	زبد البحر

storm (sea storm)	ʻāṣifa (f)	عاصفة
hurricane	iʻṣār (m)	إعصار
tsunami	tsunāmi (m)	تسونامي
calm (dead ~)	hudūʼ (m)	هدوء
quiet, calm (adj)	hādiʼ	هادئ

| pole | quṭb (m) | قطب |
| polar (adj) | quṭby | قطبيّ |

latitude	ʻarḍ (m)	عرض
longitude	ṭūl (m)	طول
parallel	mutawāzi (m)	متواز
equator	χaṭṭ al istiwāʼ (m)	خط الإستواء

sky	samāʼ (f)	سماء
horizon	ufuq (m)	أفق
air	hawāʼ (m)	هواء

lighthouse	manāra (f)	منارة
to dive (vi)	γāṣ	غاص
to sink (ab. boat)	γariq	غرق
treasures	kunūz (pl)	كنوز

199. Seas' and Oceans' names

| Atlantic Ocean | al muḥīṭ al aṭlasiy (m) | المحيط الأطلسيّ |
| Indian Ocean | al muḥīṭ al hindiy (m) | المحيط الهنديّ |

| Pacific Ocean | al muḥīṭ al hādi' (m) | المحيط الهادئ |
| Arctic Ocean | al muḥīṭ il mutaʒammid aʃ ʃimāliy (m) | المحيط المتجمّد الشماليّ |

Black Sea	al baḥr al aswad (m)	البحر الأسود
Red Sea	al baḥr al aḥmar (m)	البحر الأحمر
Yellow Sea	al baḥr al aṣfar (m)	البحر الأصفر
White Sea	al baḥr al abyaḍ (m)	البحر الأبيض

Caspian Sea	baḥr qazwīn (m)	بحر قزوين
Dead Sea	al baḥr al mayyit (m)	البحر الميّت
Mediterranean Sea	al baḥr al abyaḍ al mutawassiṭ (m)	البحر الأبيض المتوسّط

| Aegean Sea | baḥr ʔʒah (m) | بحر إيجة |
| Adriatic Sea | al baḥr al adriyatīkiy (m) | البحر الأدرياتيكيّ |

Arabian Sea	baḥr al ‘arab (m)	بحر العرب
Sea of Japan	baḥr al yabān (m)	بحر اليابان
Bering Sea	baḥr birinʒ (m)	بحر بيرينغ
South China Sea	baḥr aṣ ṣīn al ʒanūbiy (m)	بحر الصين الجنوبيّ

Coral Sea	baḥr al marʒān (m)	بحر المرجان
Tasman Sea	baḥr tasmān (m)	بحر تسمان
Caribbean Sea	al baḥr al karībiy (m)	البحر الكاريبيّ

| Barents Sea | baḥr barints (m) | بحر بارينس |
| Kara Sea | baḥr kara (m) | بحر كارا |

North Sea	baḥr aʃ ʃimāl (m)	بحر الشمال
Baltic Sea	al baḥr al balṭīq (m)	البحر البلطيق
Norwegian Sea	baḥr an narwīʒ (m)	بحر النرويج

200. Mountains

mountain	ʒabal (m)	جبل
mountain range	silsilat ʒibāl (f)	سلسلة جبال
mountain ridge	qimam ʒabaliyya (pl)	قمم جبليّة

summit, top	qimma (f)	قمّة
peak	qimma (f)	قمة
foot (~ of the mountain)	asfal (m)	أسفل
slope (mountainside)	munḥadar (m)	منحدر

volcano	burkān (m)	بركان
active volcano	burkān naʃīṭ (m)	بركان نشط
dormant volcano	burkān xāmid (m)	بركان خامد

| eruption | θawrān (m) | ثوران |
| crater | fūhat al burkān (f) | فوهة البركان |

magma	māɣma (f)	ماغما
lava	ḥumam burkāniyya (pl)	حمم بركانيّة
molten (~ lava)	munṣahira	منصهرة
canyon	talʿa (m)	تلعة
gorge	wādi ḍayyiq (m)	واد ضيّق
crevice	ʃaqq (m)	شقّ
abyss (chasm)	hāwiya (f)	هاوية
pass, col	mamarr ӡabaliy (m)	ممرّ جبليّ
plateau	haḍba (f)	هضبة
cliff	ӡurf (m)	جرف
hill	tall (m)	تلّ
glacier	nahr ӡalīdiy (m)	نهر جليديّ
waterfall	ʃallāl (m)	شلّال
geyser	fawwāra ḥārra (m)	فوّارة حارّة
lake	buḥayra (f)	بحيرة
plain	sahl (m)	سهل
landscape	manẓar ṭabīʿiy (m)	منظر طبيعيّ
echo	ṣada (m)	صدى
alpinist	mutasalliq al ӡibāl (m)	متسلّق الجبال
rock climber	mutasalliq ṣuxūr (m)	متسلّق صخور
to conquer (in climbing)	taɣallab ʿala	تغلّب على
climb (an easy ~)	tasalluq (m)	تسلّق

201. Mountains names

The Alps	ӡibāl al alb (pl)	جبال الألب
Mont Blanc	mūn blūn (m)	مون بلون
The Pyrenees	ӡibāl al barānis (pl)	جبال البرانس
The Carpathians	ӡibāl al karbāt (pl)	جبال الكاريات
The Ural Mountains	ӡibāl al ʾūrāl (pl)	جبال الأورال
The Caucasus Mountains	ӡibāl al qawqāz (pl)	جبال القوقاز
Mount Elbrus	ӡabal ilbrūs (m)	جبل إلبروس
The Altai Mountains	ӡibāl altāy (pl)	جبال ألتاي
The Tian Shan	ӡibāl tian ʃan (pl)	جبال تيان شان
The Pamir Mountains	ӡibāl bamīr (pl)	جبال بامير
The Himalayas	himalāya (pl)	هيمالايا
Mount Everest	ӡabal ivirist (m)	جبل افرست
The Andes	ӡibāl al andīz (pl)	جبال الأنديز
Mount Kilimanjaro	ӡabal kilimanӡāru (m)	جبل كليمنجارو

202. Rivers

river	nahr (m)	نهر
spring (natural source)	'ayn (m)	عين
riverbed (river channel)	maȝra an nahr (m)	مجرى النهر
basin (river valley)	ḥawḍ (m)	حوض
to flow into ...	ṣabb fi ...	صبَّ في...
tributary	rāfid (m)	رافد
bank (of river)	ḍiffa (f)	ضفَّة
current (stream)	tayyār (m)	تيَّار
downstream (adv)	f ittiȝāh maȝra an nahr	في إتجاه مجرى النهر
upstream (adv)	ḍidd at tayyār	ضد التيَّار
inundation	ɣamr (m)	غمر
flooding	fayaḍān (m)	فيضان
to overflow (vi)	fāḍ	فاض
to flood (vt)	ɣamar	غمر
shallow (shoal)	miyāh ḍaḥla (f)	مياه ضحلة
rapids	munḥadar an nahr (m)	منحدر النهر
dam	sadd (m)	سدّ
canal	qanāt (f)	قناة
reservoir (artificial lake)	xazzān mā'iy (m)	خزَّان مائيّ
sluice, lock	hawīs (m)	هويس
water body (pond, etc.)	masṭaḥ mā'iy (m)	مسطح مائيّ
swamp (marshland)	mustanqa' (m)	مستنقع
bog, marsh	mustanqa' (m)	مستنقع
whirlpool	dawwāma (f)	دوَّامة
stream (brook)	ȝadwal mā'iy (m)	جدول مائيّ
drinking (ab. water)	aʃ ʃurb	الشرب
fresh (~ water)	'aðb	عذب
ice	ȝalīd (m)	جليد
to freeze over (ab. river, etc.)	taȝammad	تجمَّد

203. Rivers' names

Seine	nahr as sīn (m)	نهر السين
Loire	nahr al lua:r (m)	نهر اللوار
Thames	nahr at tīmz (m)	نهر التيمز
Rhine	nahr ar rayn (m)	نهر الراين
Danube	nahr ad danūb (m)	نهر الدانوب

Volga	nahr al vulɣa (m)	نهر الفولغا
Don	nahr ad dūn (m)	نهر الدون
Lena	nahr līna (m)	نهر لينا

Yellow River	an nahr al aṣfar (m)	النهر الأصفر
Yangtze	nahr al yanɣtsi (m)	نهر اليانغتسي
Mekong	nahr al mikunɣ (m)	نهر الميكونغ
Ganges	nahr al ɣānʒ (m)	نهر الغانج

Nile River	nahr an nīl (m)	نهر النيل
Congo River	nahr al kunɣu (m)	نهر الكونغو
Okavango River	nahr ukavanʒu (m)	نهر اوكافانجو
Zambezi River	nahr az zambizi (m)	نهر الزمبيزي
Limpopo River	nahr limbubu (m)	نهر ليمبوبو
Mississippi River	nahr al mississibbi (m)	نهر الميسيسيبي

204. Forest

| forest, wood | ɣāba (f) | غابة |
| forest (as adj) | ɣāba | غابة |

thick forest	ɣāba kaθīfa (f)	غابة كثيفة
grove	ɣāba ṣaɣīra (f)	غابة صغيرة
forest clearing	minṭaqa uzīlat minha al aʃʒār (f)	منطقة أزيلت منها الأشجار

| thicket | aʒama (f) | أجمة |
| scrubland | ʃuʒayrāt (pl) | شجيرات |

| footpath (troddenpath) | mamarr (m) | ممرّ |
| gully | wādi ḍayyiq (m) | واد ضيّق |

tree	ʃaʒara (f)	شجرة
leaf	waraqa (f)	ورقة
leaves (foliage)	waraq (m)	ورق

fall of leaves	tasāquṭ al awrāq (m)	تساقط الأوراق
to fall (ab. leaves)	saqaṭ	سقط
top (of the tree)	ra's (m)	رأس

branch	ɣuṣn (m)	غصن
bough	ɣuṣn (m)	غصن
bud (on shrub, tree)	burʻum (m)	برعم
needle (of pine tree)	ʃawka (f)	شوكة
pine cone	kūz aṣ ṣanawbar (m)	كوز الصنوبر

hollow (in a tree)	ʒawf (m)	جوف
nest	ʻuʃʃ (m)	عشّ
burrow (animal hole)	ʒuḥr (m)	جحر
trunk	ʒiðʻ (m)	جذع

root	ʒiðr (m)	جذر
bark	liḥā' (m)	لحاء
moss	ṭuḥlub (m)	طحلب

to uproot (remove trees or tree stumps)	iqtalaʿ	إقتلع
to chop down	qataʿ	قطع
to deforest (vt)	azāl al ɣābāt	أزال الغابات
tree stump	ʒiðʿ aʃ ʃaʒara (m)	جذع الشجرة

campfire	nār muxayyam (m)	نار مخيّم
forest fire	ḥarīq ɣāba (m)	حريق غابة
to extinguish (vt)	atfa'	أطفأ

forest ranger	ḥāris al ɣāba (m)	حارس الغابة
protection	ḥimāya (f)	حماية
to protect (~ nature)	ḥama	حمى
poacher	sāriq aṣ ṣayd (m)	سارق الصيد
steel trap	maṣyada (f)	مصيدة

| to gather, to pick (vt) | ʒamaʿ | جمع |
| to lose one's way | tāh | تاه |

205. Natural resources

natural resources	θarawāt ṭabīʿiyya (pl)	ثروات طبيعيّة
minerals	maʿādin (pl)	معادن
deposits	makāmin (pl)	مكامن
field (e.g., oilfield)	ḥaql (m)	حقل

to mine (extract)	istaxraʒ	إستخرج
mining (extraction)	istixrāʒ (m)	إستخراج
ore	xām (m)	خام
mine (e.g., for coal)	manʒam (m)	منجم
shaft (mine ~)	manʒam (m)	منجم
miner	ʿāmil manʒam (m)	عامل منجم

| gas (natural ~) | ɣāz (m) | غاز |
| gas pipeline | xaṭṭ anābīb ɣāz (m) | خط أنابيب غاز |

oil (petroleum)	naft (m)	نفط
oil pipeline	anābīb an naft (pl)	أنابيب النفط
oil well	bi'r an naft (m)	بئر النفط
derrick (tower)	ḥaffāra (f)	حفّارة
tanker	nāqilat an naft (f)	ناقلة النفط

sand	raml (m)	رمل
limestone	ḥaʒar kalsiy (m)	حجر كلسيّ
gravel	ḥaṣa (m)	حصى
peat	xaθθ faḥm nabātiy (m)	خثّ فحم نباتيّ

clay	ṭīn (m)	طين
coal	faḥm (m)	فحم
iron (ore)	ḥadīd (m)	حديد
gold	ðahab (m)	ذهب
silver	fiḍḍa (f)	فضّة
nickel	nikil (m)	نيكل
copper	nuḥās (m)	نحاس
zinc	zink (m)	زنك
manganese	manɣanīz (m)	منغنيز
mercury	zi'baq (m)	زئبق
lead	ruṣāṣ (m)	رصاص
mineral	ma'dan (m)	معدن
crystal	ballūra (f)	بلّورة
marble	ruχām (m)	رخام
uranium	yurānuim (m)	يورانيوم

The Earth. Part 2

206. Weather

weather	ṭaqs (m)	طقس
weather forecast	naʃra ʒawwiyya (f)	نشرة جويّة
temperature	ḥarāra (f)	حرارة
thermometer	tirmūmitr (m)	ترمومتر
barometer	barūmitr (m)	بارومتر
humid (adj)	raṭib	رطب
humidity	ruṭūba (f)	رطوبة
heat (extreme ~)	ḥarāra (f)	حرارة
hot (torrid)	ḥārr	حارّ
it's hot	al ʒaww ḥārr	الجوّ حارّ
it's warm	al ʒaww dāfi'	الجوّ دافئ
warm (moderately hot)	dāfi'	دافئ
it's cold	al ʒaww bārid	الجوّ بارد
cold (adj)	bārid	بارد
sun	ʃams (f)	شمس
to shine (vi)	aḍā'	أضاء
sunny (day)	muʃmis	مشمس
to come up (vi)	ʃaraq	شرق
to set (vi)	ɣarab	غرب
cloud	saḥāba (f)	سحابة
cloudy (adj)	ɣā'im	غائم
rain cloud	saḥābat maṭar (f)	سحابة مطر
somber (gloomy)	ɣā'im	غائم
rain	maṭar (m)	مطر
it's raining	innaha tamṭur	إنّها تمطر
rainy (~ day, weather)	mumṭir	ممطر
to drizzle (vi)	raðð	رذّ
pouring rain	maṭar munhamir (f)	مطر منهمر
downpour	maṭar ɣazīr (m)	مطر غزير
heavy (e.g., ~ rain)	ʃadīd	شديد
puddle	birka (f)	بركة
to get wet (in rain)	ibtall	إبتلّ
fog (mist)	ḍabāb (m)	ضباب
foggy	muḍabbab	مضبّب

| snow | θalʒ (m) | ثلج |
| it's snowing | innaha taθluʒ | إنّها تثلج |

207. Severe weather. Natural disasters

thunderstorm	ʿāṣifa raʿdiyya (f)	عاصفة رعديّة
lightning (~ strike)	barq (m)	برق
to flash (vi)	baraq	برق

thunder	raʿd (m)	رعد
to thunder (vi)	raʿad	رعد
it's thundering	tarʿad as samāʾ	ترعد السماء

| hail | maṭar bard (m) | مطر برد |
| it's hailing | tamṭur as samāʾ bardan | تمطر السماء برداً |

| to flood (vt) | ɣamar | غمر |
| flood, inundation | fayaḍān (m) | فيضان |

earthquake	zilzāl (m)	زلزال
tremor, quake	hazza arḍiyya (f)	هزّة أرضيّة
epicenter	markaz az zilzāl (m)	مركز الزلزال

| eruption | θawrān (m) | ثوران |
| lava | ḥumam burkāniyya (pl) | حمم بركانيّة |

| twister, tornado | iʿṣār (m) | إعصار |
| typhoon | ṭūfān (m) | طوفان |

hurricane	iʿṣār (m)	إعصار
storm	ʿāṣifa (f)	عاصفة
tsunami	tsunāmi (m)	تسونامي

cyclone	iʿṣār (m)	إعصار
bad weather	ṭaqs sayyiʾ (m)	طقس سيّء
fire (accident)	ḥarīq (m)	حريق
disaster	kāriθa (f)	كارثة
meteorite	ḥaʒar nayzakiy (m)	حجر نيزكيّ

avalanche	inhiyār θalʒiy (m)	إنهيار ثلجيّ
snowslide	inhiyār θalʒiy (m)	إنهيار ثلجيّ
blizzard	ʿāṣifa θalʒiyya (f)	عاصفة ثلجيّة
snowstorm	ʿāṣifa θalʒiyya (f)	عاصفة ثلجيّة

208. Noises. Sounds

| silence (quiet) | ṣamt (m) | صمت |
| sound | ṣawt (m) | صوت |

noise	ḍawḍā' (f)	ضوضاء
to make noise	'amal aḍ ḍawḍā'	عمل الضوضاء
noisy (adj)	muz'iʒ	مزعج

loudly (to speak, etc.)	bi ṣawt 'āli	بصوت عال
loud (voice, etc.)	'āli	عال
constant (e.g., ~ noise)	mustamirr	مستمرّ

cry, shout (n)	ṣarχa (f)	صرخة
to cry, to shout (vi)	ṣaraχ	صرخ
whisper	hamsa (f)	همسة
to whisper (vi, vt)	hamas	همس

| barking (dog's ~) | nubāḥ (m) | نباح |
| to bark (vi) | nabaḥ | نبح |

groan (of pain, etc.)	anīn (m)	أنين
to groan (vi)	anna	أنّ
cough	su'āl (m)	سعال
to cough (vi)	sa'al	سعل

whistle	taṣfīr (m)	تصفير
to whistle (vi)	ṣaffar	صفّر
knock (at the door)	ṭarq, daqq (m)	طرق، دقّ
to knock (at the door)	daqq	دقّ

| to crack (vi) | farqa' | فرقع |
| crack (cracking sound) | farqa'a (f) | فرقعة |

siren	ṣaffārat inðār (f)	صفّارة إنذار
whistle (factory ~, etc.)	ṣafīr (m)	صفير
to whistle (ab. train)	ṣaffar	صفّر
honk (car horn sound)	tazmīr (m)	تزمير
to honk (vi)	zammar	زمّر

209. Winter

winter (n)	ʃitā' (m)	شتاء
winter (as adj)	ʃitawiy	شتويّ
in winter	fiʃ ʃitā'	في الشتاء

snow	θalʒ (m)	ثلج
it's snowing	innaha taθluʒ	إنّها تثلج
snowfall	tasāquṭ aθ θulūʒ (m)	تساقط الثلوج
snowdrift	rukma θalʒiyya (f)	ركمة ثلجيّة

snowflake	nudfat θalʒ (f)	ندفة ثلج
snowball	kurat θalʒ (f)	كرة ثلج
snowman	raʒul θalʒ (m)	رجل ثلج
icicle	qiṭ'at ʒalīd (f)	قطعة جليد

December	disimbar (m)	ديسمبر
January	yanāyir (m)	يناير
February	fibrāyir (m)	فبراير
frost (severe ~, freezing cold)	ṣaqī' (m)	صقيع
frosty (weather, air)	ṣāqi'	صاقع
below zero (adv)	taḥt aṣ ṣifr	تحت الصفر
first frost	ṣaqī' (m)	صقيع
hoarfrost	ṣaqī' (m)	صقيع
cold (cold weather)	bard (m)	برد
it's cold	al ʒaww bārid	الجوّ بارد
fur coat	mi'taf farw (m)	معطف فرو
mittens	quffāz muɣlaq (m)	قفّاز مغلق
to get sick	maraḍ	مرض
cold (illness)	bard (m)	برد
to catch a cold	aṣābahu al bard	أصابه البرد
ice	ʒalīd (m)	جليد
black ice	ʒalīd (m)	جليد
to freeze over (ab. river, etc.)	taʒammad	تجمّد
ice floe	ṭāfiya ʒalīdiyya (f)	طافية جليديّة
skis	zallāʒāt (pl)	زلّاجات
skier	mutazalliʒ bil iski (m)	متزلّج بالإسكي
to ski (vi)	tazallaʒ	تزلّج
to skate (vi)	tazaḥlaq 'alal ʒalīd	تزحلق على الجليد

Fauna

210. Mammals. Predators

predator	ḥayawān muftaris (m)	حيوان مفترس
tiger	namir (m)	نمر
lion	asad (m)	أسد
wolf	ði'b (m)	ذئب
fox	θa'lab (m)	ثعلب
jaguar	namir amrīkiy (m)	نمر أمريكيّ
leopard	fahd (m)	فهد
cheetah	namir ṣayyād (m)	نمر صيّاد
black panther	namir aswad (m)	نمر أسود
puma	būma (m)	بوما
snow leopard	namir aθ θulūʒ (m)	نمر الثلوج
lynx	waʃaq (m)	وشق
coyote	qayūṭ (m)	قيوط
jackal	ibn 'āwa (m)	ابن آوى
hyena	ḍabu' (m)	ضبع

211. Wild animals

animal	ḥayawān (m)	حيوان
beast (animal)	ḥayawān (m)	حيوان
squirrel	sinʒāb (m)	سنجاب
hedgehog	qumfuð (m)	قنفذ
hare	arnab barriy (m)	أرنب برّيّ
rabbit	arnab (m)	أرنب
badger	ɣarīr (m)	غرير
raccoon	rākūn (m)	راكون
hamster	qidād (m)	قداد
marmot	marmuṭ (m)	مرموط
mole	χuld (m)	خلد
mouse	fa'r (m)	فأر
rat	ʒurað (m)	جرذ
bat	χuffāʃ (m)	خفّاش
ermine	qāqum (m)	قاقم
sable	sammūr (m)	سمّور

marten	dalaq (m)	دلق
weasel	ibn 'irs (m)	إبن عرس
mink	mink (m)	منك
beaver	qundus (m)	قندس
otter	quḍā'a (f)	قضاعة
horse	ḥiṣān (m)	حصان
moose	mūz (m)	موظ
deer	ayyil (m)	أيّل
camel	ʒamal (m)	جمل
bison	bisūn (m)	بيسون
aurochs	θawr barriy (m)	ثور بريّ
buffalo	ʒāmūs (m)	جاموس
zebra	ḥimār zarad (m)	حمار زرد
antelope	ẓabiy (m)	ظبي
roe deer	yaḥmūr (m)	يحمور
fallow deer	ayyil asmar urubbiy (m)	أيّل أسمر أوروبيّ
chamois	ʃamwāh (f)	شامواه
wild boar	xinzīr barriy (m)	خنزير بريّ
whale	ḥūt (m)	حوت
seal	fuqma (f)	فقمة
walrus	faẓẓ (m)	فظّ
fur seal	fuqmat al firā' (f)	فقمة الفراء
dolphin	dilfin (m)	دلفين
bear	dubb (m)	دبّ
polar bear	dubb quṭbiy (m)	دبّ قطبيّ
panda	bānda (m)	باندا
monkey	qird (m)	قرد
chimpanzee	ʃimbanzi (m)	شيمبانزي
orangutan	urangutān (m)	أورنغوتان
gorilla	ɣurīlla (f)	غوريلا
macaque	qird al makāk (m)	قرد المكاك
gibbon	ʒibbūn (m)	جيبون
elephant	fīl (m)	فيل
rhinoceros	xartīt (m)	خرتيت
giraffe	zarāfa (f)	زرافة
hippopotamus	faras an nahr (m)	فرس النهر
kangaroo	kanɣar (m)	كنغر
koala (bear)	kuala (m)	كوالا
mongoose	nims (m)	نمس
chinchilla	ʃinʃīla (f)	شنشيلة
skunk	ẓaribān (m)	ظربان
porcupine	nīṣ (m)	نيص

212. Domestic animals

cat	qiṭṭa (f)	قطّة
tomcat	ðakar al qiṭṭ (m)	ذكر القطّ
dog	kalb (m)	كلب

horse	ḥiṣān (m)	حصان
stallion (male horse)	faḥl al xayl (m)	فحل الخيل
mare	unθa al faras (f)	أنثى الفرس

cow	baqara (f)	بقرة
bull	θawr (m)	ثور
ox	θawr (m)	ثور

sheep (ewe)	xarūf (f)	خروف
ram	kabʃ (m)	كبش
goat	māʿiz (m)	ماعز
billy goat, he-goat	ðakar al māʿið (m)	ذكر الماعز

| donkey | ḥimār (m) | حمار |
| mule | baɣl (m) | بغل |

pig, hog	xinzīr (m)	خنزير
piglet	xannūṣ (m)	خنّوص
rabbit	arnab (m)	أرنب

| hen (chicken) | daʒāʒa (f) | دجاجة |
| rooster | dīk (m) | ديك |

duck	baṭṭa (f)	بطّة
drake	ðakar al baṭṭ (m)	ذكر البطّ
goose	iwazza (f)	إوزّة

| tom turkey, gobbler | dīk rūmiy (m) | ديك رومي |
| turkey (hen) | daʒāʒ rūmiy (m) | دجاج رومي |

domestic animals	ḥayawānāt dawāʒin (pl)	حيوانات دواجن
tame (e.g., ~ hamster)	alīf	أليف
to tame (vt)	allaf	ألّف
to breed (vt)	rabba	ربّى

farm	mazraʿa (f)	مزرعة
poultry	ṭuyūr dāʒina (pl)	طيور داجنة
cattle	māʃiya (f)	ماشية
herd (cattle)	qaṭīʿ (m)	قطيع

stable	isṭabl xayl (m)	إسطبل خيل
pigpen	ḥaẓīrat al xanāzīr (f)	حظيرة الخنازير
cowshed	zirībat al baqar (f)	زريبة البقر
rabbit hutch	qunn al arānib (m)	قنّ الأرانب
hen house	qunn ad daʒāʒ (m)	قن الدجاج

213. Dogs. Dog breeds

dog	kalb (m)	كلب
sheepdog	kalb ra'y (m)	كلب رعي
German shepherd	kalb ar rā'i al almāniy (m)	كلب الراعي الألمانيّ
poodle	būdli (m)	بودل
dachshund	daʃhund (m)	دشهند
bulldog	bulduɣ (m)	بلدغ
boxer	buksir (m)	بوكسر
mastiff	mastīf (m)	ماستيف
Rottweiler	rut vāylir (m)	روت فايلر
Doberman	dubirmān (m)	دوبرمان
basset	bāsit (m)	باسيت
bobtail	bubteyl (m)	بوبتيل
Dalmatian	kalb dalmāsiy (m)	كلب دلماسي
cocker spaniel	kukkir spaniil (m)	كوكر سبانييل
Newfoundland	nyu faundland (m)	نيوفاوندلاند
Saint Bernard	san birnār (m)	سنبرنار
husky	haski (m)	هاسكي
Chow Chow	tʃaw tʃaw (m)	تشاوتشاو
spitz	ʃbītz (m)	شبيتز
pug	bāk (m)	باك

214. Sounds made by animals

barking (n)	nubāḥ (m)	نباح
to bark (vi)	nabaḥ	نبح
to meow (vi)	mā'	ماء
to purr (vi)	χarχar	خرخر
to moo (vi)	χār	خار
to bellow (bull)	χār	خار
to growl (vi)	damdam	دمدم
howl (n)	'uwā' (m)	عواء
to howl (vi)	'awa	عوى
to whine (vi)	'awa	عوى
to bleat (sheep)	ma'ma'	مأمأ
to oink, to grunt (pig)	qaba'	قبع
to squeal (vi)	ṣāḥ	صاح
to croak (vi)	naqq	نقّ
to buzz (insect)	ṭann	طنّ
to chirp (crickets, grasshopper)	zaqzaq	زقزق

215. Young animals

cub	ʒarw (m)	جرو
kitten	qiṭṭa sayīra (f)	قطة صغيرة
baby mouse	fa'r ṣayīr (m)	فأر صغير
puppy	ʒarw (m)	جرو

leveret	xirniq (m)	خرنق
baby rabbit	arnab sayīr (m)	أرنب صغير
wolf cub	dayfal ṣayīr að ði'ab (m)	دغفل صغير الذئب
fox cub	haʒras ṣayīr aθ θa'lab (m)	هجرس صغير الثعلب
bear cub	daysam ṣayīr ad dubb (m)	ديسم صغير الدبّ

lion cub	ʃibl al asad (m)	شبل الأسد
tiger cub	ʃibl an namir (m)	شبل النمر
elephant calf	sayīr al fīl (m)	صغير الفيل

piglet	xannūṣ (m)	خنّوص
calf (young cow, bull)	'iʒl (m)	عجل
kid (young goat)	ʒaday (m)	جدي
lamb	ḥaml (m)	حمل
fawn (young deer)	raʃa' ṣayīr al ayyil (m)	رشأ صغير الأيّل
young camel	ṣayīr al ʒamal (m)	صغير الجمل

snakelet (baby snake)	ṣayīr aθ θu'bān (m)	صغير الثعبان
froglet (baby frog)	ḍifḍa' ṣayīr (m)	ضفدع صغير

baby bird	farx (m)	فرخ
chick (of chicken)	katkūt (m)	كتكوت
duckling	farax baṭṭ (m)	فرخ بطّ

216. Birds

bird	ṭā'ir (m)	طائر
pigeon	ḥamāma (f)	حمامة
sparrow	'uṣfūr (m)	عصفور
tit (great tit)	qurquf (m)	قرقف
magpie	'aq'aq (m)	عقعق

raven	yurāb aswad (m)	غراب أسود
crow	yurāb (m)	غراب
jackdaw	zāy (m)	زاغ
rook	yurāb al qayẓ (m)	غراب القيظ

duck	baṭṭa (f)	بطّة
goose	iwazza (f)	إوزّة
pheasant	tadarruʒ (m)	تدرج
eagle	nasr (m)	نسر
hawk	bāz (m)	باز

falcon	ṣaqr (m)	صقر
vulture	raχam (m)	رخم
condor (Andean ~)	kundūr (m)	كندور

swan	timma (m)	تمّة
crane	kurkiy (m)	كركي
stork	laqlaq (m)	لقلق

parrot	babaγā' (m)	ببغاء
hummingbird	ṭannān (m)	طنّان
peacock	ṭāwūs (m)	طاووس

ostrich	na'āma (f)	نعامة
heron	balaʃūn (m)	بلشون
flamingo	nuḥām wardiy (m)	نحام ورديّ
pelican	baʒa'a (f)	بجعة

| nightingale | bulbul (m) | بلبل |
| swallow | sunūnū (m) | سنونو |

thrush	sumna (m)	سمنة
song thrush	summuna muγarrida (m)	سمنة مغرّدة
blackbird	ʃaḥrūr aswad (m)	شحرور أسود

swift	samāma (m)	سمامة
lark	qubbara (f)	قبّرة
quail	sammān (m)	سمّان

woodpecker	naqqār al χaʃab (m)	نقّار الخشب
cuckoo	waqwāq (m)	وقواق
owl	būma (f)	بومة
eagle owl	būm urāsiy (m)	بوم أوراسيّ
wood grouse	dīk il χalanʒ (m)	ديك الخلنج
black grouse	ṭayhūʒ aswad (m)	طيهوج أسود
partridge	ḥaʒal (m)	حجل

starling	zurzūr (m)	زرزور
canary	kanāriy (m)	كناريّ
hazel grouse	ṭayhūʒ il bunduq (m)	طيهوج البندق
chaffinch	ʃurʃūr (m)	شرشور
bullfinch	diγnāʃ (m)	دغناش

seagull	nawras (m)	نورس
albatross	al qaṭras (m)	القطرس
penguin	biṭrīq (m)	بطريق

217. Birds. Singing and sounds

| to sing (vi) | γanna | غنّى |
| to call (animal, bird) | nāda | نادى |

| to crow (rooster) | ṣāḥ | صاح |
| cock-a-doodle-doo | kukukuku | كوكوكوكو |

to cluck (hen)	qaraq	قرق
to caw (vi)	naʻaq	نعق
to quack (duck)	baṭbaṭ	بطبط
to cheep (vi)	ṣaʾṣaʾ	صأصأ
to chirp, to twitter	zaqzaq	زقزق

218. Fish. Marine animals

bream	abramīs (m)	أبراميس
carp	ʃabbūṭ (m)	شبّوط
perch	farx (m)	فرخ
catfish	qarmūṭ (m)	قرموط
pike	samak al karāki (m)	سمك الكراكي

| salmon | salmūn (m) | سلمون |
| sturgeon | ḥaʃʃ (m) | حفش |

herring	rinʒa (f)	رنجة
Atlantic salmon	salmūn aṭlasiy (m)	سلمون أطلسيّ
mackerel	usqumriy (m)	أسقمريّ
flatfish	samak mufalṭaḥ (f)	سمك مفلطح

zander, pike perch	samak sandar (m)	سمك سندر
cod	qudd (m)	قدّ
tuna	tūna (f)	تونة
trout	salmūn muraqqaṭ (m)	سلمون مرقّط
eel	ḥankalīs (m)	حنكليس
electric ray	raʻʻād (m)	رعّاد
moray eel	murāy (m)	موراي
piranha	birāna (f)	بيرانا

shark	qirʃ (m)	قرش
dolphin	dilfīn (m)	دلفين
whale	ḥūt (m)	حوت

crab	salṭaʻūn (m)	سلطعون
jellyfish	qindīl al baḥr (m)	قنديل البحر
octopus	uxṭubūṭ (m)	أخطبوط

starfish	naʒmat al baḥr (f)	نجمة البحر
sea urchin	qumfuð al baḥr (m)	قنفذ البحر
seahorse	ḥiṣān al baḥr (m)	فرس البحر

oyster	maḥār (m)	محار
shrimp	ʒambari (m)	جمبريّ
lobster	istakūza (f)	إستكوزا
spiny lobster	karkand ʃāik (m)	كركند شائك

219. Amphibians. Reptiles

snake	θu'bān (m)	ثعبان
venomous (snake)	sāmm	سامّ
viper	af'a (f)	أفعى
cobra	kūbra (m)	كوبرا
python	biθūn (m)	بيثون
boa	buwā' (f)	بواء
grass snake	θu'bān al 'uʃb (m)	ثعبان العشب
rattle snake	af'a al ʒalʒala (f)	أفعى الجلجلة
anaconda	anakūnda (f)	أناكوندا
lizard	siḥliyya (f)	سحليّة
iguana	iɣwāna (f)	إغوانة
monitor lizard	waral (m)	ورل
salamander	samandar (m)	سمندر
chameleon	ḥirbā' (f)	حرباء
scorpion	'aqrab (m)	عقرب
turtle	sulaḥfāt (f)	سلحفاة
frog	ḍifḍa' (m)	ضفدع
toad	ḍifḍa' aṭ ṭīn (m)	ضفدع الطين
crocodile	timsāḥ (m)	تمساح

220. Insects

insect, bug	ḥaʃara (f)	حشرة
butterfly	farāʃa (f)	فراشة
ant	namla (f)	نملة
fly	ðubāba (f)	ذبابة
mosquito	namūsa (f)	ناموسة
beetle	χunfusa (f)	خنفسة
wasp	dabbūr (m)	دبّور
bee	naḥla (f)	نحلة
bumblebee	naḥla ṭannāna (f)	نحلة طنّانة
gadfly (botfly)	na'ra (f)	نعرة
spider	'ankabūt (m)	عنكبوت
spiderweb	nasīʒ 'ankabūt (m)	نسيج عنكبوت
dragonfly	ya'sūb (m)	يعسوب
grasshopper	ʒarād (m)	جراد
moth (night butterfly)	'itta (f)	عتّة
cockroach	ṣurṣūr (m)	صرصور
tick	qurāda (f)	قرادة

flea	buryūθ (m)	برغوث
midge	ba'ūḍa (f)	بعوضة
locust	ʒarād (m)	جراد
snail	ḥalzūn (m)	حلزون
cricket	ṣarrār al layl (m)	صرّار الليل
lightning bug	yarā'a muḍī'a (f)	يراعة مضيئة
ladybug	da'sūqa (f)	دعسوقة
cockchafer	χunfusa kabīra (f)	خنفسة كبيرة
leech	'alaqa (f)	علقة
caterpillar	yasrū' (m)	يسروع
earthworm	dūda (f)	دودة
larva	yaraqa (f)	يرقة

221. Animals. Body parts

beak	minqār (m)	منقار
wings	aʒniḥa (pl)	أجنحة
foot (of bird)	riʒl (f)	رجل
feathers (plumage)	rīʃ (m)	ريش
feather	rīʃa (f)	ريشة
crest	tāʒ (m)	تاج
gills	χayāʃīm (pl)	خياشيم
spawn	bayḍ as samak (pl)	بيض السمك
larva	yaraqa (f)	يرقة
fin	zi'nifa (f)	زعنفة
scales (of fish, reptile)	ḥarāfiʃ (pl)	حرافش
fang (canine)	nāb (m)	ناب
paw (e.g., cat's ~)	qadam (f)	قدم
muzzle (snout)	χaṭm (m)	خطم
mouth (of cat, dog)	fam (m)	فم
tail	ðayl (m)	ذيل
whiskers	ʃawārib (pl)	شوارب
hoof	ḥāfir (m)	حافر
horn	qarn (m)	قرن
carapace	dir' (m)	درع
shell (of mollusk)	maḥāra (f)	محارة
eggshell	qiʃrat bayḍa (f)	قشرة بيضة
animal's hair (pelage)	ʃa'r (m)	شعر
pelt (hide)	ʒild (m)	جلد

222. Actions of animals

to fly (vi)	ṭār	طار
to fly in circles	ḥallaq	حلّق
to fly away	ṭār	طار
to flap (~ the wings)	rafraf	رفرف
to peck (vi)	naqar	نقر
to sit on eggs	qaʿad ʿalal bayḍ	قعد على البيض
to hatch out (vi)	faqas	فقس
to build a nest	bana ʿiʃʃa	بنى عشّة
to slither, to crawl	zaḥaf	زحف
to sting, to bite (insect)	lasaʿ	لسع
to bite (ab. animal)	ʿaḍḍ	عضّ
to sniff (vt)	taʃammam	تشمّم
to bark (vi)	nabaḥ	نبح
to hiss (snake)	hashas	هسهس
to scare (vt)	χawwaf	خوّف
to attack (vt)	haʒam	هجم
to gnaw (bone, etc.)	qaraḍ	قرض
to scratch (with claws)	χadaʃ	خدش
to hide (vi)	istaχbaʾ	إختبأ
to play (kittens, etc.)	laʿib	لعب
to hunt (vi, vt)	iṣṭād	إصطاد
to hibernate (vi)	kān di subāt aʃ ʃitāʾ	كان في سبات الشتاء
to go extinct	inqaraḍ	إنقرض

223. Animals. Habitats

habitat	mawṭin (m)	موطن
migration	hiʒra (f)	هجرة
mountain	ʒabal (m)	جبل
reef	ʃiʿāb (pl)	شعاب
cliff	ʒurf (m)	جرف
forest	ɣāba (f)	غابة
jungle	adɣāl (pl)	أدغال
savanna	savānna (f)	سافانّا
tundra	tundra (f)	تندرا
steppe	sahb (m)	سهب
desert	ṣaḥrāʾ (f)	صحراء
oasis	wāḥa (f)	واحة
sea	baḥr (m)	بحر

lake	buḥayra (f)	بحيرة
ocean	muḥīṭ (m)	محيط
swamp (marshland)	mustanqa' (m)	مستنقع
freshwater (adj)	al miyāh al 'aðba	المياه العذبة
pond	birka (f)	بركة
river	nahr (m)	نهر
den (bear's ~)	wakr (m)	وكر
nest	'uʃʃ (m)	عشّ
hollow (in a tree)	ʒawf (m)	جوف
burrow (animal hole)	ʒuḥr (m)	جحر
anthill	'uʃʃ naml (m)	عشّ نمل

224. Animal care

zoo	ḥadīqat al ḥayawān (f)	حديقة حيوان
nature preserve	maḥmiyya ṭabi'iyya (f)	محميّة طبيعيّة
breeder (cattery, kennel, etc.)	murabba (m)	مربّى
open-air cage	qafṣ fil hawā' aṭ ṭalq (m)	قفص في الهواء الطلق
cage	qafṣ (m)	قفص
doghouse (kennel)	bayt al kalb (m)	بيت الكلب
dovecot	burʒ al ḥamām (m)	برج الحمام
aquarium (fish tank)	ḥawḍ samak (m)	حوض سمك
dolphinarium	ḥawḍ dilfīn (m)	حوض دلفين
to breed (animals)	rabba	ربّى
brood, litter	ðurriyya (f)	ذرّيّة
to tame (vt)	allaf	ألّف
to train (animals)	darrab	درّب
feed (fodder, etc.)	'alaf (m)	علف
to feed (vt)	aṭ'am	أطعم
pet store	maḥall ḥayawānāt (m)	محلّ حيوانات
muzzle (for dog)	kimāma (f)	كمامة
collar (e.g., dog ~)	ṭawq (m)	طوق
name (of animal)	ism (m)	إسم
pedigree (of dog)	silsilat an nasab (f)	سلسلة النسب

225. Animals. Miscellaneous

pack (wolves)	qaṭī' (m)	قطيع
flock (birds)	sirb (m)	سرب
shoal, school (fish)	sirb (m)	سرب
herd (horses)	qaṭī' (m)	قطيع

| male (n) | ðakar (m) | ذكر |
| female (n) | unθa (f) | أنثى |

hungry (adj)	ʒaw'ān	جوعان
wild (adj)	barriy	بري
dangerous (adj)	χaṭīr	خطير

226. Horses

| horse | ḥiṣān (m) | حصان |
| breed (race) | sulāla (f) | سلالة |

| foal | muhr (m) | مهر |
| mare | unθa al faras (f) | أنثى الفرس |

mustang	mustān (m)	موستان
pony	ḥiṣān qazam (m)	حصان قزم
draft horse	ḥiṣān an naql (m)	حصان النقل

| mane | 'urf (m) | عرف |
| tail | ðayl (m) | ذيل |

hoof	ḥāfir (m)	حافر
horseshoe	na'l (m)	نعل
to shoe (vt)	na''al	نعّل
blacksmith	ḥaddād (m)	حدّاد

saddle	sarʒ (m)	سرج
stirrup	rikāb (m)	ركاب
bridle	liʒām (m)	لجام
reins	'inān (m)	عنان
whip (for riding)	kurbāʒ (m)	كرباج

rider	fāris (m)	فارس
to saddle up (vt)	asraʒ	أسرج
to mount a horse	rakib ḥiṣān	جلس على سرج

gallop	rimāḥa (f)	رماحة
to gallop (vi)	'ada bil ḥiṣān	عدا بالحصان
trot (n)	χabab (m)	خبب
at a trot (adv)	χābban	خابًا
to go at a trot	inṭalaq rākiḍan	إنطلق راكضا

| racehorse | ḥiṣān sibāq (m) | حصان سباق |
| horse racing | sibāq al χayl (m) | سباق الخيل |

stable	isṭabl χayl (m)	إسطبل خيل
to feed (vt)	aṭ'am	أطعم
hay	qaʃʃ (m)	قش
to water (animals)	saqa	سقى

to wash (horse)	naẓẓaf	نظّف
horse-drawn cart	'arabat χayl (f)	عربة خيل
to graze (vi)	irta'a	إرتعى
to neigh (vi)	ṣahal	صهل
to kick (about horse)	rafas	رفس

Flora

227. Trees

tree	ʃaʒara (f)	شجرة
deciduous (adj)	nafdiyya	نفضيّة
coniferous (adj)	ṣanawbariyya	صنوبريّة
evergreen (adj)	dā'imat al xudra	دائمة الخضرة
apple tree	ʃaʒarat tuffāḥ (f)	شجرة تفّاح
pear tree	ʃaʒarat kummaθra (f)	شجرة كمّثرى
cherry tree	ʃaʒarat karaz (f)	شجرة كرز
plum tree	ʃaʒarat barqūq (f)	شجرة برقوق
birch	batūla (f)	بتولا
oak	ballūṭ (f)	بلّوط
linden tree	ʃaʒarat zayzafūn (f)	شجرة زيزفون
aspen	ḥawr raʒrāʒ (m)	حور رجراج
maple	qayqab (f)	قيقب
spruce	ratinaʒ (f)	راتينج
pine	ṣanawbar (f)	صنوبر
larch	arziyya (f)	أرزيّة
fir tree	tannūb (f)	تنّوب
cedar	arz (f)	أرز
poplar	ḥawr (f)	حور
rowan	ɣubayrā' (f)	غبيراء
willow	ṣafsāf (f)	صفصاف
alder	ʒār il mā' (m)	جار الماء
beech	zān (m)	زان
elm	dardār (f)	دردار
ash (tree)	marān (f)	مران
chestnut	kastanā' (f)	كستناء
magnolia	maɣnūliya (f)	مغنوليا
palm tree	naxla (f)	نخلة
cypress	sarw (f)	سرو
mangrove	ayka sāḥiliyya (f)	أيكة ساحليّة
baobab	bāubāb (f)	باوباب
eucalyptus	ukaliptus (f)	أوكاليبتوس
sequoia	siqūya (f)	سيكويا

228. Shrubs

bush	ʃuʒayra (f)	شجيرة
shrub	ʃuʒayrāt (pl)	شجيرات
grapevine	karma (f)	كرمة
vineyard	karam (m)	كرم
raspberry bush	tūt al ʻullayq al aḥmar (m)	توت العلّيق الأحمر
redcurrant bush	kiʃmiʃ aḥmar (m)	كشمش أحمر
gooseberry bush	ʻinab aθ θaʻlab (m)	عنب الثعلب
acacia	sanṭ (f)	سنط
barberry	amīr barīs (m)	أمير باريس
jasmine	yāsmīn (m)	ياسمين
juniper	ʻarʻar (m)	عرعر
rosebush	ʃuʒayrat ward (f)	شجيرة ورد
dog rose	ward ʒabaliy (m)	ورد جبليّ

229. Mushrooms

mushroom	fuṭr (f)	فطر
edible mushroom	fuṭr ṣāliḥ lil akl (m)	فطر صالح للأكل
poisonous mushroom	fuṭr sāmm (m)	فطر سامّ
cap (of mushroom)	ṭarbūʃ al fuṭr (m)	طربوش الفطر
stipe (of mushroom)	sāq al fuṭr (m)	ساق الفطر
cep (Boletus edulis)	fuṭr bulīṭ maʼkūl (m)	فطر بوليط مأكول
orange-cap boletus	fuṭr aḥmar (m)	فطر أحمر
birch bolete	fuṭr bulīṭ (m)	فطر بوليط
chanterelle	fuṭr kwīzi (m)	فطر كويزي
russula	fuṭr russūla (m)	فطر روسّولا
morel	fuṭr al ɣūʃna (m)	فطر الغوشنة
fly agaric	fuṭr amānīt aṭ ṭāʼir as sāmm (m)	فطر أمانيت الطائر السامّ
death cap	fuṭr amānīt falusyāniy as sāmm (m)	فطر أمانيت فالوسياني السامّ

230. Fruits. Berries

fruit	θamra (f)	ثمرة
fruits	θamr (m)	ثمر
apple	tuffāḥa (f)	تفّاحة
pear	kummaθra (f)	كمّثرى
plum	barqūq (m)	برقوق

strawberry (garden ~)	farawla (f)	فراولة
cherry	karaz (m)	كرز
grape	'inab (m)	عنب
raspberry	tūt al 'ullayq al aḥmar (m)	توت العليق الأحمر
blackcurrant	'inab aθ θa'lab al aswad (m)	عنب الثعلب الأسود
redcurrant	kiʃmiʃ aḥmar (m)	كشمش أحمر
gooseberry	'inab aθ θa'lab (m)	عنب الثعلب
cranberry	tūt aḥmar barriy (m)	توت أحمر برِّيّ
orange	burtuqāl (m)	برتقال
mandarin	yūsufiy (m)	يوسفي
pineapple	ananās (m)	أناناس
banana	mawz (m)	موز
date	tamr (m)	تمر
lemon	laymūn (m)	ليمون
apricot	miʃmiʃ (f)	مشمش
peach	durrāq (m)	دراق
kiwi	kiwi (m)	كيوي
grapefruit	zinbā' (m)	زنباع
berry	ḥabba (f)	حبّة
berries	ḥabbāt (pl)	حبّات
cowberry	'inab aθ θawr (m)	عنب الثور
wild strawberry	farāwla barriyya (f)	فراولة برِّية
bilberry	'inab al aḥrāʒ (m)	عنب الأحراج

231. Flowers. Plants

flower	zahra (f)	زهرة
bouquet (of flowers)	bāqat zuhūr (f)	باقة زهور
rose (flower)	warda (f)	وردة
tulip	tulīb (f)	توليب
carnation	qurumful (m)	قرنفل
gladiolus	dalbūθ (f)	دلبوث
cornflower	turunʃāh (m)	ترنشاه
harebell	ʒarīs (m)	جريس
dandelion	hindibā' (f)	هندباء
camomile	babunʒ (m)	بابونج
aloe	aluwwa (m)	ألوّة
cactus	ṣabbār (m)	صبّار
rubber plant, ficus	tīn (m)	تين
lily	sawsan (m)	سوسن
geranium	ibrat ar rā'i (f)	إبرة الراعي

hyacinth	zanbaq (f)	زنبق
mimosa	mimūza (f)	ميموزا
narcissus	narʒis (f)	نرجس
nasturtium	abu xanʒar (f)	أبو خنجر
orchid	saḥlab (f)	سحلب
peony	fawniya (f)	فاوانيا
violet	banafsaʒ (f)	بنفسج
pansy	banafsaʒ muθallaθ (m)	بنفسج مثلث
forget-me-not	'āðān al fa'r (pl)	آذان الفأر
daisy	uqḥuwān (f)	أقحوان
poppy	xaʃxāʃ (f)	خشخاش
hemp	qinnab (m)	قنب
mint	na'nā' (m)	نعناع
lily of the valley	sawsan al wādi (m)	سوسن الوادي
snowdrop	zahrat al laban (f)	زهرة اللبن
nettle	qarrāṣ (m)	قرّاص
sorrel	ḥammāḍ (m)	حمّاض
water lily	nilūfar (m)	نيلوفر
fern	saraxs (m)	سرخس
lichen	uʃna (f)	أشنة
greenhouse (tropical ~)	daffi'a (f)	دفيئة
lawn	'uʃb (m)	عشب
flowerbed	ʒunaynat zuhūr (f)	جنينة زهور
plant	nabāt (m)	نبات
grass	'uʃb (m)	عشب
blade of grass	'uʃba (f)	عشبة
leaf	waraqa (f)	ورقة
petal	waraqat az zahra (f)	ورقة الزهرة
stem	sāq (f)	ساق
tuber	darnat nabāt (f)	درنة نبات
young plant (shoot)	nabta saɣīra (f)	نبتة صغيرة
thorn	ʃawka (f)	شوكة
to blossom (vi)	nawwar	نوّر
to fade, to wither	ðabal	ذبل
smell (odor)	rā'iḥa (f)	رائحة
to cut (flowers)	qaṭa'	قطع
to pick (a flower)	qaṭaf	قطف

232. Cereals, grains

grain	ḥubūb (pl)	حبوب
cereal crops	maḥāṣīl al ḥubūb (pl)	محاصيل الحبوب

ear (of barley, etc.)	sumbula (f)	سنبلة
wheat	qamḥ (m)	قمح
rye	ʒāwdār (m)	جاودار
oats	ʃūfān (m)	شوفان
millet	duxn (m)	دخن
barley	ʃaʿīr (m)	شعير

corn	ðura (f)	ذرة
rice	urz (m)	أرز
buckwheat	ḥinṭa sawdā' (f)	حنطة سوداء

pea plant	bisilla (f)	بسلة
kidney bean	faṣūliya (f)	فاصوليا
soy	fūl aṣ ṣūya (m)	فول الصويا
lentil	ʿadas (m)	عدس
beans (pulse crops)	fūl (m)	فول

233. Vegetables. Greens

| vegetables | xuḍār (pl) | خضار |
| greens | xuḍrawāt waraqiyya (pl) | خضروات ورقية |

tomato	ṭamāṭim (f)	طماطم
cucumber	xiyār (m)	خيار
carrot	ʒazar (m)	جزر
potato	baṭāṭis (f)	بطاطس
onion	baṣal (m)	بصل
garlic	θūm (m)	ثوم

cabbage	kurumb (m)	كرنب
cauliflower	qarnabīṭ (m)	قرنبيط
Brussels sprouts	kurumb brūksil (m)	كرنب بروكسل
broccoli	brūkuli (m)	بروكلي

beetroot	banʒar (m)	بنجر
eggplant	bātinʒān (m)	باذنجان
zucchini	kūsa (f)	كوسة
pumpkin	qarʿ (m)	قرع
turnip	lift (m)	لفت

parsley	baqdūnis (m)	بقدونس
dill	ʃabat (m)	شبت
lettuce	xass (m)	خسّ
celery	karafs (m)	كرفس
asparagus	halyūn (m)	هليون
spinach	sabānix (m)	سبانخ

pea	bisilla (f)	بسلة
beans	fūl (m)	فول
corn (maize)	ðura (f)	ذرة

kidney bean	faṣūliya (f)	فاصوليا
pepper	filfil (m)	فلفل
radish	fiȝl (m)	فجل
artichoke	χurʃūf (m)	خرشوف

REGIONAL GEOGRAPHY

Countries. Nationalities

234. Western Europe

Europe	urūbba (f)	أوروبّا
European Union	al ittiḥād al urubbiy (m)	الإتّحاد الأوروبّيّ
European (n)	urūbbiy (m)	أوروبّيّ
European (adj)	urūbbiy	أوروبّي
Austria	an nimsa (f)	النمسا
Austrian (masc.)	nimsāwy (m)	نمساويّ
Austrian (fem.)	nimsāwiyya (f)	نمساويّة
Austrian (adj)	nimsāwiy	نمساويّ
Great Britain	briṭāniya al 'uẓma (f)	بريطانيا العظمى
England	inʒiltirra (f)	إنجلترا
British (masc.)	briṭāniy (m)	بريطانيّ
British (fem.)	briṭāniyya (f)	بريطانيّة
English, British (adj)	inʒlīziy	إنجليزيّ
Belgium	balʒīka (f)	بلجيكا
Belgian (masc.)	balʒīkiy (m)	بلجيكيّ
Belgian (fem.)	balʒīkiyya (f)	بلجيكيّة
Belgian (adj)	balʒīkiy	بلجيكيّ
Germany	almāniya (f)	ألمانيا
German (masc.)	almāniy (m)	ألمانيّ
German (fem.)	almāniyya (f)	ألمانيّة
German (adj)	almāniy	ألمانيّ
Netherlands	hulanda (f)	هولندا
Holland	hulanda (f)	هولندا
Dutch (masc.)	hulandiy (m)	هولنديّ
Dutch (fem.)	hulandiyya (f)	هولنديّة
Dutch (adj)	hulandiy	هولنديّ
Greece	al yūnān (f)	اليونان
Greek (masc.)	yunāniy (m)	يونانيّ
Greek (fem.)	yunāniyya (f)	يونانيّة
Greek (adj)	yunāniy	يونانيّ
Denmark	ad danimārk (f)	الدانمارك
Dane (masc.)	danimārkiy (m)	دانماركيّ

Dane (fem.)	dānimarkiyya (f)	دانماركيّة
Danish (adj)	danimārkiy	دانماركيّ
Ireland	irlanda (f)	أيرلندا
Irish (masc.)	irlandiy (m)	أيرلنديّ
Irish (fem.)	irlandiyya (f)	أيرلنديّة
Irish (adj)	irlandiy	أيرلنديّ
Iceland	'āyslanda (f)	آيسلندا
Icelander (masc.)	'āyslandiy (m)	آيسلنديّ
Icelander (fem.)	'āyslandiyya (f)	آيسلنديّة
Icelandic (adj)	'āyslandiy	آيسلنديّ
Spain	isbāniya (f)	إسبانيا
Spaniard (masc.)	isbāniy (m)	إسبانيّ
Spaniard (fem.)	isbāniyya (f)	إسبانيّة
Spanish (adj)	isbāniy	إسبانيّ
Italy	iṭāliya (f)	إيطاليا
Italian (masc.)	iṭāliy (m)	إيطاليّ
Italian (fem.)	iṭāliyya (f)	إيطاليّة
Italian (adj)	iṭāliy	إيطاليّ
Cyprus	qubruṣ (f)	قبرص
Cypriot (masc.)	qubruṣiy (m)	قبرصيّ
Cypriot (fem.)	qubruṣiyya (f)	قبرصيّة
Cypriot (adj)	qubruṣiy	قبرصيّ
Malta	malṭa (f)	مالطا
Maltese (masc.)	mālṭiy (m)	مالطيّ
Maltese (fem.)	malṭiyya (f)	مالطيّة
Maltese (adj)	mālṭiy	مالطيّ
Norway	an nirwīʒ (f)	النرويج
Norwegian (masc.)	nurwīʒiy (m)	نرويجيّ
Norwegian (fem.)	nurwīʒiyya (f)	نرويجيّة
Norwegian (adj)	nurwīʒiy	نرويجيّ
Portugal	al burtuɣāl (f)	البرتغال
Portuguese (masc.)	burtuɣāliy (m)	برتغاليّ
Portuguese (fem.)	burtuɣāliyya (f)	برتغاليّة
Portuguese (adj)	burtuɣāliy	برتغاليّ
Finland	finlanda (f)	فنلندا
Finn (masc.)	finlandiy (m)	فنلنديّ
Finn (fem.)	finlandiyya (f)	فنلنديّة
Finnish (adj)	finlandiy	فنلنديّ
France	faransa (f)	فرنسا
French (masc.)	faransiy (m)	فرنسيّ
French (fem.)	faransiyya (f)	فرنسيّة
French (adj)	faransiy	فرنسيّ

Sweden	as suwayd (f)	السويد
Swede (masc.)	suwaydiy (m)	سويدي
Swede (fem.)	suwaydiyya (f)	سويدية
Swedish (adj)	suwaydiy	سويدي

Switzerland	swīsra (f)	سويسرا
Swiss (masc.)	swisriy (m)	سويسري
Swiss (fem.)	swisriyya (f)	سويسرية
Swiss (adj)	swisriy	سويسري

Scotland	iskutlanda (f)	اسكتلندا
Scottish (masc.)	iskutlandiy (m)	اسكتلندي
Scottish (fem.)	iskutlandiyya (f)	اسكتلندية
Scottish (adj)	iskutlandiy	اسكتلندي

Vatican	al vatikān (m)	الفاتيكان
Liechtenstein	liʃtinʃtāyn (m)	ليشتنشتاين
Luxembourg	luksimburɣ (f)	لوكسمبورغ
Monaco	munāku (f)	موناكو

235. Central and Eastern Europe

Albania	albāniya (f)	ألبانيا
Albanian (masc.)	albāniy (m)	ألباني
Albanian (fem.)	albāniyya (f)	ألبانية
Albanian (adj)	albāniy	ألباني

Bulgaria	bulɣāriya (f)	بلغاريا
Bulgarian (masc.)	bulɣāriy (m)	بلغاري
Bulgarian (fem.)	bulɣāriyya (f)	بلغارية
Bulgarian (adj)	bulɣāriy	بلغاري

Hungary	al maʒar (f)	المجر
Hungarian (masc.)	maʒariy (m)	مجري
Hungarian (fem.)	maʒariyya (f)	مجرية
Hungarian (adj)	maʒariy	مجري

Latvia	lātviya (f)	لاتفيا
Latvian (masc.)	lātviy (m)	لاتفي
Latvian (fem.)	lātviyya (f)	لاتفية
Latvian (adj)	lātviy	لاتفي

Lithuania	litwāniya (f)	ليتوانيا
Lithuanian (masc.)	litwāniy (m)	ليتواني
Lithuanian (fem.)	litwāniyya (f)	ليتوانية
Lithuanian (adj)	litwāny	ليتواني

Poland	bulanda (f)	بولندا
Pole (masc.)	bulandiy (m)	بولندي
Pole (fem.)	bulandiyya (f)	بولندية

Polish (adj)	bulandiy	بولندي
Romania	rumāniya (f)	رومانيا
Romanian (masc.)	rumāniy (m)	روماني
Romanian (fem.)	rumāniyya (f)	رومانية
Romanian (adj)	rumāniy	روماني

Serbia	ṣirbiya (f)	صربيا
Serbian (masc.)	ṣirbiy (m)	صربي
Serbian (fem.)	ṣirbiyya (f)	صربية
Serbian (adj)	ṣirbiy	صربي

Slovakia	sluvākiya (f)	سلوفاكيا
Slovak (masc.)	sluvākiy (m)	سلوفاكي
Slovak (fem.)	sluvākiyya (f)	سلوفاكية
Slovak (adj)	sluvākiy	سلوفاكي

Croatia	kruātiya (f)	كرواتيا
Croatian (masc.)	kruātiy (m)	كرواتي
Croatian (fem.)	kruātiyya (f)	كرواتية
Croatian (adj)	kruātiy	كرواتي

Czech Republic	atʃ tʃīk (f)	التشيك
Czech (masc.)	tʃīkiy (m)	تشيكي
Czech (fem.)	tʃīkiyya (f)	تشيكية
Czech (adj)	tʃīkiy	تشيكي

Estonia	istūniya (f)	إستونيا
Estonian (masc.)	istūniy (m)	إستوني
Estonian (fem.)	istūniyya (f)	إستونية
Estonian (adj)	istūniy	إستوني

Bosnia and Herzegovina	al busna wal hirsuk (f)	البوسنة والهرسك
Macedonia (Republic of ~)	maqdūniya (f)	مقدونيا
Slovenia	sluvīniya (f)	سلوفينيا
Montenegro	al ӡabal al aswad (m)	الجبل الأسود

236. Former USSR countries

Azerbaijan	aðarbiӡān (m)	أذربيجان
Azerbaijani (masc.)	aðarbiӡāniy (m)	أذربيجاني
Azerbaijani (fem.)	aðarbiӡāniyya (f)	أذربيجانية
Azerbaijani, Azeri (adj)	aðarbiӡāniy	أذربيجاني

Armenia	armīniya (f)	أرمينيا
Armenian (masc.)	armaniy (m)	أرمني
Armenian (fem.)	armaniyya (f)	أرمنية
Armenian (adj)	armaniy	أرمني

| Belarus | bilarūs (f) | بيلاروس |
| Belarusian (masc.) | bilarūsiy (m) | بيلاروسي |

Belarusian (fem.)	bilārūsiyya (f)	بيلاروسيّة
Belarusian (adj)	bilarūsiy	بيلاروسيّ
Georgia	ʒūrʒiya (f)	جورجيا
Georgian (masc.)	ʒurʒiy (m)	جورجيّ
Georgian (fem.)	ʒurʒiyya (f)	جورجيّة
Georgian (adj)	ʒurʒiy	جورجيّ
Kazakhstan	kazaxstān (f)	كازاخستان
Kazakh (masc.)	kazaxstāniy (m)	كازاخستانيّ
Kazakh (fem.)	kazaxstāniyya (f)	كازاخستانيّة
Kazakh (adj)	kazaxstāniy	كازاخستانيّ
Kirghizia	qiryizistān (f)	قيرغيزستان
Kirghiz (masc.)	qiryizistāny (m)	قيرغيزستانيّ
Kirghiz (fem.)	qiryizistāniyya (f)	قيرغيزستانيّة
Kirghiz (adj)	qiryizistāniy	قيرغيزستانيّ
Moldova, Moldavia	muldāviya (f)	مولدافيا
Moldavian (masc.)	muldāviy (m)	مولدافيّ
Moldavian (fem.)	muldāviyya (f)	مولدافيّة
Moldavian (adj)	muldāviy	مولدافيّ
Russia	rūsiya (f)	روسيا
Russian (masc.)	rūsiy (m)	روسيّ
Russian (fem.)	rūsiyya (f)	روسيّة
Russian (adj)	rūsiy	روسيّ
Tajikistan	ṭaʒīkistān (f)	طاجيكستان
Tajik (masc.)	ṭaʒīkiy (m)	طاجيكيّ
Tajik (fem.)	ṭaʒīkiyya (f)	طاجيكيّة
Tajik (adj)	ṭaʒīkiy	طاجيكيّ
Turkmenistan	turkmānistān (f)	تركمانستان
Turkmen (masc.)	turkmāniy (m)	تركمانيّ
Turkmen (fem.)	turkmāniyya (f)	تركمانيّة
Turkmenian (adj)	turkmāniy	تركمانيّ
Uzbekistan	uzbikistān (f)	أوزبكستان
Uzbek (masc.)	uzbikiy (m)	أوزبكيّ
Uzbek (fem.)	uzbikiyya (f)	أوزبكيّة
Uzbek (adj)	uzbikiy	أوزبكيّ
Ukraine	ukrāniya (f)	أوكرانيا
Ukrainian (masc.)	ukrāniy (m)	أوكرانيّ
Ukrainian (fem.)	ukrāniyya (f)	أوكرانيّة
Ukrainian (adj)	ukrāniy	أوكرانيّ

237. Asia

Asia	'āsiya (f)	آسيا
Asian (adj)	'āsyawiy	آسيويّ

Vietnam	vitnām (f)	فيتنام
Vietnamese (masc.)	vitnāmiy (m)	فيتنامي
Vietnamese (fem.)	vitnāmiyya (f)	فيتنامية
Vietnamese (adj)	vitnāmiy	فيتنامي

India	al hind (f)	الهند
Indian (masc.)	hindiy (m)	هندي
Indian (fem.)	hindiyya (f)	هندية
Indian (adj)	hindiy	هندي

Israel	isrā'īl (f)	إسرائيل
Israeli (masc.)	isra'īliy (m)	إسرائيلي
Israeli (fem.)	isrā'īliyya (f)	إسرائيلية
Israeli (adj)	isrā'īliy	إسرائيلي

Jew (n)	yahūdiy (m)	يهودي
Jewess (n)	yahūdiyya (f)	يهودية
Jewish (adj)	yahūdiy	يهودي

China	aş şīn (f)	الصين
Chinese (masc.)	şīniy (m)	صيني
Chinese (fem.)	şīniyya (f)	صينية
Chinese (adj)	şīniy	صيني

Korean (masc.)	kūriy (m)	كوري
Korean (fem.)	kuriyya (f)	كورية
Korean (adj)	kūriy	كوري

Lebanon	lubnān (f)	لبنان
Lebanese (masc.)	lubnāniy (m)	لبناني
Lebanese (fem.)	lubnāniyya (f)	لبنانية
Lebanese (adj)	lubnāniy	لبناني

Mongolia	manɣūliya (f)	منغوليا
Mongolian (masc.)	manɣūliy (m)	منغولي
Mongolian (fem.)	manɣūliyya (f)	منغولية
Mongolian (adj)	manɣūliy	منغولي

Malaysia	malīziya (f)	ماليزيا
Malaysian (masc.)	malīziy (m)	ماليزي
Malaysian (fem.)	malīziyya (f)	ماليزية
Malaysian (adj)	malīziy	ماليزي

Pakistan	bakistān (f)	باكستان
Pakistani (masc.)	bakistāniy (m)	باكستاني
Pakistani (fem.)	bakistāniyya (f)	باكستانية
Pakistani (adj)	bakistāniy	باكستاني

Saudi Arabia	as sa'ūdiyya (f)	السعودية
Arab (masc.)	'arabiy (m)	عربي
Arab (fem.)	'arabiyya (f)	عربية
Arab, Arabic (adj)	'arabiy	عربي

Thailand	taylānd (f)	تايلاند
Thai (masc.)	taylāndiy (m)	تايلاندي
Thai (fem.)	taylandiyya (f)	تايلاندية
Thai (adj)	taylāndiy	تايلاندي

Taiwan	taywān (f)	تايوان
Taiwanese (masc.)	taywāniy (m)	تايواني
Taiwanese (fem.)	taywāniyya (f)	تايوانية
Taiwanese (adj)	taywāniy	تايواني

Turkey	turkiya (f)	تركيا
Turk (masc.)	turkiy (m)	تركي
Turk (fem.)	turkiyya (f)	تركية
Turkish (adj)	turkiy	تركي

Japan	al yabān (f)	اليابان
Japanese (masc.)	yabāniy (m)	ياباني
Japanese (fem.)	yabāniyya (f)	يابانية
Japanese (adj)	yabāniy	ياباني

Afghanistan	afɣanistān (f)	أفغانستان
Bangladesh	banʒladīʃ (f)	بنجلاديش
Indonesia	indunīsiya (f)	إندونيسيا
Jordan	al urdun (m)	الأردن

Iraq	al ʿirāq (m)	العراق
Iran	'īrān (f)	إيران
Cambodia	kambūdya (f)	كمبوديا
Kuwait	al kuwayt (f)	الكويت

Laos	lawus (f)	لاوس
Myanmar	myanmār (f)	ميانمار
Nepal	nibāl (f)	نيبال
United Arab Emirates	al imārāt al ʿarabiyya al muttaḥida (pl)	الإمارات العربية المتحدة

Syria	sūriya (f)	سوريا
Palestine	filisṭīn (f)	فلسطين
South Korea	kuriya al ʒanūbiyya (f)	كوريا الجنوبية
North Korea	kūria aʃ ʃimāliyya (f)	كوريا الشمالية

238. North America

United States of America	al wilāyāt al muttaḥida al amrīkiyya (pl)	الولايات المتحدة الأمريكية
American (masc.)	amrīkiy (m)	أمريكي
American (fem.)	amrīkiyya (f)	أمريكية
American (adj)	amrīkiy	أمريكي
Canada	kanada (f)	كندا
Canadian (masc.)	kanadiy (m)	كندي

| Canadian (fem.) | kanadiyya (f) | كنديّة |
| Canadian (adj) | kanadiy | كنديّ |

Mexico	al maksīk (f)	المكسيك
Mexican (masc.)	maksīkiy (m)	مكسيكيّ
Mexican (fem.)	maksīkiyya (f)	مكسيكيّة
Mexican (adj)	maksīkiy	مكسيكيّ

239. Central and South America

Argentina	arʒantīn (f)	الأرجنتين
Argentinian (masc.)	arʒantīniy (m)	أرجنتينيّ
Argentinian (fem.)	arʒantīniyya (f)	أرجنتينيّة
Argentinian (adj)	arʒantīniy	أرجنتينيّ

Brazil	al brazīl (f)	البرازيل
Brazilian (masc.)	brazīliy (m)	برازيليّ
Brazilian (fem.)	brazīliyya (f)	برازيليّة
Brazilian (adj)	brazīliy	برازيليّ

Colombia	kulumbiya (f)	كولومبيا
Colombian (masc.)	kulumbiy (m)	كولومبيّ
Colombian (fem.)	kulumbiyya (f)	كولومبيّة
Colombian (adj)	kulumbiy	كولومبيّ

Cuba	kūba (f)	كوبا
Cuban (masc.)	kūbiy (m)	كوبيّ
Cuban (fem.)	kūbiyya (f)	كوبيّة
Cuban (adj)	kūbiy	كوبيّ

Chile	tʃīli (f)	تشيلي
Chilean (masc.)	tʃīliy (m)	تشيليّ
Chilean (fem.)	tʃīliyya (f)	تشيليّة
Chilean (adj)	tʃīliy	تشيليّ

Bolivia	bulīviya (f)	بوليفيا
Venezuela	vinizwiyla (f)	فنزويلا
Paraguay	baraɣwāy (f)	باراغواي
Peru	biru (f)	بيرو

Suriname	surinām (f)	سورينام
Uruguay	uruɣwāy (f)	الأوروغواي
Ecuador	al iqwadūr (f)	الإكوادور

The Bahamas	ʒuzur bahāmas (pl)	جزر باهاماس
Haiti	haīti (f)	هايتي
Dominican Republic	ʒumhūriyyat ad duminikan (f)	جمهوريّة الدومينيكان
Panama	banama (f)	بنما
Jamaica	ʒamāyka (f)	جامايكا

240. Africa

Egypt	miṣr (f)	مصر
Egyptian (masc.)	miṣriy (m)	مصريّ
Egyptian (fem.)	miṣriyya (f)	مصريّة
Egyptian (adj)	miṣriy	مصريّ
Morocco	al maɣrib (m)	المغرب
Moroccan (masc.)	maɣribiy (m)	مغربيّ
Moroccan (fem.)	maɣribiyya (f)	مغربيّة
Moroccan (adj)	maɣribiy	مغربيّ
Tunisia	tūnis (f)	تونس
Tunisian (masc.)	tūnisiy (m)	تونسيّ
Tunisian (fem.)	tūnisiyya (f)	تونسيّة
Tunisian (adj)	tūnisiy	تونسيّ
Ghana	ɣāna (f)	غانا
Zanzibar	zanʒibār (f)	زنجبار
Kenya	kiniya (f)	كينيا
Libya	lībiya (f)	ليبيا
Madagascar	madaɣaʃqar (f)	مدغشقر
Namibia	namībiya (f)	ناميبيا
Senegal	as siniɣāl (f)	السنغال
Tanzania	tanzāniya (f)	تنزانيا
South Africa	ʒumhūriyyat afrīqiya al ʒanūbiyya (f)	جمهريّة أفريقيا الجنوبيّة
African (masc.)	afrīqiy (m)	أفريقيّ
African (fem.)	afrīqiyya (f)	أفريقيّة
African (adj)	afrīqiy	أفريقيّ

241. Australia. Oceania

Australia	usturāllya (f)	أستراليا
Australian (masc.)	usturāliy (m)	أستراليّ
Australian (fem.)	usturāliyya (f)	أستراليّة
Australian (adj)	usturāliy	أستراليّ
New Zealand	nyu zilanda (f)	نيوزيلندا
New Zealander (masc.)	nyu zilandiy (m)	نيوزيلنديّ
New Zealander (fem.)	nyu zilandiyya (f)	نيوزيلنديّة
New Zealand (as adj)	nyu zilandiy	نيوزيلنديّ
Tasmania	tasmāniya (f)	تاسمانيا
French Polynesia	bulinīziya al faransiyya (f)	بولينزيا الفرنسيّة

242. Cities

Amsterdam	amstirdām (f)	أمستردام
Ankara	anqara (f)	أنقرة
Athens	aθīna (f)	أثينا
Baghdad	baɣdād (f)	بغداد
Bangkok	bankūk (f)	بانكوك
Barcelona	barʃalūna (f)	برشلونة
Beijing	bikīn (f)	بيكين
Beirut	bayrūt (f)	بيروت
Berlin	birlīn (f)	برلين
Mumbai (Bombay)	bumbāy (f)	بومباى
Bonn	būn (f)	بون
Bordeaux	burdu (f)	بوردو
Bratislava	bratislāva (f)	براتيسلافا
Brussels	brūksil (f)	بروكسل
Bucharest	buxarist (f)	بوخارست
Budapest	budabist (f)	بودابست
Cairo	al qāhira (f)	القاهرة
Kolkata (Calcutta)	kalkutta (f)	كلكتا
Chicago	ʃikāɣu (f)	شيكاغو
Copenhagen	kubinhāʒin (f)	كوبنهاجن
Dar-es-Salaam	dar as salām (f)	دار السلام
Delhi	dilhi (f)	دلهي
Dubai	dibay (f)	دبي
Dublin	dablin (f)	دبلن
Düsseldorf	dusildurf (f)	دوسلدورف
Florence	flurinsa (f)	فلورنسا
Frankfurt	frankfurt (f)	فرانكفورت
Geneva	ʒinīv (f)	جنيف
The Hague	lahāy (f)	لاهاى
Hamburg	hamburɣ (m)	هامبورغ
Hanoi	hanuy (f)	هانوى
Havana	havāna (f)	هافانا
Helsinki	hilsinki (f)	هلسنكي
Hiroshima	hiruʃīma (f)	هيروشيما
Hong Kong	hunɣ kunɣ (f)	هونغ كونغ
Istanbul	istanbūl (f)	إسطنبول
Jerusalem	al quds (f)	القدس
Kyiv	kiyiv (f)	كييف
Kuala Lumpur	kuala lumpur (f)	كوالالمبور
Lisbon	liʃbūna (f)	لشبونة
London	lundun (f)	لندن
Los Angeles	lus anʒilis (f)	لوس أنجلوس

Lyons	liyūn (f)	ليون
Madrid	madrīd (f)	مدريد
Marseille	marsīliya (f)	مرسيليا
Mexico City	madīnat maksiku (f)	مدينة مكسيكو
Miami	mayāmi (f)	ميامي
Montreal	muntriyāl (f)	مونتريال
Moscow	musku (f)	موسكو
Munich	myūniҳ (f)	ميونخ

Nairobi	nayrūbi (f)	نيروبي
Naples	nabuli (f)	نابولي
New York	nyu yūrk (f)	نيويورك
Nice	nīs (f)	نيس
Oslo	uslu (f)	أوسلو
Ottawa	uttawa (f)	أوتاوا

Paris	barīs (f)	باريس
Prague	brāҳ (f)	براغ
Rio de Janeiro	riu di ʒaniyru (f)	ريو دي جانيرو
Rome	rūma (f)	روما

Saint Petersburg	sant bitirsburҳ (f)	سانت بطرسبرغ
Seoul	siūl (f)	سيول
Shanghai	ʃanҳhāy (f)	شانغهاي
Singapore	sinɣafūra (f)	سنغافورة
Stockholm	stukhūlm (f)	ستوكهولم
Sydney	sidniy (f)	سيدني

Taipei	taybay (f)	تايبيه
Tokyo	ṭukyu (f)	طوكيو
Toronto	turūntu (f)	تورونتو

Venice	al bunduqiyya (f)	البندقيّة
Vienna	vyīna (f)	فيينا
Warsaw	warsaw (f)	وارسو
Washington	wāʃinṭun (f)	واشنطن

243. Politics. Government. Part 1

politics	siyāsa (f)	سياسة
political (adj)	siyāsiy	سياسيّ
politician	siyāsiy (m)	سياسي

state (country)	dawla (f)	دولة
citizen	muwāṭin (m)	مواطن
citizenship	ʒinsiyya (f)	جنسيّة

national emblem	ʃi'ār waṭaniy (m)	شعار وطنيّ
national anthem	naʃīd waṭaniy (m)	نشيد وطنيّ
government	ḥukūma (f)	حكومة

head of state	ra's ad dawla (m)	رأس الدولة
parliament	barlamān (m)	برلمان
party	ḥizb (m)	حزب
capitalism	ra'smāliyya (f)	رأسماليّة
capitalist (adj)	ra'smāliy	رأسماليّ
socialism	iʃtirākiyya (f)	إشتراكيّة
socialist (adj)	iʃtirākiy	إشتراكيّ
communism	ʃuyūʿiyya (f)	شيوعيّة
communist (adj)	ʃuyūʿiy	شيوعيّ
communist (n)	ʃuyūʿiy (m)	شيوعيّ
democracy	dimuqraṭiyya (f)	ديموقراطيّة
democrat	dimuqrāṭiy (m)	ديموقراطيّ
democratic (adj)	dimuqrāṭiy	ديموقراطيّ
Democratic party	al ḥizb ad dimukrāṭiy (m)	الحزب الديموقراطيّ
liberal (n)	libirāliy (m)	ليبيراليّ
liberal (adj)	libirāliy	ليبيراليّ
conservative (n)	muḥāfiz (m)	محافظ
conservative (adj)	muḥāfiz	محافظ
republic (n)	ʒumhūriyya (f)	جمهوريّة
republican (n)	ʒumhūriy (m)	جمهوريّ
Republican party	al ḥizb al ʒumhūriy (m)	الحزب الجمهوريّ
elections	intiχābāt (pl)	إنتخابات
to elect (vt)	intaχab	إنتخب
elector, voter	nāχib (m)	ناخب
election campaign	ḥamla intiχābiyya (f)	حملة إنتخابيّة
voting (n)	taṣwīt (m)	تصويت
to vote (vi)	ṣawwat	صوّت
suffrage, right to vote	ḥaqq al intiχāb (m)	حقّ الإنتخاب
candidate	muraʃʃaḥ (m)	مرشّح
to be a candidate	raʃʃaḥ nafsahu	رشّح نفسه
campaign	ḥamla (f)	حملة
opposition (as adj)	muʿāriḍ	معارض
opposition (n)	muʿāraḍa (f)	معارضة
visit	ziyāra (f)	زيارة
official visit	ziyāra rasmiyya (f)	زيارة رسميّة
international (adj)	duwaliy	دوليّ
negotiations	mubāḥaθāt (pl)	مباحثات
to negotiate (vi)	aʒra mubāḥaθāt	أجرى مباحثات

244. Politics. Government. Part 2

society	muʒtamaʻ (m)	مجتمع
constitution	dustūr (m)	دستور
power (political control)	sulṭa (f)	سلطة
corruption	fasād (m)	فساد
law (justice)	qānūn (m)	قانون
legal (legitimate)	qānūniy	قانونيّ
justice (fairness)	ʻadāla (f)	عدالة
just (fair)	ʻādil	عادل
committee	laʒna (f)	لجنة
bill (draft law)	maʃrūʻ qānūn (m)	مشروع قانون
budget	mīzāniyya (f)	ميزانيّة
policy	siyāsa (f)	سياسة
reform	iṣlāḥ (m)	إصلاح
radical (adj)	radikāliy	راديكاليّ
power (strength, force)	quwwa (f)	قوّة
powerful (adj)	qawiy	قويّ
supporter	muʼayyid (m)	مؤيّد
influence	taʼθīr (m)	تأثير
regime (e.g., military ~)	niẓām ḥukm (m)	نظام حكم
conflict	χilāf (m)	خلاف
conspiracy (plot)	muʼāmara (f)	مؤامرة
provocation	istifzāz (m)	إستفزاز
to overthrow (regime, etc.)	asqaṭ	أسقط
overthrow (of government)	isqāṭ (m)	إسقاط
revolution	θawra (f)	ثورة
coup d'état	inqilāb (m)	إنقلاب
military coup	inqilāb ʻaskariy (m)	انقلاب عسكريّ
crisis	azma (f)	أزمة
economic recession	rukūd iqtiṣādiy (m)	ركود إقتصاديّ
demonstrator (protester)	mutaẓāhir (m)	متظاهر
demonstration	muẓāhara (f)	مظاهرة
martial law	al aḥkām al ʻurfiyya (pl)	الأحكام العرفيّة
military base	qaʻida ʻaskariyya (f)	قاعدة عسكريّة
stability	istiqrār (m)	إستقرار
stable (adj)	mustaqirr	مستقرّ
exploitation	istiɣlāl (m)	إستغلال
to exploit (workers)	istaɣall	إستغلّ
racism	ʻunṣuriyya (f)	عنصريّة
racist	ʻunṣuriy (m)	عنصريّ

| fascism | fāʃiyya (f) | فاشيّة |
| fascist | fāʃiy (m) | فاشيّ |

245. Countries. Miscellaneous

foreigner	aʒnabiy (m)	أجنبيّ
foreign (adj)	aʒnabiy	أجنبيّ
abroad (in a foreign country)	fil χāriʒ	في الخارج

emigrant	nāziḥ (m)	نازح
emigration	nuziḥ (m)	نزوح
to emigrate (vi)	nazūḥ	نزح

the West	al ɣarb (m)	الغرب
the East	aʃ ʃarq (m)	الشرق
the Far East	aʃ ʃarq al aqsa (m)	الشرق الأقصى

civilization	ḥaḍāra (f)	حضارة
humanity (mankind)	al baʃariyya (f)	البشريّة
the world (earth)	al ʿālam (m)	العالم
peace	salām (m)	سلام
worldwide (adj)	ʿālamiy	عالميّ

homeland	waṭan (m)	وطن
people (population)	ʃaʿb (m)	شعب
population	sukkān (pl)	سكّان

people (a lot of ~)	nās (pl)	ناس
nation (people)	umma (f)	أمّة
generation	ʒīl (m)	جيل

territory (area)	arḍ (f)	أرض
region	mintaqa (f)	منطقة
state (part of a country)	wilāya (f)	ولاية

tradition	taqlīd (m)	تقليد
custom (tradition)	ʿāda (f)	عادة
ecology	ʿilm al bīʔa (m)	علم البيئة

Indian (Native American)	hindiy aḥmar (m)	هنديّ أحمر
Gypsy (masc.)	ɣaʒariy (m)	غجريّ
Gypsy (fem.)	ɣaʒariyya (f)	غجريّة
Gypsy (adj)	ɣaʒariy	غجريّ

empire	imbiraṭuriyya (f)	امبراطوريّة
colony	mustaʿmara (f)	مستعمرة
slavery	ʿubūdiyya (f)	عبوديّة
invasion	ɣazw (m)	غزو
famine	maʒāʿa (f)	مجاعة

246. Major religious groups. Confessions

religion	dīn (m)	دين
religious (adj)	dīniy	ديني
faith, belief	'īmān (m)	إيمان
to believe (in God)	'āman	آمن
believer	mu'min (m)	مؤمن
atheism	al ilḥād (m)	الإلحاد
atheist	mulḥid (m)	ملحد
Christianity	al masīḥiyya (f)	المسيحيّة
Christian (n)	masīḥiy (m)	مسيحي
Christian (adj)	masīḥiy	مسيحي
Catholicism	al kaθūlikiyya (f)	الكاثوليكيّة
Catholic (n)	kaθulīkiy (m)	كاثوليكي
Catholic (adj)	kaθulīkiy	كاثوليكي
Protestantism	al brutistantiyya (f)	البروتستانتية
Protestant Church	al kanīsa al brutistantiyya (f)	الكنيسة البروتستانتيّة
Protestant (n)	brutistantiy (m)	بروتستانتيّ
Orthodoxy	urθuðuksiyya (f)	الأرثوذكسيّة
Orthodox Church	al kanīsa al urθuðuksiyya (f)	الكنيسة الأرثوذكسيّة
Orthodox (n)	urθuðuksiy (m)	أرثوذكسيّ
Presbyterianism	maʃīxiyya (f)	المشيخيّة
Presbyterian Church	al kanīsa al maʃīxiyya (f)	الكنيسة المشيخيّة
Presbyterian (n)	maʃīxiy (m)	مشيخي
Lutheranism	al kanīsa al luθiriyya (f)	الكنيسة اللوثريّة
Lutheran (n)	luθiriy (m)	لوثريّ
Baptist Church	al kanīsa al maʿmadāniyya (f)	الكنيسة المعمدانيّة
Baptist (n)	maʿmadāniy (m)	معمدانيّ
Anglican Church	al kanīsa al anʒlikāniyya (f)	الكنيسة الإنجليكانيّة
Anglican (n)	anʒlikāniy (m)	أنجليكانيّ
Mormonism	al murumūniyya (f)	المورمونيّة
Mormon (n)	masīḥiy murmūn (m)	مسيحي مرمون
Judaism	al yahūdiyya (f)	اليهودية
Jew (n)	yahūdiy (m)	يهوديّ
Buddhism	al būðiyya (f)	البوذيّة
Buddhist (n)	būðiy (m)	بوذيّ

| Hinduism | al hindūsiyya (f) | الهندوسيّة |
| Hindu (n) | hindūsiy (m) | هندوسيّ |

Islam	al islām (m)	الإسلام
Muslim (n)	muslim (m)	مسلم
Muslim (adj)	islāmiy	إسلاميّ

Shiah Islam	al maðhab aʃ ʃiʻiy (m)	المذهب الشيعيّ
Shiite (n)	ʃiʻiy (m)	شيعيّ
Sunni Islam	al maðhab as sunniy (m)	المذهب السنّيّ
Sunnite (n)	sunniy (m)	سنّيّ

247. Religions. Priests

| priest | qissīs (m), kāhin (m) | قسّيس, كاهن |
| the Pope | al bāba (m) | البابا |

monk, friar	rāhib (m)	راهب
nun	rāhiba (f)	راهبة
pastor	qissīs (m)	قسّيس

abbot	ra'īs ad dayr (m)	رئيس الدير
vicar (parish priest)	viqār (m)	فيقار
bishop	usquf (m)	أسقف
cardinal	kardināl (m)	كاردينال

preacher	tabʃīr (m)	تبشير
preaching	xuṭba (f)	خطبة
parishioners	ra'iyyat al abraʃiyya (f)	رعية الأبرشيّة

| believer | mu'min (m) | مؤمن |
| atheist | mulḥid (m) | ملحد |

248. Faith. Christianity. Islam

| Adam | 'ādam (m) | آدم |
| Eve | ḥawā' (f) | حوّاء |

God	allah (m)	الله
the Lord	ar rabb (m)	الربّ
the Almighty	al qadīr (m)	القدير

sin	ðamb (m)	ذنب
to sin (vi)	aðnab	أذنب
sinner (masc.)	muðnib (m)	مذنب
sinner (fem.)	muðniba (f)	مذنبة
hell	al ʒaḥīm (f)	الجحيم
paradise	al ʒanna (f)	الجنّة

| Jesus | yasū' (m) | يسوع |
| Jesus Christ | yasū' al masīḥ (m) | يسوع المسيح |

the Holy Spirit	ar rūḥ al qudus (m)	الروح القدس
the Savior	al masīḥ (m)	المسيح
the Virgin Mary	maryam al 'aðrā' (f)	مريم العذراء

the Devil	aʃ ʃayṭān (m)	الشيطان
devil's (adj)	ʃayṭāniy	شيطانيّ
Satan	aʃ ʃayṭān (m)	الشيطان
satanic (adj)	ʃayṭāniy	شيطانيّ

angel	malāk (m)	ملاك
guardian angel	malāk ḥāris (m)	ملاك حارس
angelic (adj)	malā'ikiy	ملائكيّ

apostle	rasūl (m)	رسول
archangel	al malak ar ra'īsiy (m)	الملك الرئيسي
the Antichrist	al masīḥ ad daʒʒāl (m)	المسيح الدجّال

Church	al kanīsa (f)	الكنيسة
Bible	al kitāb al muqaddas (m)	الكتاب المقدّس
biblical (adj)	tawrātiy	توراتيّ

Old Testament	al 'ahd al qadīm (m)	العهد القديم
New Testament	al 'ahd al ʒadīd (m)	العهد الجديد
Gospel	inʒīl (m)	إنجيل
Holy Scripture	al kitāb al muqaddas (m)	الكتاب المقدّس
Heaven	al ʒanna (f)	الجنّة

Commandment	waṣiyya (f)	وصيّة
prophet	nabiy (m)	نبيّ
prophecy	nubū'a (f)	نبوءة

Allah	allah (m)	الله
Mohammed	muḥammad (m)	محمّد
the Koran	al qur'ān (m)	القرآن

mosque	masʒid (m)	مسجد
mullah	mulla (m)	مَلّا
prayer	ṣalāt (f)	صلاة
to pray (vi, vt)	ṣalla	صلّى

pilgrimage	ḥaʒʒ (m)	حجّ
pilgrim	ḥāʒʒ (m)	حاجّ
Mecca	makka al mukarrama (f)	مكة المكرّمة

church	kanīsa (f)	كنيسة
temple	ma'bad (m)	معبد
cathedral	katidrā'iyya (f)	كاتدرائيّة
Gothic (adj)	qūṭiy	قوطيّ
synagogue	kanīs ma'bad yahūdiy (m)	كنيس معبد يهوديّ

mosque	masʒid (m)	مسجد
chapel	kanīsa sayīra (f)	كنيسة صغيرة
abbey	dayr (m)	دير
convent	dayr (m)	دير
monastery	dayr (m)	دير
bell (church ~s)	ʒaras (m)	جرس
bell tower	burʒ al ʒaras (m)	برج الجرس
to ring (ab. bells)	daqq	دق
cross	ṣalīb (m)	صليب
cupola (roof)	qubba (f)	قبّة
icon	ʾīkūna (f)	ايقونة
soul	nafs (f)	نفس
fate (destiny)	maṣīr (m)	مصير
evil (n)	ʃarr (m)	شرّ
good (n)	χayr (m)	خير
vampire	maṣṣāṣ dimāʾ (m)	مصّاص دماء
witch (evil ~)	sāḥira (f)	ساحرة
demon	ʃayṭān (m)	شيطان
spirit	rūḥ (m)	روح
redemption (giving us ~)	takfīr (m)	تكفير
to redeem (vt)	kaffar ʾan	كفّر عن
church service, mass	qaddās (m)	قدّاس
to say mass	alqa χuṭba bil kanīsa	ألقى خطبة بالكنيسة
confession	iʾtirāf (m)	إعتراف
to confess (vi)	iʾtaraf	إعترف
saint (n)	qiddīs (m)	قدّيس
sacred (holy)	muqaddas (m)	مقدّس
holy water	māʾ muqaddas (m)	ماء مقدّس
ritual (n)	ṭuqūs (pl)	طقوس
ritual (adj)	ṭuqūsiy	طقوسيّ
sacrifice	ðabīḥa (f)	ذبيحة
superstition	χurāfa (f)	خرافة
superstitious (adj)	muʾmin bil χurāfāt (m)	مؤمن بالخرافات
afterlife	al ʾāχira (f)	الآخرة
eternal life	al ḥayāt al abadiyya (f)	الحياة الأبدية

MISCELLANEOUS

249. Various useful words

background (green ~)	χalfiyya (f)	خلفيّة
balance (of situation)	tawāzun (m)	توازن
barrier (obstacle)	ḥāʒiz (m)	حاجز
base (basis)	asās (m)	أساس
beginning	bidāya (f)	بداية
category	fiʼa (f)	فئة
cause (reason)	sabab (m)	سبب
choice	iχtiyār (m)	إختيار
coincidence	ṣudfa (f)	صدفة
comfortable (~ chair)	murīḥ	مريح
comparison	muqārana (f)	مقارنة
compensation	taʻwīḍ (m)	تعويض
degree (extent, amount)	daraʒa (f)	درجة
development	tanmiya (f)	تنمية
difference	farq (m)	فرق
effect (e.g., of drugs)	taʼθīr (m)	تأثير
effort (exertion)	ʒuhd (m)	جهد
element	ʻunṣur (m)	عنصر
end (finish)	nihāya (f)	نهاية
example (illustration)	miθāl (m)	مثال
fact	ḥaqīqa (f)	حقيقة
frequent (adj)	mutakarrir (m)	متكرّر
growth (development)	numuww (m)	نمو
help	musāʻada (f)	مساعدة
ideal	miθāl (m)	مثال
kind (sort, type)	nawʻ (m)	نوع
labyrinth	tayh (m)	تيه
mistake, error	χaṭaʼ (m)	خطأ
moment	laḥẓa (f)	لحظة
object (thing)	mawḍūʻ (m)	موضوع
obstacle	ʻaqba (f)	عقبة
original (original copy)	aṣl (m)	أصل
part (~ of sth)	ʒuzʼ (m)	جزء
particle, small part	ʒuzʼ (m)	جزء
pause (break)	istirāḥa (f)	إستراحة

position	mawqif (m)	موقف
principle	mabda' (m)	مبدأ
problem	muʃkila (f)	مشكلة
process	'amaliyya (f)	عمليّة
progress	taqaddum (m)	تقدّم
property (quality)	xaṣṣa (f)	خاصّة
reaction	radd fiʿl (m)	ردّ فعل
risk	muxāṭara (f)	مخاطرة
secret	sirr (m)	سرّ
series	silsila (f)	سلسلة
shape (outer form)	ʃakl (m)	شكل
situation	ḥāla (f), waḍʿ (m)	حالة، وضع
solution	ḥall (m)	حلّ
standard (adj)	qiyāsiy	قياسيّ
standard (level of quality)	qiyās (m)	قياس
stop (pause)	istirāḥa (f)	إستراحة
style	uslūb (m)	أسلوب
system	niẓām (m)	نظام
table (chart)	ʒadwal (m)	جدول
tempo, rate	surʿa (f)	سرعة
term (word, expression)	muṣṭalaḥ (m)	مصطلح
thing (object, item)	ʃay' (m)	شيء
truth (e.g., moment of ~)	ḥaqīqa (f)	حقيقة
turn (please wait your ~)	dawr (m)	دور
type (sort, kind)	nawʿ (m)	نوع
urgent (adj)	ʿāʒil	عاجل
urgently (adv)	ʿāʒilan	عاجلًا
utility (usefulness)	manfaʿa (f)	منفعة
variant (alternative)	ʃakl muxtalif (m)	شكل مختلف
way (means, method)	ṭarīqa (f)	طريقة
zone	minṭaqa (f)	منطقة

250. Modifiers. Adjectives. Part 1

additional (adj)	iḍāfiy	إضافيّ
ancient (~ civilization)	qadīm	قديم
artificial (adj)	ṣināʿiy	صناعيّ
back, rear (adj)	xalfiy	خلفيّ
bad (adj)	sayyi'	سيئ
beautiful (~ palace)	ʒamīl	جميل
beautiful (person)	ʒamīl	جميل
big (in size)	kabīr	كبير

bitter (taste)	murr	مرّ
blind (sightless)	a'ma	أعمى
calm, quiet (adj)	hādi'	هادئ
careless (negligent)	muhmil	مهمل
caring (~ father)	muhtamm	مهتمّ
central (adj)	markaziy	مركزيّ
cheap (low-priced)	raχīṣ	رخيص
cheerful (adj)	farḥān	فرحان
children's (adj)	lil aṭfāl	للأطفال
civil (~ law)	madaniy	مدنيّ
clandestine (secret)	sirriy	سرّيّ
clean (free from dirt)	naẓīf	نظيف
clear (explanation, etc.)	wāḍiḥ	واضح
clever (smart)	ðakiy	ذكيّ
close (near in space)	qarīb	قريب
closed (adj)	muɣlaq	مغلق
cloudless (sky)	ṣāfi	صاف
cold (drink, weather)	bārid	بارد
compatible (adj)	mutawāfiq	متوافق
contented (satisfied)	rāḍi	راض
continuous (uninterrupted)	mutawāṣil	متواصل
cool (weather)	qarīr	قرير
dangerous (adj)	χaṭīr	خطير
dark (room)	muẓlim	مظلم
dead (not alive)	mayyit	ميّت
dense (fog, smoke)	kaθīf	كثيف
destitute (extremely poor)	mu'dim	معدم
different (not the same)	muχtalif	مختلف
difficult (decision)	ṣa'b	صعب
difficult (problem, task)	ṣa'b	صعب
dim, faint (light)	bāhit	باهت
dirty (not clean)	wasiχ	وسخ
distant (in space)	ba'īd	بعيد
dry (clothes, etc.)	ʒāff	جافّ
easy (not difficult)	sahl	سهل
empty (glass, room)	χāli	خال
even (e.g., ~ surface)	musaṭṭaḥ	مسطّح
exact (amount)	daqīq	دقيق
excellent (adj)	mumtāz	ممتاز
excessive (adj)	mufriṭ	مفرط
expensive (adj)	ɣāli	غال
exterior (adj)	χāriʒiy	خارجيّ
far (the ~ East)	ba'īd	بعيد

fast (quick)	sarīʿ	سريع
fatty (food)	dasim	دسم
fertile (land, soil)	χaṣib	خصب
flat (~ panel display)	musaṭṭaḥ	مسطّح
foreign (adj)	aʒnabiy	أجنبي
fragile (china, glass)	haʃʃ	هشّ
free (at no cost)	maʒʒāniy	مجّانيّ
free (unrestricted)	ḥurr	حر
fresh (~ water)	ʿaðb	عذب
fresh (e.g., ~ bread)	ṭāziʒ	طازج
frozen (food)	muʒammad	مجمّد
full (completely filled)	malyān	مليان
gloomy (house, forecast)	muẓlim	مظلم
good (book, etc.)	ʒayyid	جيّد
good, kind (kindhearted)	ṭayyib	طيّب
grateful (adj)	ʃākir	شاكر
happy (adj)	saʿīd	سعيد
hard (not soft)	ʒāmid	جامد
heavy (in weight)	taqīl	ثقيل
hostile (adj)	muʿādin	معاد
hot (adj)	sāχin	ساخن
huge (adj)	ḍaχm	ضخم
humid (adj)	raṭib	رطب
hungry (adj)	ʒawʿān	جوعان
ill (sick, unwell)	marīḍ	مريض
immobile (adj)	θābit	ثابت
important (adj)	muhimm	مهمّ
impossible (adj)	mustaḥīl	مستحيل
incomprehensible	ɣayr wāḍiḥ	غير واضح
indispensable (adj)	ḍarūriy	ضروريّ
inexperienced (adj)	qalīl al χibra	قليل الخبرة
insignificant (adj)	ɣayr muhimm	غير مهمّ
interior (adj)	dāχiliy	داخليّ
joint (~ decision)	muʃtarak	مشترك
last (e.g., ~ week)	māḍi	ماض
last (final)	ʾāχir	آخر
left (e.g., ~ side)	al yasār	اليسار
legal (legitimate)	qānūniy, ʃarʿiy	قانونيّ، شرعيّ
light (in weight)	χafīf	خفيف
light (pale color)	fātiḥ	فاتح
limited (adj)	maḥdūd	محدود
liquid (fluid)	sāʾil	سائل
long (e.g., ~ hair)	ṭawīl	طويل

| loud (voice, etc.) | 'āli | عال |
| low (voice) | munχafiḍ | منخفض |

251. Modifiers. Adjectives. Part 2

main (principal)	ra'īsi	رئيسي
matt, matte	munṭafi'	منطفئ
meticulous (job)	mutqan	متقن
mysterious (adj)	ɣarīb	غريب
narrow (street, etc.)	ḍayyiq	ضيّق

native (~ country)	aṣliy	أصليّ
nearby (adj)	qarīb	قريب
nearsighted (adj)	qaṣīr an naẓar	قصير النظر
needed (necessary)	lāzim	لازم
negative (~ response)	salbiy	سلبيّ

neighboring (adj)	muʒāwir	مجاور
nervous (adj)	'aṣabiy	عصبيّ
new (adj)	ʒadīd	جديد
next (e.g., ~ week)	muqbil	مقبل

nice (kind)	laṭīf	لطيف
nice (voice)	laṭīf	لطيف
normal (adj)	'ādiy	عاديّ
not big (adj)	ɣayr kabīr	غير كبير
not difficult (adj)	ɣayr ṣa'b	غير صعب

obligatory (adj)	ḍarūriy	ضروريّ
old (house)	qadīm	قديم
open (adj)	maftūḥ	مفتوح
opposite (adj)	muqābil	مقابل

ordinary (usual)	'ādiy	عاديّ
original (unusual)	aṣliy	أصليّ
past (recent)	māḍi	ماض
permanent (adj)	dā'im	دائم
personal (adj)	ʃaχṣiy	شخصيّ

polite (adj)	mu'addab	مؤدّب
poor (not rich)	faqīr	فقير
possible (adj)	mumkin	ممكن
present (current)	ḥāḍir	حاضر
previous (adj)	māḍi	ماض

principal (main)	asāsiy	أساسيّ
private (~ jet)	ʃaχṣiy	شخصيّ
probable (adj)	muḥtamal	محتمل
prolonged (e.g., ~ applause)	mumtadd	ممتدّ

public (open to all)	'āmm	عامّ
punctual (person)	daqīq	دقيق
quiet (tranquil)	hādi'	هادئ
rare (adj)	nādir	نادر
raw (uncooked)	nayy	نيّ
right (not left)	al yamīn	اليمين
right, correct (adj)	ṣaḥīḥ	صحيح
ripe (fruit)	nāḍiʒ	ناضج
risky (adj)	xaṭir	خطر
sad (~ look)	ḥazīn	حزين
sad (depressing)	ḥazīn	حزين
safe (not dangerous)	'āmin	آمن
salty (food)	māliḥ	مالح
satisfied (customer)	rāḍi	راض
second hand (adj)	musta'mal	مستعمل
shallow (water)	ḍaḥl	ضحل
sharp (blade, etc.)	ḥādd	حادّ
short (in length)	qaṣīr	قصير
short, short-lived (adj)	qaṣīr	قصير
significant (notable)	muhimm	مهمّ
similar (adj)	ʃabīh	شبيه
simple (easy)	basīṭ	بسيط
skinny	naḥīf	نحيف
small (in size)	ṣayīr	صغير
smooth (surface)	amlas	أملس
soft (~ toys)	ṭariy	طريّ
solid (~ wall)	matīn	متين
sour (flavor, taste)	ḥāmiḍ	حامض
spacious (house, etc.)	wāsi'	واسع
special (adj)	xāṣṣ	خاصّ
straight (line, road)	mustaqīm	مستقيم
strong (person)	qawiy	قويّ
stupid (foolish)	yabiy	غبيّ
suitable (e.g., ~ for drinking)	ṣāliḥ	صالح
sunny (day)	muʃmis	مشمس
superb, perfect (adj)	mumtāz	ممتاز
swarthy (adj)	asmar	أسمر
sweet (sugary)	musakkar	مسكّر
tan (adj)	asmar	أسمر
tasty (delicious)	laðīð	لذيذ
tender (affectionate)	ḥanūn	حنون
the highest (adj)	a'la	أعلى
the most important	ahamm	أهمّ

the nearest	aqrab	أقرب
the same, equal (adj)	mumāθil	مماثل
thick (e.g., ~ fog)	kaθīf	كثيف
thick (wall, slice)	θaxīn	ثخين
thin (person)	naḥīf	نحيف
tight (~ shoes)	ḍayyiq	ضيّق
tired (exhausted)	ta'bān	تعبان
tiring (adj)	mut'ib	متعب
transparent (adj)	ʃaffāf	شفّاف
unclear (adj)	ɣayr wāḍiḥ	غير واضح
unique (exceptional)	farīd	فريد
various (adj)	muxtalif	مختلف
warm (moderately hot)	dāfi'	دافئ
wet (e.g., ~ clothes)	mablūl	مبلول
whole (entire, complete)	kāmil	كامل
wide (e.g., ~ road)	wāsi'	واسع
young (adj)	ʃābb	شاب

MAIN 500 VERBS

252. Verbs A-C

to accompany (vt)	rāfaq	رافق
to accuse (vt)	ittaham	إتّهم
to acknowledge (admit)	i'taraf	إعترف
to act (take action)	'amal	عمل
to add (supplement)	aḍāf	أضاف
to address (speak to)	χāṭab	خاطب
to admire (vi)	u'ȝab bi	أعجب بـ
to advertise (vt)	a'lan	أعلن
to advise (vt)	naṣaḥ	نصح
to affirm (assert)	aṣarr	أصرّ
to agree (say yes)	ittafaq	إتّفق
to aim (to point a weapon)	ṣawwab	صوّب
to allow (sb to do sth)	samaḥ	سمح
to amputate (vt)	batar	بتر
to answer (vi, vt)	aȝāb	أجاب
to apologize (vi)	i'taðar	إعتذر
to appear (come into view)	ẓahar	ظهر
to applaud (vi, vt)	ṣaffaq	صفّق
to appoint (assign)	'ayyan	عيّن
to approach (come closer)	iqtarab	إقترب
to arrive (ab. train)	waṣal	وصل
to ask (~ sb to do sth)	ṭalab	طلب
to aspire to ...	sa'a	سعى
to assist (help)	sā'ad	ساعد
to attack (mil.)	haȝam	هجم
to attain (objectives)	balaɣ	بلغ
to avenge (get revenge)	intaqam	إنتقم
to avoid (danger, task)	taȝannab	تجنّب
to award (give medal to)	manaḥ	منح
to battle (vi)	qātal	قاتل
to be (vi)	kān	كان
to be a cause of ...	sabbab	سبّب
to be afraid	χāf	خاف
to be angry (with ...)	za'al	زعل

to be at war	ḥārab	حارب
to be based (on ...)	iʻtamad	إعتمد
to be bored	ʃaʻar bil malal	شعر بالملل
to be convinced	iqtanaʻ	إقتنع
to be enough	kafa	كفى
to be envious	ḥasad	حسد
to be indignant	istāʼ	إستاء
to be interested in ...	ihtamm	إهتمّ
to be lost in thought	ʃaṭaḥ bi muxayyilatih	شطح بمخيّلته
to be lying (~ on the table)	kān mawʒūdan	كان موجودًا
to be needed	kānat hunāk ḥāʒa ila	كانت هناك حاجة إلى
to be perplexed (puzzled)	iḥtār	إحتار
to be preserved	baqiya	بقي
to be required	kān maṭlūb	كان مطلوبًا
to be surprised	indahaʃ	إندهش
to be worried	qalaq	قلق
to beat (to hit)	ḍarab	ضرب
to become (e.g., ~ old)	aṣbaḥ	أصبح
to behave (vi)	taṣarraf	تصرّف
to believe (think)	iʻtaqad	إعتقد
to belong to ...	xaṣṣ	خصّ
to berth (moor)	rasa	رسا
to blind (other drivers)	aʻma	أعمى
to blow (wind)	habb	هبّ
to blush (vi)	iḥmarr	إحمرّ
to boast (vi)	tabāha	تباهى
to borrow (money)	istalaf	إستلف
to break (branch, toy, etc.)	kasar	كسر
to breathe (vi)	tanaffas	تنفّس
to bring (sth)	ata bi	أتى بـ
to burn (paper, logs)	ḥaraq	حرق
to buy (purchase)	iʃtara	إشترى
to call (~ for help)	istaɣāθ	إستغاث
to call (yell for sb)	nāda	نادى
to calm down (vt)	ṭamʼan	طمأن
can (v aux)	istaṭāʻ	إستطاع
to cancel (call off)	alɣa	ألغى
to cast off (of a boat or ship)	aqlaʻ	أقلع
to catch (e.g., ~ a ball)	amsak	أمسك
to change (~ one's opinion)	ɣayyar	غيّر
to change (exchange)	ṣaraf	صرف
to charm (vt)	fatan	فتن
to choose (select)	ixtār	إختار

to chop off (with an ax)	qata'	قطع
to clean (e.g., kettle from scale)	nazzaf	نظف
to clean (shoes, etc.)	nazzaf	نظف
to clean up (tidy)	rattab	رتّب
to close (vt)	aɣlaq	أغلق
to comb one's hair	tamaʃʃaṭ	تمشّط
to come down (the stairs)	nazil	نزل
to come out (book)	ṣadar	صدر
to compare (vt)	qāran	قارن
to compensate (vt)	'awwaḍ	عوّض
to compete (vi)	nāfas	نافس
to compile (~ a list)	ʒamma'	جمّع
to complain (vi, vt)	ʃaka	شكا
to complicate (vt)	'aqqad	عقّد
to compose (music, etc.)	laḥḥan	لحّن
to compromise (reputation)	faḍah	فضح
to concentrate (vi)	tarakkaz	تركّز
to confess (criminal)	i'taraf	إعترف
to confuse (mix up)	iχtalaṭ	إختلط
to congratulate (vt)	hanna'	هنّأ
to consult (doctor, expert)	istaʃār ...	إستشار...
to continue (~ to do sth)	istamarr	إستمرّ
to control (vt)	taḥakkam	تحكّم
to convince (vt)	aqna'	أقنع
to cooperate (vi)	ta'āwan	تعاون
to coordinate (vt)	nassaq	نسّق
to correct (an error)	ṣaḥḥaḥ	صحّح
to cost (vt)	kallaf	كلّف
to count (money, etc.)	'add	عدّ
to count on ...	i'tamad 'ala ...	إعتمد على...
to crack (ceiling, wall)	taʃaqqaq	تشقّق
to create (vt)	χalaq	خلق
to crush, to squash (~ a bug)	fa'aṣ	فعص
to cry (weep)	baka	بكى
to cut off (with a knife)	qata'	قطع

253. Verbs D-G

to dare (~ to do sth)	aqdam	أقدم
to date from ...	raʒa' tarīχuhu ila	رجع تاريخه إلى

to deceive (vi, vt)	xada‘	خدع
to decide (~ to do sth)	qarrar	قرّر
to decorate (tree, street)	zayyan	زيّن
to dedicate (book, etc.)	karras	كرّس
to defend (a country, etc.)	dāfa‘	دافع
to defend oneself	dāfa‘ ‘an nafsih	دافع عن نفسه
to demand (request firmly)	ṭālib	طالب
to denounce (vt)	waʃa	وشى
to deny (vt)	ankar	أنكر
to depend on ...	ta‘allaq bi ...	تعلّق بـ....
to deprive (vt)	ḥaram	حرم
to deserve (vt)	istaḥaqq	إستحقّ
to design (machine, etc.)	ṣammam	صمّم
to desire (want, wish)	raɣib	رغب
to despise (vt)	iḥtaqar	إحتقر
to destroy (documents, etc.)	atlaf	أتلف
to differ (from sth)	ixtalaf	إختلف
to dig (tunnel, etc.)	ḥafar	حفر
to direct (point the way)	waʒʒah	وجّه
to disappear (vi)	ixtafa	إختفى
to discover (new land, etc.)	iktaʃaf	إكتشف
to discuss (vt)	nāqaʃ	ناقش
to distribute (leaflets, etc.)	wazza‘	وزّع
to disturb (vt)	az‘aʒ	أزعج
to dive (vi)	ɣāṣ	غاص
to divide (math)	qasam	قسم
to do (vt)	‘amal	عمل
to do the laundry	ɣasal	غسل
to double (increase)	ḍā‘af	ضاعف
to doubt (have doubts)	ʃakk fi	شكّ في
to draw a conclusion	istantaʒ	إستنتج
to dream (daydream)	ḥalam	حلم
to dream (in sleep)	ḥalam	حلم
to drink (vi, vt)	ʃarib	شرب
to drive a car	qād sayyāra	قاد سيّارة
to drive away (scare away)	ṭarad	طرد
to drop (let fall)	awqa‘	أوقع
to drown (ab. person)	ɣariq	غرق
to dry (clothes, hair)	ʒaffaf	جفّف
to eat (vi, vt)	akal	أكل
to eavesdrop (vi)	tanaṣṣat	تنصّت

to emit (diffuse - odor, etc.)	fāḥ	فاح
to enjoy oneself	istamtaʿ	إستمتع
to enter (on the list)	saʒʒal	سجّل
to enter (room, house, etc.)	daxal	دخل
to entertain (amuse)	salla	سلّى
to equip (fit out)	ʒahhaz	جهّز
to examine (proposal)	baḥas fi	بحث في
to exchange (sth)	tabādal	تبادل
to excuse (forgive)	ʿaðar	عذر
to exist (vi)	kān mawʒūdᵃ	كان موجودًا
to expect (anticipate)	tawaqqaʿ	توقّع
to expect (foresee)	tanabba'	تنبّأ
to expel (from school, etc.)	faṣal	فصل
to explain (vt)	ʃaraḥ	شرح
to express (vt)	ʿabbar	عبّر
to extinguish (a fire)	atfa'	أطفأ
to fall in love (with ...)	aḥabb	أحبّ
to feed (provide food)	aṭʿam	أطعم
to fight (against the enemy)	qātal	قاتل
to fight (vi)	taʿārak	تعارك
to fill (glass, bottle)	mala'	ملأ
to find (~ lost items)	waʒad	وجد
to finish (vt)	atamm	أتمّ
to fish (angle)	iṣṭād as samak	إصطاد السمك
to fit (ab. dress, etc.)	nāsab	ناسب
to flatter (vt)	ʒāmal	جامل
to fly (bird, plane)	ṭār	طار
to follow ... (come after)	tabaʿ	تبع
to forbid (vt)	manaʿ	منع
to force (compel)	aʒbar	أجبر
to forget (vi, vt)	nasiy	نسي
to forgive (pardon)	ʿafa	عفا
to form (constitute)	ʃakkal	شكّل
to get dirty (vi)	tawassax	توسّخ
to get infected (with ...)	inʿada	إنعدى
to get irritated	inzaʿaʒ	إنزعج
to get married	tazawwaʒ	تزوج
to get rid of ...	taxallaṣ min ...	تخلّص من...
to get tired	taʿib	تعب
to get up (arise from bed)	qām	قام

to give (vt)	aʿṭa	أعطى
to give a bath (to bath)	ḥammam	حمّم
to give a hug, to hug (vt)	ʿānaq	عانق
to give in (yield to)	istaslam	إستسلم
to glimpse (vt)	lamaḥ	لمح
to go (by car, etc.)	sāfar	سافر
to go (on foot)	maʃa	مشى
to go for a swim	sabaḥ	سبح
to go out (for dinner, etc.)	χaraȝ	خرج
to go to bed (go to sleep)	nām	نام
to greet (vt)	sallam ʿala	سلّم على
to grow (plants)	anbat	أنبت
to guarantee (vt)	ḍaman	ضمن
to guess (the answer)	χamman	خمّن

254. Verbs H-M

to hand out (distribute)	wazzaʿ ʿala	وزّع على
to hang (curtains, etc.)	ʿallaq	علّق
to have (vt)	malak	ملك
to have a try	ḥāwal	حاول
to have breakfast	afṭar	أفطر
to have dinner	taʿaʃʃa	تعشّى
to have lunch	taɣadda	تغدّى
to head (group, etc.)	raʾs	رأس
to hear (vt)	samiʿ	سمع
to heat (vt)	saχχan	سخّن
to help (vt)	sāʿad	ساعد
to hide (vt)	χabaʾ	خبأ
to hire (e.g., ~ a boat)	istaʾȝar	إستأجر
to hire (staff)	wazzaf	وظّف
to hope (vi, vt)	tamanna	تمنّى
to hunt (for food, sport)	iṣṭād	إصطاد
to hurry (vi)	istaȝal	إستعجل
to imagine (to picture)	taṣawwar	تصوّر
to imitate (vt)	qallad	قلّد
to implore (vt)	tawassal	توسّل
to import (vt)	istawrad	إستورد
to increase (vi)	izdād	إزداد
to increase (vt)	zayyad	زيّد
to infect (vt)	aʿda	أعدى
to influence (vt)	aθθar	أثّر
to inform (e.g., ~ the police about)	aχbar	أخبر

to inform (vt)	aχbar	أخبر
to inherit (vt)	wariθ	ورث
to inquire (about …)	istafsar	إستفسر
to insert (put in)	adχal	أدخل
to insinuate (imply)	lamaḥ	لمح
to insist (vi, vt)	aṣarr	أصرّ
to inspire (vt)	alham	ألهم
to instruct (teach)	ʻallam	علّم
to insult (offend)	ahān	أهان
to interest (vt)	hamm	همّ
to intervene (vi)	tadaχχal	تدخّل
to introduce (sb to sb)	ʻarraf	عرّف
to invent (machine, etc.)	iχtaraʻ	إخترع
to invite (vt)	daʻa	دعا
to iron (clothes)	kawa	كوى
to irritate (annoy)	azʻaʒ	أزعج
to isolate (vt)	ʻazal	عزل
to join (political party, etc.)	inḍamm ila	إنضمّ إلى
to joke (be kidding)	mazaḥ	مزح
to keep (old letters, etc.)	iḥtafaz	إحتفظ
to keep silent	sakat	سكت
to kill (vt)	qatal	قتل
to knock (at the door)	daqq	دقّ
to know (sb)	ʻaraf	عرف
to know (sth)	ʻaraf	عرف
to laugh (vi)	ḍaḥik	ضحك
to launch (start up)	aṭlaq	أطلق
to leave (~ for Mexico)	ɣādar	غادر
to leave (forget sth)	nasiya	نسي
to leave (spouse)	tarak	ترك
to liberate (city, etc.)	ḥarrar	حرّر
to lie (~ on the floor)	raqad	رقد
to lie (tell untruth)	kaðib	كذب
to light (campfire, etc.)	aʃʻal	أشعل
to light up (illuminate)	aḍāʼ	أضاء
to like (I like …)	aʻʒab	أعجب
to limit (vt)	ḥaddad	حدّد
to listen (vi)	istamaʻ	إستمع
to live (~ in France)	sakan	سكن
to live (exist)	ʻāʃ	عاش
to load (gun)	ḥaʃa	حشا
to load (vehicle, etc.)	ʃaḥan	شحن
to look (I'm just ~ing)	nazar	نظر
to look for … (search)	baḥaθ	بحث

to look like (resemble)	kān ʃabīhan	كان شبهًا
to lose (umbrella, etc.)	faqad	فقد
to love (e.g., ~ dancing)	aḥabb	أحبَّ

to love (sb)	aḥabb	أحبَّ
to lower (blind, head)	anzal	أنزل
to make (~ dinner)	ḥaḍḍar	حضَّر
to make a mistake	axṭaʼ	أخطأ
to make angry	azʻal	أزعل

to make easier	sahhal	سهَّل
to make multiple copies	ṣawwar	صوَّر
to make the acquaintance	taʻarraf	تعرَّف
to make use (of …)	istanfaʻ	إستنفع
to manage, to run	adār	أدار

to mark (make a mark)	ʻallam	علَّم
to mean (signify)	ʻana	عنى
to memorize (vt)	ḥafaẓ	حفظ
to mention (talk about)	ðakar	ذكر
to miss (school, etc.)	ɣāb	غاب

to mix (combine, blend)	xalaṭ	خلط
to mock (make fun of)	saxar	سخر
to move (to shift)	ḥarrak	حرَّك
to multiply (math)	ḍarab	ضرب
must (v aux)	kān yaʒib ʻalayh	كان يجب عليه

255. Verbs N-R

to name, to call (vt)	samma	سمَّى
to negotiate (vi)	aʒra mubāḥaθāt	أجرى مباحثات
to note (write down)	katab mulāḥaza	كتب ملاحظة
to notice (see)	lāḥaẓ	لاحظ

to obey (vi, vt)	ṭāʻ	طاع
to object (vi, vt)	iʻtaraḍ	إعترض
to observe (see)	rāqab	راقب
to offend (vt)	asāʼ	أساء
to omit (word, phrase)	ḥaðaf	حذف

to open (vt)	fataḥ	فتح
to order (in restaurant)	ṭalab	طلب
to order (mil.)	amar	أمر
to organize (concert, party)	naẓẓam	نظَّم
to overestimate (vt)	bāliɣ fit taqdīr	بالغ في التقدير
to own (possess)	malak	ملك
to participate (vi)	iʃtarak	إشترك
to pass through (by car, etc.)	marr bi	مرَّ بـ

to pay (vi, vt)	dafaʻ	دفع
to peep, spy on	waṣwaṣ	وصوص
to penetrate (vt)	daχal	دخل
to permit (vt)	samaḥ	سمح
to pick (flowers)	qaṭaf	قطف
to place (put, set)	waḍaʻ	وضع
to plan (~ to do sth)	χaṭṭaṭ	خطّط
to play (actor)	maθθal	مثّل
to play (children)	laʻib	لعب
to point (~ the way)	aʃār	أشار
to pour (liquid)	ṣabb	صبّ
to pray (vi, vt)	ṣalla	صلّى
to prefer (vt)	faḍḍal	فضّل
to prepare (~ a plan)	aʻadd	أعدّ
to present (sb to sb)	qaddam	قدّم
to preserve (peace, life)	ḥafaẓ	حفظ
to prevail (vt)	ɣalab	غلب
to progress (move forward)	taqaddam	تقدّم
to promise (vt)	waʻad	وعد
to pronounce (vt)	naṭaq	نطق
to propose (vt)	iqtaraḥ, ʻaraḍ	إقترح , عرض
to protect (e.g., ~ nature)	ḥama	حمى
to protest (vi)	iḥtaʒʒ	إحتجّ
to prove (vt)	aθbat	أثبت
to provoke (vt)	istafazz	إستفزّ
to pull (~ the rope)	ʃadd	شدّ
to punish (vt)	ʻāqab	عاقب
to push (~ the door)	dafaʻ	دفع
to put away (vt)	ʃāl	شال
to put in order	naẓẓam	نظّم
to put, to place	waḍaʻ	وضع
to quote (cite)	istaʃhad	إستشهد
to reach (arrive at)	waṣal	وصل
to read (vi, vt)	qara'	قرأ
to realize (a dream)	ḥaqqaq	حقّق
to recognize (identify sb)	ʻaraf	عرف
to recommend (vt)	naṣaḥ	نصح
to recover (~ from flu)	ʃufiy	شفي
to redo (do again)	aʻād	أعاد
to reduce (speed, etc.)	qallal	قلّل
to refuse (~ sb)	rafaḍ	رفض
to regret (be sorry)	nadim	ندم

to reinforce (vt)	'azzaz	عزّز
to remember (Do you ~ me?)	taðakkar	تذكّر
to remember (I can't ~ her name)	taðakkar	تذكّر
to remind of ...	ðakkar	ذكّر
to remove (~ a stain)	azāl	أزال
to remove (~ an obstacle)	azāl	أزال
to rent (sth from sb)	ista'ʒar	إستأجِر
to repair (mend)	aṣlaḥ	أصلح
to repeat (say again)	karrar	كرّر
to report (make a report)	qaddam taqrīr	قدّم تقريرًا
to reproach (vt)	lām	لام
to reserve, to book	haʒaz	حجز
to restrain (hold back)	mana'	منع
to return (come back)	'ād	عاد
to risk, to take a risk	χāṭar	خاطر
to rub out (erase)	masaḥ	مسح
to run (move fast)	ʒara	جرى
to rush (hurry sb)	a'ʒʒal	عجّل

256. Verbs S-W

to satisfy (please)	arḍa	أرضى
to save (rescue)	anqað	أنقذ
to say (~ thank you)	qāl	قال
to scold (vt)	wabbaχ	وبّخ
to scratch (with claws)	χadaʃ	خدش
to select (to pick)	iχtār	إختار
to sell (goods)	bā'	باع
to send (a letter)	arsal	أرسل
to send back (vt)	a'ād	أعاد
to sense (~ danger)	ʃa'r bi	شعر بـ
to sentence (vt)	ḥakam	حكم
to serve (in restaurant)	χadam	خدم
to settle (a conflict)	sawwa	سوّى
to shake (vt)	hazz	هزّ
to shave (vi)	ḥalaq	حلق
to shine (gleam)	lam'	لمع
to shiver (with cold)	irta'aʃ	إرتعش
to shoot (vi)	aṭlaq an nār	أطلق النار
to shout (vi)	ṣaraχ	صرخ

to show (to display)	'araḍ	عرض
to shudder (vi)	irta'aʃ	إرتعش
to sigh (vi)	tanahhad	تنهّد
to sign (document)	waqqa'	وقّع
to signify (mean)	'ana	عنى
to simplify (vt)	bassaṭ	بسّط
to sin (vi)	aðnab	أذنب
to sit (be sitting)	ʒalas	جلس
to sit down (vi)	ʒalas	جلس
to smell (emit an odor)	fāḥ	فاح
to smell (inhale the odor)	iʃtamm	إشتمّ
to smile (vi)	ibtasam	إبتسم
to snap (vi, ab. rope)	inqata'	إنقطع
to solve (problem)	ḥall	حلّ
to sow (seed, crop)	baðar	بذر
to spill (liquid)	dalaq	دلق
to spill out, scatter (flour, etc.)	saqaṭ	سقط
to spit (vi)	bazaq	بزق
to stand (toothache, cold)	taḥammal	تحمّل
to start (begin)	bada'	بدأ
to steal (money, etc.)	saraq	سرق
to stop (for pause, etc.)	waqaf	وقف
to stop (please ~ calling me)	tawaqqaf	توقّف
to stop talking	sakat	سكت
to stroke (caress)	masaḥ	مسح
to study (vt)	daras	درس
to suffer (feel pain)	'āna	عانى
to support (cause, idea)	ayyad	أيّد
to suppose (assume)	iftaraḍ	إفترض
to surface (ab. submarine)	ṣa'id ilas saṭḥ	صعد إلى السطح
to surprise (amaze)	adhaʃ	أدهش
to suspect (vt)	iʃtabah fi	إشتبه في
to swim (vi)	sabaḥ	سبح
to take (get hold of)	axað	أخذ
to take a bath	istaḥamm	إستحمّ
to take a rest	istarāḥ	إستراح
to take away (e.g., about waiter)	ðahab bi	ذهب بـ
to take off (airplane)	aqla'	أقلع
to take off (painting, curtains, etc.)	naza'	نزع

to take pictures	ṣawwar	صوّر
to talk to ...	takallam ma'a ...	تكلّم مع...
to teach (give lessons)	'allam	علّم
to tear off, to rip off (vt)	qaṭa'	قطع
to tell (story, joke)	ḥaddaθ	حدّث
to thank (vt)	ʃakar	شكر
to think (believe)	i'taqad	إعتقد
to think (vi, vt)	ẓann	ظنّ
to threaten (vt)	ḥaddad	هدّد
to throw (stone, etc.)	rama	رمى
to tie to ...	rabaṭ bi ...	ربط بـ...
to tie up (prisoner)	rabaṭ	ربط
to tire (make tired)	at'ab	أتعب
to touch (one's arm, etc.)	lamas	لمس
to tower (over ...)	irtafa'	إرتفع
to train (animals)	darrab	درّب
to train (sb)	darrab	درّب
to train (vi)	tadarrab	تدرّب
to transform (vt)	ḥawwal	حوّل
to translate (vt)	tarʒam	ترجم
to treat (illness)	'ālaʒ	عالج
to trust (vt)	waθiq	وثق
to try (attempt)	ḥāwal	حاول
to turn (e.g., ~ left)	in'aṭaf	إنعطف
to turn away (vi)	a'raḍ 'an	أعرض عن
to turn off (the light)	atfa'	أطفأ
to turn on (computer, etc.)	fataḥ, ʃaɣɣal	فتح, شغّل
to turn over (stone, etc.)	qalab	قلب
to underestimate (vt)	istaxaff	إستخفّ
to underline (vt)	waḍa' xaṭṭ taḥt	وضع خطّا تحت
to understand (vt)	fahim	فهم
to undertake (vt)	qām bi	قام بـ
to unite (vt)	waḥḥad	وحّد
to untie (vt)	fakk	فكّ
to use (phrase, word)	istaxdam	إستخدم
to vaccinate (vt)	laqqaḥ	لقّح
to vote (vi)	ṣawwat	صوّت
to wait (vt)	intaẓar	إنتظر
to wake (sb)	ayqaẓ	أيقظ
to want (wish, desire)	arād	أراد
to warn (of the danger)	ḥaððar	حذّر
to wash (clean)	ɣasal	غسل

to water (plants)	saqa	سقى
to wave (the hand)	lawwaḥ	لوّح
to weigh (have weight)	wazan	وزن
to work (vi)	ʻamal	عمل
to worry (make anxious)	aqlaq	أقلق
to worry (vi)	qalaq	قلق
to wrap (parcel, etc.)	laff	لفَّ
to wrestle (sport)	ṣāraʻ	صارع
to write (vt)	katab	كتب
to write down	katab	كتب